Literary culture in Cuba

Manchester University Press

Literary culture in Cuba

Revolution, nation-building and the book

Par Kumaraswami and Antoni Kapcia,
with Meesha Nehru

Manchester University Press

Copyright © Antoni Kapcia, Par Kumaraswami and Meesha Nehru 2012

The right of Antoni Kapcia, Par Kumaraswami and Meesha Nehru to be identified as the authors of this work has been asserted by them in accordance with the Copyright, Designs and Patents Act 1988.

Published by Manchester University Press
Altrincham Street, Manchester M1 7JA, UK
www.manchesteruniversitypress.co.uk

British Library Cataloguing-in-Publication Data is available

Library of Congress Cataloging-in-Publication Data is available

ISBN 978 0 7190 9995 3 *paperback*

First published by Manchester University Press in hardback 2012

This edition first published 2016

The publisher has no responsibility for the persistence or accuracy of URLs for any external or third-party internet websites referred to in this book, and does not guarantee that any content on such websites is, or will remain, accurate or appropriate.

Printed by Lightning Source

Contents

Acknowledgments	*page* vii
Acronyms and abbreviations	xi
Spanish words and phrases with particular Cuban usage	xiii
List of figures	xiv
Introduction	1
1 Locating literary culture in the trajectory of the Revolution	11
2 Understanding literary culture in the Revolution	33
3 1959–61: The first flush of revolution	63
4 1961–89: The years of radicalisation and consolidation	82
5 1990s–2000s: The years of crisis and reassessment	132
6 The path to becoming a writer in contemporary Cuba: The role of the Centro de Formación Literaria Onelio Jorge Cardoso and the movement of *talleres literarios* (by Meesha Nehru)	178
7 The history of a novel: Alberto Ajón León's *¿Qué bolá? (What's Up?)*	194
8 The Feria Internacional del Libro de La Habana	215
Conclusion	233
List of interviewees	241
Bibliography	245
Index	259

Acknowledgements

Although a great many people have contributed in some form or other to the preparation and completion of this study (not least the many Cubans – around 150 – who so willingly agreed to be interviewed by us between 2004 and 2011, or who gave us access to their organisations or archives), the authors would especially like to acknowledge the support of the following people and institutions.

Firstly, we have to thank the great many Cuban colleagues (many of them already friends and many having since become friends) who contributed in a variety of ways, with advice, contacts, materials, repeated discussions or interviews, arrangements, and endless hospitality. Two deserve special thanks and praise: Xiomara García Cao and Ana Curbeira Cancela; already good friends to us both, they proved to be invaluable researchers for, and key contributors to, the project, both in Cuba and in the UK. We also owe special thanks to Alberto Ajón León, who kindly and willingly helped us throughout our research on his novel (the subject of Chapter 7).

Beyond them, a great many others became or remained constant sources of willing and perceptive support; we would especially like to thank: Fernando León Jacomino, Fernando Martínez Heredia, Esther Pérez, Ambrosio Fornet, Luisa Campuzano, Yannis Lobaina González, Sergio Chaple, Rafael Hernández, the late Mercedes Santos Moray, Mirta Yáñez, Daniel García Santos, Rafael Rodríguez Beltrán and Roberto Fernández Retamar. In the UK, we owe special thanks to Meesha Nehru, whose part in the project, as doctoral researcher and then contributor to this book, was essential.

Beyond these individuals, there are a great many institutions whose support should be acknowledged gratefully. Firstly, we thank the Leverhulme Trust, who provided the funding for the project behind this book, and who, throughout, showed a willingness to be understanding and flexible as the inevitable obstacles and delays arose.

Secondly, we owe thanks to our respective institutions, the Universities of Manchester and Nottingham (and, before that, Heriot-Watt University), and, within them, to our colleagues in our respective departments, whose understanding and support is much appreciated.

In Cuba, we wish gratefully to acknowledge the sustained support which also came from colleagues at the University of Havana, and especially from José Carlos Vázquez López, Laura Monteagudo, Cristina Díaz and the many colleagues from the Facultad de Lenguas Extranjeras. However, thanks should also go to the many other Cuban institutions which proved especially welcoming, helpful and willing to share knowledge and perceptions with us. These especially include two which were fundamental to the research and idea of the project.

Firstly, we thank the Instituto Cubano de Investigación Cultural Juan Marinello, and especially Pablo Pacheco, whose ready and enthusiastic welcome for the original proposal made him in one sense the godfather of the project. We also gratefully acknowledge the support from his successors, Rolando González Patricio and Elena Socarrás, and the input from the Instituto's research staff, especially Cecilia Linares Fleites, who contributed invaluably in the early stages of the research. The second institution to thank is the Instituto Cubano del Libro, and especially its directors with whom we worked (Iroel Sánchez Espinosa and Suleika Romay), but also Laura Betancourt (who in the early stages provided invaluable guidance), Rubiel García (who clarified several important questions towards the end) and, most importantly, Jacqueline Laguardia, of the Observatorio Cubano del Libro y la Literatura.

Beyond these two we extend our thanks to other Cuban institutions: the Ministerio de Cultura (and especially Fernando Rojas); the Biblioteca Nacional José Martí (and particularly those associated with its several reading programmes); Casa de las Américas; the Centro Onelio Jorge Cardoso. None of this would, of course, have been possible without the sustained support of the Cuban Consulate in London.

Finally, each of us would like to thank our respective friends and families.

Par: To Colin Davidson, whose tolerance during her regular absences in Cuba made them easier for all concerned; and especially Oscar and Anjali, without whom none of this would have been so enjoyable. Also to those individuals whose humour, support and advice will, I hope, always be at the centre of my life: Pedro Aragonés, Raji and Tim

Acknowledgements

Davenport, Saira Khan, Ann McFall, Raúl Marchena, Laura Powick, Núria Triana-Toribio.

Tony: Very special thanks also go to my partner, Jean Gilkison, the person who gave us the original idea and encouragement for the whole project, and who provided invaluable support, advice and ideas throughout the years of the research for this book.

Acronyms and abbreviations

AHS	Asociación Hermanos Saíz
AJR	Asociación de Jóvenes Rebeldes
ANAP	Asociación Nacional de Agricultores Pequeños
BNJM	Biblioteca Nacional José Martí
CDR	Comité de Defensa de la Revolución
CMEA	Council for Mutual Economic Assistance (known as Comecon)
CNC	Consejo Nacional de Cultura
CPLL	Centros Provinciales del Libro y la Literatura
CTC	Central de Trabadajores de Cuba
CUC	Cuban convertible peso
DNL	Distribuidora Nacional de Libros
FAR	Fuerzas Armadas Revolucionarias
FEEM	Federación de Estudiantes de la Enseñanza Media
FEU	Federación de Estudiantes de Cuba
FILH	Feria Internacional del Libro de La Habana (also 'Feria')
FMC	Federación de Mujeres Cubanas
ICAIC	Instituto Cubano de Artes e Industrias Cinematográficas
ICL	Instituto Cubano del Libro (post-1976)
IL	Instituto del Libro (pre-1976)
ILL	Instituto de Literatura y Lingüística
ISA	Instituto Superior de Arte
MINCULT	Ministerio de Cultura
MINED	Ministerio de Educación
MN	*Moneda nacional* (Cuban peso)
OCLL	Observatorio Cubano del Libro y la Literatura
OPP	Organos de Poder Popular
ORI	Organizaciones Revolucionarias Integradas (1961–62)
PCC	Partido Comunista de Cuba (post-1965)

PSP	Partido Socialista Popular (communist party 1944–61)
PURSC	Partido Unido de la Revolución Socialista de Cuba (1962–65)
SET	Sistema de Ediciones Territoriales
UJC	Unión de Jóvenes Comunistas
UMAP	Unidad Militar de Ayuda a la Producción
UNEAC	Unión de Escritores y Artistas de Cuba

NB Throughout the book, initials are also used to indicate interviewees, for example [RFR] or [AGN]. The full list of such abbreviations and the names to which they refer is at the end of the book, before the Bibliography.

Spanish words and phrases with particular Cuban usage

asesor (cultural/literario)	Advisor, instructor
balsero	Literally 'rafter'; term for illegal emigrant
caravana	The itinerary of the Feria del Libro outside Havana
colchón editorial	The backlog of manuscripts or published books that have not been distributed
consejo asesor	Advisory editorial committee
comunitario	Locally focused
cubanidad	Cuban-ness
cuenta propia	Self-employment
egresado	Graduate
guerrillerismo	Guerrilla mentality
instructor de arte	Cultural instructor
jineterismo	Hustling or prostitution
país de honor	Country honoured (Havana Book Fair)
parametración	Imposition of strict limits (on expression)
sábado del libro	Saturday book launch
zafra	Sugar harvest

List of figures

Figure 1. Organisational structure of Letras Cubanas   196

Introduction

Most studies of the Cuban Revolution since the mid-1960s (when its emerging shape began to allow the first serious considerations of the transformation (Seers, 1964; Fagen, 1969; Huberman and Sweezy, 1968; O'Connor, 1971), as opposed to polemical responses, either for (Frank, 1961; Sartre, 1961; Mills, 1960) or against (Pflaum, 1961; Weyl, 1961), have tended to focus on the political, economic or social patterns of the process of change. As a result, apart from the periodic collections of essays that offer a broad 'compendium' of the Revolution's many dimensions (Mesa-Lago, 1971; Bonachea and Valdés, 1972; Suchlicki, 1972; Halebsky and Kirk, 1985; Chomsky et al, 2003; Brenner, 2005), which usually include a section on culture, most approaches have tended to neglect the cultural dimension or to accord it a secondary status. In the latter case, culture is often seen as an interesting, if perhaps revealing, side issue, usually acknowledging the more outstanding post-1959 cultural developments (in cinema or music) or, alternatively, highlighting one of the better-known *causes célèbres* of the expected conflict between communist state and intellectual freedom (the *caso Padilla* (Padilla affair), or Reinaldo Arenas, most typically). Conversely, studies of modern Cuban culture have often tended to consider the Revolution's political, economic or social transformation as a backdrop to the cultural patterns analysed, as the context for a specific development or as a restrictive environment, creating opportunities but also tensions and conflicts (see Chapter 2). In other words, rarely have such studies seen culture as central to the other transformations.

However, this neglect is puzzling, not least because previous revolutions (notably those in Russia and Mexico) included significant attempts to build a cultural revolution into the whole process of change. Moreover, two of the Revolution's first institutions (the Instituto Cubano de Artes e Industrias Cinematográficas (ICAIC), and Casa de las

Américas, created in March and April 1959 respectively) were cultural, indicating that, by some leaders at least, culture was considered a priority. Subsequent cultural developments bringing positive international attention to Cuba (cinema or popular music, for example) might also suggest the Revolution's success in creating an infrastructure and environment for cultural expansion.

In fact, any examination of the relationship between culture and the motives, patterns, effects and underlying ideology of the wider transformation shows clearly that that relationship has been neither accidental nor incidental, but at the very least reflecting a deeper inter-connection. After all, the official centrality accorded to the ideas, writings and example of the *héroe nacional*, José Martí (visible everywhere), and the ubiquitous repetition of his words, *el único modo de ser libre es ser culto* (the only way to be free is to be educated, and cultured) would suggest that he believed (as, presumably, do at least some of those following his footsteps since 1953) that culture was fundamental to a genuine social liberation.

However, if that seems true of culture in general, it is clear that, within that context, literature seems to have enjoyed a special place of prestige, authority and centrality. Not only were the Imprenta Nacional (national printing house) and the Editorial Nacional (national publishing house), also officially known as the Editora Nacional, early creations of the Revolution, but the leading cultural protagonists of the first few years (apart from Alfredo Guevara in cinema and Alicia Alonso in ballet) who helped to shape the contours of the whole cultural revolution, were mostly writers, such as Alejo Carpentier, José Lezama Lima, or Nicolás Guillén. Moreover, as culture developed in the 1960s, literature seemed to be especially privileged; the remarkable initiative of the *instructores de arte* (cultural teachers) – the Revolution's cultural 'shock troops', sent out into the fields, schools and factories to train Cubans to develop their artistic or musical talents (in the belief that any Cuban had both the right and ability to be culturally skilled) – excluded literature, implying that literary talent might be uniquely innate, rather than teachable. Indeed, as this study explains, it was only after a decade of change that the same principle began to be applied to literature as well, in the form of the *talleres literarios* (literary workshops).

However, here we find another apparent reality, seeming to contradict that 'special place': over the decades, it has often seemed to be writers (rather than musicians, dramatists or artists) who have been singled out by the political authorities for close attention, strict regulation and even punishment. These included the main protagonists of the *Lunes* affair of 1961 (see Chapter 3), the young activists of the Puente group (Chapter 4), and the main *cause célèbre* of the late 1960s and early 1970s (presaging the clampdown of the *quinquenio gris* (the grey five-year period) of 1971–76), the marginalisation and eventual detention and 'confession' of the poet Heberto Padilla (Chapter 4). That clampdown seemed mostly to target writers, while the next generation suffering from discrimination on grounds of artistic or sexual preference included the well-known case of Arenas. While this impression might of course simply reflect our own limited knowledge or the success of studies highlighting those cases – since theatre did in fact see several actors and playwrights suffer in the *quinquenio* (Gallardo, 2009) – this propensity for literature to draw special critical attention and fear of those in authority does seem to have confirmed expectations, arising from our perceptions of culture under communism, where writers (such as Milosz, Pasternak and Solzhenitsyn) were especially targeted.

Given this apparently contradictory landscape, therefore, some key questions arise: why does this contradiction exist (if what we see is in fact accurate) and what does it mean for our understanding of the role of literature in the Revolution and also of the nature of the Revolution? This study attempts to provide some possible answers, by following a particular line of argument.

Because of the need to develop such answers, going to the heart of the intimate relationship between literature and the Revolution, that line of argument is to examine the subject within very clear contexts. The first context is the need to understand post-1959 Cuban literature not as represented by those authors or texts traditionally attracting external attention (not least because such attention may well reflect external preconceptions, as much as the reality of what is being examined), but rather to consider such conventional subjects for analysis as the tip of an iceberg, below which lies the vast majority of the other texts and other writers not attracting this attention, as much the outcome of the Revolution–literature relationship as Arenas, Padilla or the best-known contemporary writers, Leonardo Padura Fuentes or Pedro Juan Gutiérrez. For the sheer volume of writing talent which has emerged in Cuba says something about the context in which writers have written and operated, but it also reminds us that, beyond the famous, lies a huge hinterland of hidden stories, experiences and decisions – not least the decision to stay in Cuba and continue working within a revolutionary project.

Secondly, we need to understand literature in Cuba as, anyway, going beyond text or author, regardless of the latter's identity, and, instead, to see it in a wider context: of what we see here as literary culture, namely the whole set of processes, institutions, policies, spaces and the 'circuit of culture' (Du Gay, 1997) affecting writing, reading and books. Indeed that is clearly the subject of this study.

Finally, we need to understand this literary culture within the context of the Revolution's trajectory from 1959, with all its ideological underpinnings, imperatives, debates and tensions, although, within that, we need to understand that this culture had its own trajectory, evolution, imperatives, debates and tensions, bearing some direct relationship to the Revolution's wider patterns of evolution but also to its own momentum. For this reason the authors' different disciplines (cultural studies and history) have been brought into play, to create what we believe is a necessary interdisciplinary approach and focus, specifically mixing cultural studies' use of interviews (especially in Chapters 4, 5 and 8) and cultural theory, on the one hand, with historiography's empirical awareness of a historical dimension and use of documentary evidence.

Structure of the book

This therefore explains the structure of this book. Chapter 1 outlines the Revolution's wider trajectory, as a process of political and social change over fifty years, suggesting how we might view the cultural trajectory within that. Chapter 2, set against the dominant patterns of interpretation in analyses of Cuban literature and culture since 1959, outlines the theoretical framework in which this study is located, emphasising the process's ideological continuum, the existence, nature and function of different spaces within a constantly changing context, and, most importantly, the idea of a different notion of value which, we suggest, is the essential framework for understanding the whole question.

Three chapters then examine the evolution of Cuban literary culture from 1959 to 2011. Chapter 3 examines just three years of the initial Revolution, the years of redefinition when the new literary culture emerged from experience and the developing ideological consensus. The pace, scale and depth of the early changes were so significant that they warrant detailed attention, and, in the light of the book's approach, that first period stood clearly apart from the following three decades.

Chapter 4 then covers the history of literary culture over the next twenty-eight years, since, after those initial years and despite differences between phases within those three decades, 1961–89 showed more of a common internal pattern than that whole period shared with the opening years. Nonetheless, those differences also matter, for each phase's character did mark it out from the preceding and following phases: 1961–67 saw the cultural authorities' main focus on the reader, rather than the writer (the latter having been, de facto if not officially, the prime focus in 1959–61); in 1967–76 the focus shifted to literature's social context (and purpose), namely both an internal Cuban context and an external context, in the Third World; in 1977–89, the focus shifted to the book itself, and to publishing, while correcting the neglect of the writer. However, despite these differences, nothing changed the overall emerging emphasis of the strategy for a literary culture, largely determined from 1961 and following the same principles until the crisis of 1989–94, following the collapse of the Soviet Union. Chapter 5 addresses, extensively, the mixed effects of that crisis: rapid and painful adjustment but also unexpected opportunities and development, and eventually, after 2000, a surprising and productive return to the principles of 1961, with a postscript anticipating the effects of reform under the leadership of Raúl Castro.

Three 'case studies' then follow this history, each seen as reflecting the patterns, processes and thinking of the trajectory traced, although all three refer principally to the post-1989 context. Chapter 6 (written by Meesha Nehru) analyses the unusual writers' training workshop, the Centro Onelio Jorge Cardoso, seen here as a 'case' because it arose from the characteristic *talleres literarios* of the 1970s and 1980s, and also because its development reflected the post-1991 emphasis on the infrastructure and opportunities for 'professional' writers. Chapter 7 narrates, in the context of the complexities of the Cuban publishing infrastructure of 2008–11, the story of one possibly typical work of fiction, tracing its passage from conception to reception and revealing, in the process, the many complexities, pressures and negotiations which all actors in Cuba's literary culture constantly have to confront. Finally, Chapter 8 studies the annual Havana Book Fair (the Feria Internacional del Libro de La Habana, hereafter the Feria), seen here as a revealing microcosm of that literary culture, not just for 2000–11 (to which it mostly refers) but also of the whole post-1959 project, with its special unchallenged value placed on literature, on the book and on reading.

Before examining processes after 1959, however, it is important to emphasise that the post-1959 developments did not happen in a political vacuum, and that the new valorisation of literature, writers and the book was not a totally new departure, but, instead, had a clear basis in the patterns, experiences and the thinking evident in Cuba before the Revolution.

The pre-1959 background

Most studies of literature under the Revolution tend to assume that pre-1959 Cuba was a cultural desert, with literature and writers given few opportunities and little respect. As Lourdes Casal put it, literature was seen as 'a pastime for good-for-nothings and homosexuals' (Casal, 1971: 456). While this overview was not completely inaccurate, it somewhat overstates the case, ignoring the reality that Cuba was, in this respect, not so different from most of contemporary Latin America, with some prominent exceptions; in Mexico and Argentina, for example, state initiatives and a lively literary culture, high literacy and a large internal and continental public (since their publishers dominated the wider Latin American market) combined to create a range of outlets for would-be writers. Elsewhere, however, the picture was as bleak as in Cuba, publishing being based on small-scale operations, often subsidised by writers themselves or rich patrons, leading many writers to live or publish abroad or through supportive groupings at home.

In Cuba, that was true. There were relatively few bookshops – one for every 60,000 inhabitants (Smorkaloff, 1997: 146) – and even the prestigious Biblioteca Nacional José Martí (José Martí National Library (BNJM)), unable to buy its books, relied on authors' own donations [GP].[1] Equally, there were no large-scale publishing enterprises outside the media, and those that did exist were small presses, producing geographically limited and small print-runs, or the specialist university presses in Havana, Santiago or Santa Clara [RFR]. The most prestigious small press was the Havana-based Editorial Lex, but others included two operations owned by Spanish exiles: the educational publishers Editorial Cultural, whose output – usually for private schools – included some literature [MSM], and Manuel Altoaguirre's Editorial La Verónica [LC]. In all, fewer than one million books were published annually in the 1950s, around 200 titles, mostly textbooks (Rodríguez, 2001: 65). Therefore, what existed on 1 January 1959 was 'a printing and binding industry consisting of small artisan-style letterpress printers and hand binderies, and one large modern plant producing *Selecciones*, the Spanish-language *Reader's Digest*, about a million copies of which

Introduction

were printed in Cuba for distribution throughout all of Latin America' (Shatzkin, 1985: 36). Hence, Cuban writers did what their counterparts did elsewhere. Firstly, they used small publishers, often funding small print-runs themselves (usually 500–750 copies: Shatzkin, 1985: 36); while this was more common among aspiring writers, keen to launch their literary careers, it even applied to the most established and internationally renowned writers [RFR]. Secondly, many chose to leave Cuba, for what was subsequently perceived as a self-imposed exile but which was both a pragmatic and intellectual strategy. It was pragmatic because only abroad could large-scale publishing opportunities be found, allowing writers to be professional or semi-professional; this was obviously more likely in Spanish-speaking countries, especially Spain, Mexico [RFR] or Argentina, although both Carpentier and Virgilio Piñera lived in Caracas. This emigration also had another purpose: to become part of the wider, and more prestigious, cultural community formed by European or North American culture, whose leading exponents had always determined intellectual and artistic currents, constituted the prestigious vanguard and were generally seen as the arbiters of taste. Hence, by living in Europe (especially Paris) or the United States (especially New York), a Cuban writer had access to the ideas and models of that community and could thus be as up to date as possible with the latest fashions, and, ideally, aspire to gain recognition by that community (Kapcia, 2005). This emigration also included study abroad, bringing greater prestige than graduation from a Cuban university for those whose family circumstances allowed it, or who gained a scholarship [RFR; GP]. While many chose this option in a US college or university [RFR] (Pérez, 1998: 406–11), others chose France [GP] or Spain [CL], the latter proving especially welcoming to young Cubans in search of study.

Those remaining in Cuba sought outlets and support through the well-established tradition of the groupings around *tertulias* (organised literary and philosophical gatherings) and cultural magazines. Cuba's literary culture had long been based on this tradition, usually relying on the prestige bestowed by a well-known writer (effectively the group's mentor) or on the funds and spaces provided by a moneyed patron. That had been true of the nineteenth-century *tertulias*, and also, in the twentieth-century Republic, with Fernando Ortiz and the *Grupo Minorista* (Kapcia, 2005: 45 and 77–9). Magazines arising from these groupings were by definition usually short-lived and always of limited circulation, although two – *Cuba Contemporánea* and *Revista de Avance* – had enjoyed longer lives and achieved some well-earned prestige (Wright, 1988).

In the years immediately before the Revolution, the most famous group was that around the magazine *Orígenes*, whose artistic mentor was Lezama Lima but whose material patron was José Rodríguez Feo, until the two fell out, the latter then founding *Ciclón*, with Piñera, in 1955. For Lezama, *Orígenes* was the latest of a long series of ephemeral magazines, but it became the most successful, lasting eight years and gathering most of Cuba's established and promising poets in a collective statement of aesthetic views which sought to reject the ideas of politically or socially committed art and seek a genuinely Cuban art in an approach that partly echoed the 'art for art's sake' ideas of Hispanic *modernismo*. Indeed, the place of *Orígenes* in the evolution of a literary culture before 1959 was unmatched, because not only did the group gather together many of Cuba's leading poets of a particular generation but it also created – among those of the next generation who remained associated with the group (Fernández Retamar, Pablo Armando Fernández, Fayad Jamís) – what effectively constituted one basis of the Revolution's *primera promoción* (first wave) (Goytisolo, 1970).

Ciclón was the other major magazine of the time. Filling a gap left by the disappearance of the two magazines associated with the communist party (known as the Partido Socialista Popular (PSP) from 1944) in the late 1930s and 1940s, *Mediodía* and *Gaceta del Caribe*, it largely adopted a politically committed approach, albeit never as explicit as the earlier PSP organs, which – together with the popular radio station Diez-Mil – had contributed to some public awareness of the importance of culture.

The other major grouping – of direct relevance to the Revolution's first cultural generation (and especially to ICAIC and *Lunes*, many of whose founding members came from the group) – was *Nuestro Tiempo*. Created in 1950 (largely out of the more informal Cine-Club of 1948) and based in a group of like-minded, politically aware, young writers and *cineastas*, this group not only adopted a very different posture to *Orígenes*, but was also increasingly influenced by Marxist aesthetics and by notions of the popularisation of art.

As a result, despite the evident failings of the context in which literature struggled to survive, Cuba did possess something of a literary culture by the 1950s. Indeed, the Universidad de la Habana's Escuela de Artes y Letras in the 1950s acted as a valuable forum for the appreciation not just of literature in general (and Spanish-language literature in particular) but even of Cuban literature, already studied seriously [EDL; RFR; GP]. Moreover, this culture included a strong tradition of seeking to spread appreciation of art beyond the narrow confines of the educated middle class and elite.

However, this reminds us that this literary culture was always rather narrowly defined, always somewhat exclusive – especially to the educated bourgeoisie [EDL; CL] – and generally little appreciated by the wider public, especially among the middle class where either a kind of perceived philistinism reigned [AAM] or where reading tastes tended to be driven more by North American models, increasingly publicised – in translation – by popular weekly magazines or the Spanish translation of *Reader's Digest* (Pérez, 1999). In a Cuba where the ability to read English enjoyed considerable intellectual and social prestige – perhaps more than anywhere else in Latin America – there was an inevitable gravitation towards those models, even in cultural circles; if, in the first thirty years of the century, Paris had been the Cuban writers' cultural Mecca, by the 1950s Faulkner and Hemingway were the models and New York the magnet.

That said, however, literature and literary figures did enjoy considerable prestige among Cuba's educated and cultured classes, more than any other cultural form. There were several reasons for this special place in the cultural hierarchy, starting with the historical prestige bestowed by Martí, whose status as *héroe nacional*, as well as being one of the Hispanic world's leading exponents of *modernismo*, enhanced the relationship between literature and national identity; if a poet such as Martí could enjoy the status of an *Apóstol* and die leading a cavalry charge in Cuba's final War of Independence, then poetry, and literature, might after all be more than just a pastime for effete intellectuals. Hence, as every Cuban child learned to read and quote Martí, as his verses were reproduced in textbooks, magazines or monuments – especially after 1953 (his centenary, when over 500 works on him were published (Hennessy, 1963: 354) –, a *literato* at least, if not literature per se, enjoyed a special esteem in Cuban perceptions of culture. This meant that the important exception to the general neglect of literature was the widespread awareness that, where literary activity and renown had some relationship with 'the nation', it had a social, political and national value beyond its aesthetic merit.

Literature's special place was then further enhanced as some of Cuba's writers became famous beyond the island, enjoying a prestige rarely enjoyed by Cuba's musicians, for example (although the international fame enjoyed by Wilfredo Lam and René Portocarrero potentially put the visual arts on the same plane). Thus, in addition to Martí (and, to a lesser extent, his fellow *modernista*, Julián del Casal), Cuban literature was recognised by the outside world through the work of the *negrista* poet Guillén, and the novelists Carpentier and Lezama. In a postcolonial and nationalist society, where external recognition of national expertise was especially valued, their fame added to literature's prestige.

Finally, Cuba's high levels of literacy by regional standards (although lower than the Southern Cone countries), coupled with the 'Americanised' urban middle class's willingness to engage in some sort of recreational reading, meant that appreciation of literature – even if not necessarily Cuban literature – existed in potential.

Therefore, pre-1959 might not have been the cultural desert which is often painted in broad-brush strokes. Indeed, literature enjoyed some advantages over other genres, and the makings of a literary culture did exist, however small, limited and distorted by cultural colonialism. The basis already existed, therefore, for literature to be accorded an unusual place within the Cuban cultural hierarchy and canon, and even within the processes of cultural revolution and decolonisation. The events to follow were to throw all of this into question and begin a radical and often fraught search for definitions of literary culture and revolution that created all kinds of tensions, but also opened up new opportunities.

Notes

1 References within square brackets are used throughout this study to indicate material provided in the interviews conducted by the three authors, and correspond to the list of interviews at the end of the book.

1

Locating literary culture in the trajectory of the Revolution

The Revolution's political and economic trajectory

Although historians disagree about the precise timing of the Revolution's various phases, there is some consensus. The first six to twelve months were clearly characterised by euphoria, unity and uncertainty about the process's ideological direction. However, radicalisation soon began, rooted in several factors: the 1956–58 guerrilla experience; the influence of radicals like Che Guevara or the PSP; the sense of popular empowerment created by the early reforms and growing participation; the departure of the elite and middle class; and the nationalist response to growing US hostility. This all created inevitable tensions within the revolutionary alliance, which began to splinter; by July, many liberals had left the government.

US opposition was crucial. Rooted in old prejudices and mutual misunderstanding, and in Washington's fear of the PSP, this emerged clearly with criticism of the agrarian reform of May 1959; although the reform was moderate, US sugar interests (fearing expropriation) pressured Washington into opposition. Then, after the Cuban search for trade diversification produced a Soviet–Cuban sugar–oil deal in February 1960, this opposition grew; when US oil companies (persuaded by Washington) refused to refine the Soviet oil, they were expropriated, leading in turn to Washington's reduction of Cuba's annual quota of US sugar purchases. When an angry Cuban government seized US interests, the quota ended, and, in autumn 1960, the first trade embargo was imposed, relations being finally broken in January 1961. Then, on 17–19 April 1961, came the long-expected CIA-trained émigré invasion, at the Bay of Pigs (or Playa Girón), repelled by the Cuban army, militias and local Comités de Defensa de la Revolución (CDR). Meanwhile, on 16 April, Fidel Castro first declared the Revolution to be 'socialist'.

For a short period Cuba seemed to be heading towards a Socialist Bloc model. In 1961, the three rebel groups – the guerrillas' 26 July Movement, the PSP and the small guerrilla group, Directorio Revolucionario Estudiantil – were merged in the Organizaciones Revolucionarias Integradas (ORI). Economically, the government nationalised industries and utilities, collectivised agriculture in 1963, and began receiving Soviet material and financial and human aid, Cuban–Soviet trade thus partly filling the gap left by the US withdrawal and embargo. However, this trend was interrupted by three seminal crises. Firstly, some PSP leaders' attempt in 1961–62 to influence the new Organizaciones Revolucionarias Integradas (ORI), under Aníbal Escalante, led Castro to condemn and demote them, replacing ORI by the 26 July-dominated Partido Unido de la Revolución Socialista de Cuba (PURSC, 1962–65) and then in 1965 the Partido Comunista de Cuba (PCC, hereafter 'the Party'). Secondly, in October 1962 came the Missile Crisis, resulting from Soviet offers of military protection; when Moscow agreed to remove its missiles, the Cubans felt publicly betrayed. Finally, an economic crisis followed; although partly due to excessive Cuban ambition and the costs of adjustment from traditional dependency, many blamed it on Soviet advice and lukewarm Soviet support.

What followed was a debate about a practical strategy for creating socialism in an underdeveloped economy: while more orthodox communists saw this as 'scientifically' impossible, many ex-rebels (led by Guevara) argued differently. The debate ended around 1965 with the adoption of a widespread radicalism. Economically, it began the so-called 'moral economy', moving away from Soviet nostrums towards an intense centralisation (especially in 1968, when the Revolutionary Offensive nationalised all remaining 56,000 small businesses) and, inspired by Guevara's belief in the power of consciousness, an extensive reliance on voluntary labour and belief in egalitarianism. This was all geared to a would-be record sugar harvest (*zafra*) of 10 million tons in 1970, seen as the platform for economic independence.

Politically, those same years were characterised by constant mobilisation (for labour, defence or socialisation) rather than formal structures; for example, the new Party held no national Congress. Instead, what dominated daily political life were the several 'mass organisations' created in 1959–62, to spread the Revolution and link the leaders with the grassroots. These especially included the militias, the neighbourhood CDRs (now the principal mechanism for political socialisation), and the organisations for women (the Federación de Mujeres Cubanas (FMC)), private farmers (the Asociación Nacional de Agricultores Pequeños (ANAP)), workers (CTC) and students (FEU and the Federación de Estudiantes de la Enseñanza Media (FEEM)), all of them involving and politicising most Cubans in the many collective tasks.

Internationally, Cuba was now isolated, expelled from the Organisation of American States in 1962 and under full US economic sanctions from 1963. On one side, it was assailed by one superpower, determined to destroy what many Cubans saw as the long overdue nation-building process; on the other side, many felt betrayed by the other superpower, now seen as conservative and complicit with imperialism. Hence, 1961 saw the start of an active strategy of fomenting revolution abroad, challenging both US hegemony and Soviet caution. After the secret US guarantees in 1962 not to invade Cuba, this strategy was enacted actively, driven by Guevara's theories and training pro-Cuban guerrilla groups across Latin America. Successes were few, in the face of US strengthening of the region's militaries and the Left's split between pro-Cuban radicals and pro-Moscow orthodoxy. With Guevara's death in Bolivia in 1967, it seemed to end.

This had also evolved into a wider 'Third Worldism', as the Revolution – as example, people and material – was spread to struggles in colonial Africa. In 1966, the Moscow-organised Tricontinental Conference in Havana, for Third World radical and nationalist forces, was won over by Cuban arguments, making Cuba the vanguard of anti-colonial struggles.

By 1968 this radicalism was in crisis. The economy was struggling under the unorthodox strategy, with falling production and Soviet reluctance. The Revolutionary Offensive was the last straw, and, when the 1970 *zafra* failed, unbalancing an already fragile economy, another rethink beckoned. The outcome was a sustained process of 'institutionalisation' and consolidation, replacing the previous (often haphazard) mobilisations, egalitarianism, *guerrillerismo* (guerrilla ethos) and arguments with Moscow by a return to economic orthodoxy, with more decentralisation, wage differentials and material (rather than 'moral') incentives, allowing the Socialist Bloc's trading organisation (the Council for Mutual Economic Assistance (CMEA)) to accept Cuba as a member. By 1975 a new economic system was in place, and recovery began, raising wages and living standards and introducing a degree of consumerism, based on Eastern European manufactures.

The political system also became institutionalised. In 1975, the Party held its First Congress and began to grow, increasing tenfold by the

1980s, and, in 1976, the Revolution's first Constitution was enacted. A new, Soviet-style pyramidal system of electoral representation, Organos de Poder Popular (OPP), was also created in 1976, consisting of three tiers of assembly (municipal, provincial and national), the latter indirectly elected. While the new system never formally replaced the CDRs, the latter did decline in political significance.

The political tone also began to change, with the rise of those advocating greater proximity to Soviet models and the decline of those following Guevara. Internationally, Cuba was more compliant, retreating from its former public antipathy to Soviet policies and its commitment to armed struggle. While this also reflected realism (since governments in the region and Africa were now more ready to end Cuba's isolation), it meant a significant shift in Cuba's definition of revolution.

One outcome was a tentative détente with a Carter-led United States, whose overtures in 1977 resulted in mutual partial recognition, 'interest sections' being established in third-party embassies in each other's capitals; in 1979, some Cuban-Americans were allowed to return for family visits. However, this led to popular resentment and protest over the differences between Cubans' living standards and the apparent wealth of many returning emigrants; when thousands stormed the Peruvian embassy in April 1980, seeking exit visas, the authorities responded by allowing a huge boatlift (of some 125,000) from the port of Mariel, swelling those numbers with released prisoners and some of the more problematic intellectuals.

By 1981, this moment of improved US–Cuban relations had passed, as a Reagan-led United States reinvigorated the Cold War, identifying Cuba as the force behind the revolutions in Nicaragua and Grenada. It also ended because of growing US fears about Cuba's increased international activism, especially in Angola; for a new overseas strategy had emerged, sending *internacionalistas* (Cuban teachers, experts, medical workers and even military personnel) to countries requesting such aid (ultimately affecting over forty countries). Besides easing potential frustrations among Cuba's young (whose rising expectations were otherwise not easily met) with opportunities to travel and access to hard currency, and fortifying ideological commitment among the *internacionalistas* (inevitably working in poorer countries), this strategy gained Cuba many politically useful friends across the developing world, leading to Cuba's election as leader of the Non-Aligned Movement in 1979.

Hence, when the besieged MPLA government in newly independent Angola requested Cuban help against a South African invasion (backing UNITA and FNLA rebels), Cuba immediately dispatched thousands of troops to halt the incursions; their numbers rose to over 200,000 over fourteen years, culminating in the victory at Cuito Canavale in 1988, which ended the South African threat (and ultimately the apartheid regime). Cuban troops were also sent to Ethiopia in 1979 (against a Somali invasion), with smaller contingents serving in Equatorial Guinea and Syria and with military advisors in Nicaragua, Grenada and many African countries.

The reheating of the Cold War also contributed to the rise of Gorbachev in the Soviet Union, which created clear problems for Cuba, given his determination to improve relations with Washington at the expense of support for Cuba. This added to existing Cuban fears that the strategy of Soviet-linked 'institutionalisation' had problematically created a bureaucratic, privileged and less responsive Party and an ideological weakening, with the new materialist consumerism, especially as the CMEA entered crisis. By 1984 this generated another rethink, the 'Rectification of Past Errors and Negative Tendencies', launched formally at the contentious 1986 Party Congress and targeting more than the Gorbachev threat: specifically the need to streamline economically, combat Party bureaucratisation and privilege, and return to an earlier preoccupation with 'the nation'.

However, just then the Socialist Bloc, CMEA and Soviet Union all collapsed in quick succession in 1989–91. Apart from the resulting deep psychological trauma and fears (with the United States, glimpsing the possibility of eliminating the Cuban 'problem', further tightening the embargo in 1992), the unprecedented scale of the unfolding economic crisis was beyond anyone's worst nightmare. The sudden disappearance of 90 per cent of Cuba's imports and 60 per cent of her trade, of secure sugar markets, and essential imports of oil, fertiliser and food staples, plus a 35 per cent economic collapse in three years, all affected production, energy generation and transport, bringing desperate shortages, which, with demoralising prolonged power cuts (*apagones*), short-time working and increased pressure on Cubans to find individual and often illegal ways to employment, hard currency and contraband, threatened the post-1959 basis of loyalty and commitment. When, in August 1994, disturbances broke out in Havana, protesting at the shortages and the authorities' forceful treatment of attempts to escape Cuba, the Revolution's existence seemed threatened, especially as the government's Mariel-like response (allowing Cubans to leave) produced an exodus of some 35,000 *balseros* (rafters).

After an initial strategy of battening down the hatches – declared in August 1990 as 'the Special Period in Peacetime' (effectively a war footing) – the ensuing debate focused on two things: how to save the Revolution and which elements should be saved. This debate (evident in the 1991 Party Congress and the new workplace *parlamentos obreros* (workers' parliaments)) produced an unprecedented programme of reforms: legalisation of the US dollar, now able to circulate freely as part of a 'dual currency' (driving the devalued Cuban peso (henceforth known as *moneda nacional*, or MN) from many areas of the economy); limited self-employment (*cuenta propia*); greater toleration of joint ventures with foreign investors; the conversion of state lands into cooperatives; and the shift from sugar towards mass tourism. The result was a steady growth from 1995. The debate on the 'essence' of the Revolution took longer.

Given the urgency of economic survival, political reform was postponed, leaders relying on the depths of loyalty while the immediate problems were addressed. However, there were signs of shifts. In 1992, new *barrio*-level Consejos Populares (People's Councils) were created and spread, recognising that, as the state's ability to provide weakened, most Cubans had retreated to their immediate local community for solutions; although they were administrative rather than representative, they emphasised what was called the *comunitario* (referring invariably to the local community), returning to the Revolution's 1959 roots. The National Assembly also became directly elected, reversing recently declining electoral participation. Finally, in 1993–94, the authorities reached out to groups previously seen as problematic, especially the Catholic Church and the Cuban-American community, the latter now a source of hard-currency remittances and a community in transition, its younger generation and more recent economic migrants being less intransigent politically. In fact, those years saw a renewed emphasis on *nación*, reflected in changes to the Constitution (stressing the Revolution's Cuban and *martiano* – from Martí – heritage) and the tolerance of religious believers (*creyentes*) inside the Party.

However, the opening to the emigrant community was interrupted in February 1996, when two planes piloted by Cuban-Americans (scouring the Florida Straits for illegal *balseros*) ignored US and Cuban warnings and entered Cuban airspace; when they were shot down, this forced the hitherto reluctant Clinton Administration into accepting the Helms-Burton Act, to tighten the embargo further. Taken together with Clinton's policy towards Cuba (a 'twin track' of maintaining the embargo while courting 'civil society' with cultural and academic links), this led the Cuban authorities to question US links.

However, the Fifth Party Congress in 1997 confirmed moves towards greater inclusion and participation, reflected in 1998 by the Pope's visit to Cuba, which, despite his history of destabilising and stalwart anti-communism, brought thousands of Cubans onto the streets, largely to celebrate recovery from the economic hecatomb. This mass manifestation reminded Cuba's leaders that, while 1975–89 had underplayed the mobilisations of the 1960s, the post-disturbances rally of August 1994 had possibly saved the Revolution, by strengthening flagging morale. This realisation was then enhanced in late 1999 by the six-month long campaign to bring six-year-old Elián González back to Cuba: with the first youth-led rallies of January 2000 – under the FEU and Unión de Jóvenes Comunistas (Union of Communist Youth, UJC) – came an awareness that young Cubans (rather than being 'the problem' and the Revolution's Achilles heel) could be mobilised effectively. Thus, retrospectively, a new strategy was declared to have begun in January: the *Batalla de Ideas*.

Focusing on youth, on ideological reinvigoration (to resist imperialism, the dollar and the corrosive effects of economic reforms), and on a return to the energy of the 1960s, the *Batalla* took several forms: a new UJC-run educational revolution, which saw intensive training of young Cubans to fill gaps in a range of urgently needed professional roles (e.g. nurses, teachers, social workers) and which also involved old people in higher education; a sustained effort to popularise culture, on a par with the campaigns of the 1960s; repeated mass protests against US actions; and a new 'internationalism', with thousands once again sent abroad, especially to support Chávez's 'Bolivarian revolution' in Venezuela.

Indeed, this confirmed a new reality: with the 'pink tide', a more supportive environment in Latin America had eased international pressure on Cuba. This was needed, because the new Bush Administration, indebted to the electorally crucial Cuban-American lobby after 2000, further intensified the embargo (in 2004) and began to supply the usually fragmented illegal opposition. When the Cuban authorities responded by arresting seventy-five opposition activists in spring 2003, the European Union abandoned its usual stance of critical dialogue and, for two years, followed the US line by imposing diplomatic and aid sanctions.

By 2005, however, the costs of the *Batalla* were evident, exhausting the activists on whom it relied and creating inefficiencies and growing youth alienation. Moreover, many doubted the long-term effects of such mobilisation. The problem was partly solved by Fidel Castro's illness and temporary handover to his brother, Raúl, in July 2006; for, while Fidel generally preferred such mobilisation, Raúl was seemingly more committed to participation through formal institutions, believing in a stronger Party. Indeed, the Party had been neglected for a decade (the 2002 Congress failing to materialise); therefore, once Fidel resigned formally in January 2008 (Raúl being elected president in February), the new emphasis became clear, with government changes and a drive against petty corruption, pilfering, 'labour indiscipline' and the counterproductive dependency culture. Simultaneously, formal consultation through the Party and the mass organisations was emphasised, to improve communication and restore public confidence in the system's effectiveness and accountability. Finally, in April 2011, the long-postponed Sixth Party Congress confirmed Cuba's new direction, with a programme which stressed massive cuts in government expenditure and the government payroll, and with increased self-employment and small enterprises.

The Revolution's social trajectory

This long process of political change since 1959 also saw a parallel process of social change. The most immediate change was to the class structure, produced by the exodus of the old elite and middle class from 1960; by the early 1970s, almost a million had left, mostly for the United States. While the political effects were mixed (creating an electorally powerful and solid support for the embargo, but removing a potentially damaging opposition and contributing to internal unity), the economic and social effects were also mixed, siphoning off much-needed expertise (which would take a decade and much costly investment to replace) but, by removing a whole class, changing Cuba's social character permanently.

Moreover, the properties which these people abandoned became a valuable resource, being either used as educational or community institutions, or to solve the more pressing housing needs, with thousands of shanty and slum-dwellers being moved into them in multiple-occupation patterns, completely changing the social and racial character of formerly bourgeois residential areas. Urban reforms (1959,

1960 and 1966) went further, abolishing renting and eventually making around 80 per cent of Cubans into owner-occupiers, able to pass on (but not sell) their new property. In the 1970s, volunteer-labour construction *microbrigadas* (micro-brigades) were then used to construct hundreds of apartment blocks, using prefabricated materials and creating new urban districts.

Every such reform had a racial impact, the black population having previously been disadvantaged in employment, wages and access to services. Furthermore, in 1959 discrimination was prohibited, and a strategy began to re-value Afro-Cuban culture, rescuing hitherto marginalised dance forms and acknowledging the Afro-Cuban contribution to Cuban history. Although this approach often treated black culture in 'folkloric' terms (with those advocating black consciousness being considered politically divisive), Cuba's greater involvement in Africa and the Caribbean in the 1970s had an impact in re-valorising black Cuba and the African heritage, as fundamental to Cuban history and *cubanidad* (Cuban-ness).

The other major rapid social change came in education. Firstly, massive investments saw new and refurbished schools, to redress the shortage of provision; then, in 1961, came the Literacy Campaign, realising one of the promises of 1953 and building on a 1959 literacy drive within the guerrillas' Ejército Rebelde (Rebel Army). In summer 1960, an ambitious campaign was launched to eliminate remaining illiteracy (then approximately 23 per cent) in one year, even if this meant bringing the education system to a halt (Foreign Office, 1961: 2–3). There were several aims: to eliminate an embarrassing ill (which, after two years of revolution, had not been attacked systematically); to lay 'the foundations necessary for the planned rapid build-up of a socialist state' (Foreign Office, 1961: 1); to weaken the hold of the Church (by then openly opposing radicalisation); and to strengthen the drive towards greater integration between black and white and between urban and rural Cuba (Foreign Office, 1961: 2–3). More cynical observers added other aims: given Cuba's growing isolation, to find a field of social activity more successful than any other Latin American country, to appeal to the 'peasants and the lower urban classes' (Foreign Office, 1961: 1) and, of course, to indoctrinate (Foreign Office, 1961: 2).

The scale of the task was vast: it meant educating around 800,000 people, with an education workforce depleted by emigration. Hence it was addressed with military-like detail and scope: the Comisión Nacional de Alfabetización (national literacy committee) included representatives from the Ministry of Education (MINED), the militias, the Asociación de Jóvenes Rebeldes (AJR – the 26 July Movement's youth wing), the FMC, and many other pertinent bodies. The workforce was then divided into *brigadas* (of 2,000), themselves subdivided into four *batallones* (battalions), each in turn divided into five companies, and each company into three platoons, of thirty-one *brigadistas* each (Foreign Office, 1961: 5).

On 6 June 1961, with the Campaign under way, the government nationalised all private education with effect from 8 July; in Havana alone, this brought under collective control some 150 schools (*Revolución*, 1961b: 2). Even after that, investment continued in follow-up programmes and ambitious schemes to radicalise urban youth by having them study and work in the countryside. It also contributed to the initial moves to open up universities to working-class entrants, although policy changes in the 1970s made university entrance more selective, since, with employment guaranteed to all graduates, it was argued that Cuba should not produce more graduates than it could employ.

This rural focus was also an early characteristic of the Revolution's social strategy. Besides the educational and agrarian reforms (dramatically changing rural lives), investment strategies from 1963 prioritised the countryside as the main area for the development of infrastructure, social provision and employment – even at the cost of urban Cuba (especially Havana), which stagnated in comparison.

Employment was also addressed, attacking Cuba's massive informal sector and tendency towards idle labour outside the sugar harvest (i.e. half the year). This meant three measures: the implicit permanent employment arising from the agrarian reforms, especially on the collective *granjas del pueblo* (people's farms); the growth of the public sector (as nationalisations increased and a welfare state grew), creating work in the resulting bureaucracy; and legislation in 1969–71 which outlawed wilful unemployment, or *vagancia* (idleness), as anti-social, implying an obligation to guarantee jobs for all.

There were of course inevitable downsides to this provision. Expectations rose, but there soon developed a 'dependency culture', assuming permanent state provision regardless of one's input; overstaffing led to falling productivity, inefficiency and a corrosive absenteeism (especially in 1968–70); and selective university entrance denied access to thousands of young Cubans with talent and expectations, creating a growing pool of potentially discontented youth. This latter problem was finally admitted in the 1990s, the *Batalla*'s educational impetus being partly aimed at such people, who, if completing one of the new intensive professional training courses (especially as *trabajadores sociales* (social workers), who became seen as the *Batalla*'s 'shock troops'), were guaranteed a university place.

Employment was also central to another major area of social change: women. Here, the main problems to be addressed were discrimination in employment and salaries, *machismo* and the expectations on women to do a 'double shift' (*doble jornada*) as both carer and breadwinner. Under FMC pressure, the former was tackled by campaigns to get women into work, maximising an underused resource and boosting self-esteem; in many areas women thereafter dominated, but their overall labour contribution grew too. The provision of free childcare was necessarily expanded to allow for this, and the FMC campaigned for other changes such as the legalisation of divorce and abortion, and, after the prohibition of prostitution, retraining those women affected. *Machismo* proved more deep-rooted; the 1975 Family Code stipulated men's domestic contribution, but the problem persisted, the *doble jornada* often becoming a *triple jornada* (triple shift), as political activism came into the equation.

The legalisation of divorce and abortion directly antagonised the Church. Before 1959, it had been socially weak, by Latin American standards, based in the white middle class and with many clergy being Spanish. Hence, as the Church's social base emigrated and the hierarchy began to oppose the radicalisation, Cuba's leaders felt justified in harassing and marginalising it, expelling many Spanish clergy in 1961. Eventually, Vatican pressure on the Church created a *modus vivendi* with the Revolution, and, after a brief moment of confrontation in 1992–93, Church fears about social disintegration led to a consensus with the Cuban authorities and a pattern of accommodation.

The Church's dilemma was compounded by most other religions' more conciliatory relationship with the Revolution, especially the Baptists, Methodists and Presbyterians (all traditionally based in Cuba's more pro-Revolution black population) and the largest religion, the syncretic Afro-Cuban based *santería* (literally, religion of the saints). Although, initially, some leaders dismissed *santería* as superstition, a more relaxed attitude prevailed, creating a closer relationship, and the Party's 1992 tolerance of *creyentes* was especially aimed at *santería*.

Healthcare was also dramatically improved; given the emigration of expertise, initial efforts focused on prevention, through education, inoculation and sanitation. By the 1970s, however, with a newly trained generation of personnel, the emphasis shifted to cure and greater provision, expanding medical staff, eliminating most tropical diseases and increasing life expectancy rates to First World levels. Overall, therefore, the whole social revolution was fundamental to support for the Revolution. Hence, the 1990s' crisis threatened that support, obliging the authorities to maintain at cost the levels of provision. That crisis had other deleterious effects: as the dollar and tourism created a two-tier economy, some inequality re-emerged somewhat dangerously for the Revolution; equally, the state's inability to provide full employment (though guaranteeing sixty per cent of unemployed Cubans' salaries), or the usual levels of energy or transport, undermined the old structures of community and social integration. As Cubans foraged independently, seeking individual solutions to immediate needs, in family, locality and illegality, faith in the benefactor state weakened, as did the old collectivist spirit of solidarity.

Culture and Revolution: the parallel trajectory

Within this trajectory, we can now identify the general patterns of the evolution of culture within the Revolution. Usually this tends to be interpreted according to two criteria. Firstly, it is assumed to have been determined by clearly defined official statements of cultural policy; the most notable were Fidel Castro's *Palabras a los Intelectuales* (words to the intellectuals) speech of 30 June 1961 – with its famous, but often misquoted, 'central' words: 'dentro de la Revolución, todo; contra la Revolución, nada' (inside the Revolution, everything; against the Revolution, nothing) and the Final Resolution of the notorious 1971 Congress on Education and Culture (which defined art as *un arma de la Revolución* (a weapon of the Revolution) and which also condemned homosexuality). The second criterion is the succession of apparently significant events, most obviously the closure of the *Lunes de Revolución* cultural supplement in 1961, the drawn-out *caso Padilla* in 1968–71, or the *quinquenio gris* of 1971–76.

However, this tendency overlooks two realities. Firstly, cultural policy was not always defined, especially early on, instead often resulting from a combination of empirically developed positions, constantly shifting politics and a few specific statements – the latter often reflecting or codifying, as much as determining, existing developments. Secondly, such identified 'events' are always seen outside Cuba in terms of what emerged publicly and of what either corresponded to previous expectations of art under communism (based on the Socialist Bloc experience) or, alternatively, of what contradicted those expectations. Nonetheless, some things were clear, even in 1959–60, despite the ideological uncertainty. In March 1959, ICAIC became the Revolution's first cultural institution, and, as one of the first institutions of any kind, demonstrated the importance of culture to the new Revolution. There were many significant aspects. Firstly (partly learning from Soviet, Mexican or Spanish Republican experiences), it showed the importance of film to the revolutionary project, in spreading the revolution, inculcating a new consciousness and rescuing the previously denigrated or forgotten past. Secondly, it showed the continuing influence of the pre-1959 *Nuestro Tiempo* group, whose political coherence and collective activism made them one of the few pre-revolutionary groups to survive, although formally disbanded. Finally, since ICAIC was largely the initiative of Alfredo Guevara – a PSP member but also an old student friend of Fidel Castro from 1948 – it showed the ability, in the inchoate political context, of one individual to influence policy and create a space.

Another pointer followed in April 1959, with the creation – again an individual initiative (of the leading 26 July activist Haydée Santamaría) – of the Casa de las Américas cultural centre, which clearly indicated the importance of a Latin American dimension, before that became politically explicit in 1960. Although Casa has since been best known for its literary importance, it soon housed departments for art, music and theatre, and a department for literary research, fundamental to a Cuban approach to literary theory. One outcome was that Casa became a protective space for Cuba's visual and plastic arts, proving to be the basis for the flourishing of the genre – echoing ICAIC's role in developing popular and classical music (Benedetti, 1971: 18), possibly ensuring that the visual arts did not see the same scale of exodus as literature (Benedetti, 1971: 11). Moreover, like ICAIC, Casa's wider significance also lay in its emergence out of radical approaches to the question of culture.

Beyond these two institutions, culture was the responsibility of the new MINED's Dirección de Cultura (cultural department). This partly reflected pre-1959 traditions (Raúl Roa having led a similar department in the 1940s), but also indicated an early didactic purpose to culture. By 1960, thinking had shifted enough (towards a fundamental political role for culture) to create a specific institution, the Consejo Nacional de Cultura (National Council for Culture (CNC)); taking shape in January

1961, this was an embryonic Ministry, but, lacking a prestigious and powerful national champion and, with ICAIC and Casa remaining outside its remit, it always lacked ministerial status.

Nonetheless, the CNC reflected two realities. Firstly, it indicated a growing awareness of the Revolution's need to develop a more coherent (rather than ad hoc) strategy and to give culture a more prominent role (rather than subordinate it to education); secondly, it confirmed the rise of PSP activists within the Revolution's structures. For, while filling gaps in the emerging, but still inchoate, state, and using their experience and organisation to influence grass-roots and even national leadership, so too in culture did they begin to become significant, especially people (such as José Antonio Portuondo, Mirta Aguirre, Edith García Buchaca and Joaquín Ordoqui) who, having once been active in the PSP's newspaper, *Hoy*, and its radio station, Diez Mil, already had clear ideas about the relationship between culture and socialism, based either on the 1920s' Soviet experience or, more ominously, on the more restrictive 1940s. Either way, they saw culture having a more didactic purpose.

However, they did not monopolise the field, because of the energy and cohesion of the *Nuestro Tiempo* group, which, though politically close to the PSP, espoused more unorthodox aesthetic views, focusing on the need to bring art to the people. Interestingly, the PSP influence within the CNC survived the post-Escalante clear-out, suggesting that their didactic approach to culture corresponded closely to the preferences of the 26 July Movement's leaders; this was significant because an alternative, more eclectic, approach (focused on a cultural vanguard) was offered simultaneously by *Lunes de Revolución*, already effectively setting itself up as an arbiter of the new culture.

Established in March 1959, as the Monday cultural supplement of the 26 July Movement's newspaper, *Revolución*, at the instigation of Carlos Franqui, the latter's editor, and Guillermo Cabrera Infante, the young writer and film critic, it attempted to repeat in Cuba the role of the *Revista de Occidente* in 1930s' Spain: to bring the Cubans up to date with the latest developments in, and the best of, modern world culture. In fact, *Lunes* was largely staffed by young writers and artists who, in self-imposed exile in the 1950s, had become familiar with such developments and with the new aesthetic precepts of Paris and New York, especially an eclectic belief in cultural free expression and a Sartrean notion of the intellectual's role as society's critical conscience.

However, given ICAIC's existence and once the CNC was created, the *Lunes* position reflected a debate about cultural authority. For, de

Literary culture in the trajectory of the Revolution 25

facto and explicitly, the *Lunes* group considered that their artistic ideas represented the correct approach to any 'cultural revolution', since they saw themselves as the Revolution's parallel cultural vanguard. Hence, while they challenged what they saw as the outmoded and inappropriate positions of the pre-1959 *Orígenes* group, they also challenged both ICAIC's claims and, increasingly, the CNC's arguments and purpose.

Therefore, it was significant that the dispute in May 1961 which ultimately ended *Lunes*'s existence arose from a fierce argument over a film – *PM*, made by Orlando Rodríguez and Sabá Cabrera Infante, for, as *Lunes* spread into TV and film, it encroached on ICAIC territory, generating a battle for cultural authority and power. Hence, when ICAIC (with official authority to determine film distribution) refused permission to show the film in the Rex, Havana's remaining private cinema, because of its political insensitivity and aesthetic taste, ICAIC prevailed.

That did not end the matter but, rather, started an intense debate, expressed first in three weekly Friday meetings in the BNJM, between intellectuals and government ministers and officials, from which came the *Palabras*. The usual interpretation of the speech is that it was ambiguous, solving nothing, or defining limits rather than possibilities, as seen in its 'central' words. However, the speech in reality was much more complex (Kumaraswami, 2009a) and much less ambiguous than suggested, the meaning of the *dentro-contra* ('within-against') dichotomy being much more inclusive than feared by those already and increasingly disposed to see Castro's words as confirming the supposedly baleful and restrictive influence of ICAIC, the CNC and 'communism' (Kapcia, 2005: 133–4). These fears were, of course, especially strong when what emerged was the eventual closure of *Lunes*, explicitly replaced by *Gaceta de Cuba*, the organ of the new Unión Nacional de Escritores y Artistas de Cuba (the writers' and artists' union (UNEAC)), often seen as a copy of the Soviet model.

However, UNEAC actually turned out to have a more protective than regulatory role, at least for its first seven years. For example, 1962–66 saw a series of fierce debates (overlooked by those arguing that *Palabras* ended all debate) about definitions of revolutionary culture (Pogolotti, 2006); these, although often bitter and even personal, and usually between those close to the PSP and those challenging their positions, were given ample space in *Gaceta de Cuba*, undermining the idea of UNEAC as a spineless tool of an emerging 'Stalinism'. Hence, the BNJM meetings and *Palabras* were the start, rather than the end, of debate about culture and Revolution, because the *Gaceta* debates (repeated in, and extending to, the equally 'official' *Cine Cubano* and *Cultura 64*) focused on the definition of revolutionary art, cinema and literature, the question of what was acceptable art within a socialist revolution, and the continuing (and by no means closed) question of the freedom of cultural expression. In a display of openness, they included the question of the appropriateness of western film (sparked by ICAIC's decision to show *La Dolce Vita*) – Alfredo Guevara arguing with the PSP's *Hoy* – and on the desirability of socialist realism in literature (Ambrosio Fornet arguing with the PSP's Portuondo). Then, when one such debate centred on the existence of an independent publishing house, Ediciones El Puente, with bitter recriminations inside the 'group', UNEAC stepped in to provide the latter with printing facilities and finance in 1965.

Subsequently, in 1968 (although there is still no clear evidence of this) it is widely suggested that UNEAC's president, Guillén (a long-time communist), responding to calls within UNEAC, pressured the government to close the infamous Unidades Militares de Ayuda a la Producción (military units to aid production (UMAP)) – work camps for 'misfits', such as supposedly wayward youth, homosexuals or religious Cubans. Also, in 1968, when two UNEAC prize juries awarded its poetry prize to Padilla and the theatre prize to Antón Arrufat, despite fears about politically suspect content, UNEAC still published the books, albeit with a 'disclaimer' as a preface.

Meanwhile, in 1967, after all the debates about abstract art, the French Salon de Mai exhibition was successfully brought to Havana, generating criticism of some of the exhibits but demonstrating a continuing willingness not to follow preordained categorisations of 'good' or 'acceptable' art, and even to embrace the most daring avant-garde art from the capitalist west.

Of course, UNEAC's behaviour over these issues could also be a sign of weakness rather than strength, the tolerance shown perhaps reflecting uncertainty about how to think; moreover, it took UNEAC three years to protest effectively against the UMAP. If this is true, it is revealing that weakness, rather than reputed monolithic strength, allowed opportunities to flourish.

Around this time, the decision was also taken that, rather than leave writers and artists to exist independently on the proceeds of their work, the Revolution's duty was to provide for them, not by paying royalties for their production but by paying them to work within the cultural apparatus (as editors, critics, bureaucrats, and so on), in the educational structures (typically the universities), in the media (TV or the press) or in the diplomatic service, as cultural attachés – the latter role also allowing them to represent abroad the best of contemporary Cuban culture (although another possible interpretation is that this also removed them from positions of potential influence inside Cuba, with many of those thus employed coming from the *Lunes* group).

Meanwhile, the differences between the two national newspapers (*Revolución* and *Hoy*), both remarkably allowed to flourish independently for six years, was also seemingly settled by the creation in 1965 of one single newspaper, *Granma*. While this fusion is usually seen as ending *Revolución*'s independent voice, it also, of course, ended *Hoy*'s existence, at a time when the new PCC's Central Committee was clearly dominated by ex-guerrillas rather than the PSP. Equally, the creation of *Caimán Barbudo* in 1966 was ambiguous. Ostensibly replacing the problematic El Puente as a vehicle for the younger generation, it was the cultural supplement of *Juventud Rebelde*, the UJC organ, and displayed a more explicitly militant stance than El Puente, arguing for art under socialism to be committed and popular. However, it always showed a willingness to be faithful to a notion of the aesthetic avant-garde.

One reason for this apparent contradiction is that this militancy arose not so much from Cuba's constantly redefined communism but from a shift in cultural thinking towards solidarity with the Third World. Writers such as Edmundo Desnoes (Desnoes, 1967) and Fernández Retamar (1980) intellectualised this shift, but its most explicit expression came in January 1968, with the Havana Cultural Congress, to which the Cuban authorities invited unorthodox radicals from the emerging European New Left, challenging Socialist Bloc norms. The Congress most clearly emphasised the Revolution's commitment to the processes of cultural decolonisation, for its prime target was cultural colonialism, debates focusing on the role of art and the intellectual in the processes of decolonisation.

What followed was the magazine *Pensamiento Crítico*, produced by a group of young intellectuals associated with Guevara's ideas, and adopting explicitly revolutionary positions but in unorthodox ways, admiring (and publishing) radical ideas from the New Left and the more revolutionary ideas of decolonisation, dependency theory, and from an increasingly radical Third World.

Indeed, it is within this context that one should interpret the 1967 decision to reject what was seen as the imperialist notion of copyright, confirming formally what had anyway been empirically true since the first organised strategy to pirate foreign textbooks (see Chapter 3);

although this decision also abolished royalties, that had less of an impact at the time, since writers were by then fully employed by the state. Hence, both aspects of the decision were in keeping with the Revolution's growing commitment to cultural decolonisation.

By 1971, that process had shifted further, intensified by the *zafra* crisis and the accompanying realisation that a reassessment might soon be necessary. Culturally this was manifested in the 1971 Congress on Education and Culture and the final denouement of the arguments with, and about, Padilla. However, what is conventionally seen as a new cultural 'Sovietisation' (parallel to the supposed 'Sovietisation' of economics and politics) ought perhaps to be better understood as an even more militant manifestation of the same Third Worldism, defiantly expressed just as Cuba's economic unorthodoxy was about to be forced back towards a more Soviet-oriented definition.

As for Padilla, he had been seen increasingly as 'problematic', since he had, in a 1967 article, defended the émigré Cabrera Infante's *Tres Tristes Tigres* novel, comparing it to the 'inferior' *Pasión de Urbino* by Otero; hence his problems with the 1968 UNEAC poetry jury had a specific context. By 1971, his position had worsened, as his Socialist Bloc travels (as a Prensa Latina correspondent) brought him into contact with dissident intellectuals and what he increasingly saw as the grey and repressive reality of culture in those countries. Finally, a few days before the Congress, he was detained by the authorities, accused of consorting with counter-revolutionary foreign elements, and forced to deliver a public *autocrítica* (self-criticism) to a UNEAC audience, accusing several of his friends of the same 'crimes'. This whole episode unleashed a storm of criticism from several European and Latin American intellectuals, although many of the latter soon retracted their support for the protest.

Hence, when what had been planned as a congress on education suddenly became 'Education and Culture', with an apparently hard-line approach to culture and the intellectual, probably in response to the protests from European intellectuals and their Latin American counterparts (seen as slavishly European in their thinking), confirming for the Cuban leadership a continuing problem of cultural imperialism. Hence the Congress was more about Cuba's militant cultural nationalism and an emerging strategy of a newly 'Third Worldist' cultural decolonisation than a simple repetition of a perhaps familiar Soviet-style clampdown.

That said, however, the post-1970 political reassessment had a clear cultural parallel, with less flexible protagonists of the early cultural debates moving into positions of power within the cultural apparatus, especially the CNC, now under Luis Pavón. This reality, legitimised by the 1971 Congress's positions, began what was later known as the *quinquenio gris*, which saw the previous imperative of regulation become a sustained restriction. This was when several of those previously associated with *Lunes*, who had (especially while abroad) entertained aesthetic ideas now seen as antithetical to the new ordinance, or who were evidently homosexual or Catholic, were marginalised, some being given insultingly menial tasks and many prevented from publishing. Those most affected tended to be in the theatre (Gallardo, 2009), pre-1959 writers or the Revolution's first generation; indeed, many younger artists benefitted from the spaces created by the clampdown. Moreover, the *quinquenio*'s effects were not felt equally; while local or provincial radio, for example, was relatively flexible and tolerant, television (under a Pavón-style hard-liner, Jorge Serguera) was notoriously narrow-minded and orthodox [SA].

This period formally ended in 1976, with the creation of the Ministry of Culture (MINCULT), under the former Education Minister, Armando Hart, an ex-26 July leader. Not only did MINCULT replace the CNC but Hart made it abundantly clear that he sought more space for expression and hoped to institutionalise more coherently a cultural infrastructure which, for all its appearances, had lacked coherence, entrenching people and stances in specific spaces of influence. The new strategy, however, consolidated itself slowly, resisted by those in the middle levels whose positions had come from adherence to the *pavonato* (the period of Pavón's leadership). Hence, many of the marginalised remained un-rehabilitated, especially if sexuality had been the reason for their treatment. In fact the use of the Mariel exodus to encourage some intellectuals and artists to leave Cuba (most notably Arenas) indicated the continuation of old prejudices, as well as a determination to close an embarrassing chapter.

Meanwhile, however, a more coherent cultural strategy had begun to emerge. While earlier statements of policy (1961, 1968, and 1971) had largely reflected attitudes, the 1975 Party Congress saw a detailed strategy emerge, in the final agreed *Tesis y Resoluciones*. This outlined a series of statements on culture's role in the new Cuba, and detailed several specific aspects (not least a significantly revived emphasis on the *nación*), culture's relationship to education and employment, and, equally significantly, the necessary improvement of material conditions for cultural expression. The latter included the 1977 decision to reinstate the authors' rights and royalties abolished in 1967.

Since post-Padilla external perspectives of Cuban culture remained focused on individual cultural freedom (Franco, 2002), many of these new approaches were missed. One such was the creation of the Centro de Estudios Martianos (Centre for Studies of Martí) in 1977, which rescued Martí from the relative oblivion of the previous period (when it was unclear how to locate him within the newly socialist definition). Another was the rescue of the relatively forgotten element of the *Palabras*: the *instructores de arte* movement and its offshoot, the *movimiento de aficionados* (amateurs' movement). This was the ambitious campaign of the early 1960s to spread the practice of art, music, dance and drama to all Cubans, via workshops in factories, schools and localities, which remained rather ad hoc after the initial expansion, partly because of uncertainty about culture and 'the masses': should the Revolution raise their cultural level, enabling them to appreciate 'the arts' (a perspective curiously shared by both *Lunes* and the PSP) or should they be enabled to become practitioners? Now, however, a new drive to follow the latter option saw the creation of Casas de Cultura in each *municipio* – reflecting Socialist Bloc practice and 1940s' Mexico – and also, for the first time nationally, the parallel *talleres literarios*, acknowledging that literature was not an exception and that, in principle, people could be trained to write.

Subsequent statements of cultural policy did not differ much from this 1975 platform: the 1980 and 1986 Party Congresses largely confirmed existing policy, although addressing a new concern about artists' conditions, shared with increasing openness by UNEAC. Indeed, after over a decade of relative weakness, UNEAC now came into its own, joining the post-1986 debate about, and reassessment of, identity and engaging in a 'cultural rectification' which began a rethink about the *quinquenio*, including the first coining of the term by Fornet in 1995 (1995: 15), and the reinsertion of those intellectuals and artists affected. UNEAC also began to exercise its original role as a forum for writers' and artists' concerns, expressing their complaints about conditions, echoing the 1975 Congress. The 1988 UNEAC Congress saw this emerge more fully, as the assembly heard a range of complaints about conditions and materials. This partly arose from the dynamism and political skills of the new president, Abel Prieto (who now began to become a key player in the cultural world and inside the emerging apparatus of the cultural authorities), but it also reflected the mood of the time.

However, this was all halted abruptly by the 1989–94 crisis, which had a traumatic effect on the arts. Not only could the state no longer guarantee to provide materially for Cuba's artists and writers, but the disappearance of transport, energy, paper and other consumables left the artistic community without a public, without physical spaces and without necessary materials.

That same crisis, however, also brought unexpected cultural benefits, for, given both the state's weakness and the new freedom to possess dollars, Cuba's artists were suddenly encouraged to earn hard currency through their work, either abroad (recording, performing, selling art, etc.) or inside Cuba (using the growing tourist market). Some genres could respond immediately: the visual and plastic arts boomed, selling and exhibiting abroad and at home, often following primitivist or exotic themes and aesthetics; the film industry was forced into uncomfortable but lucrative commercial collaborations with foreign production companies, increasingly catering for the overseas market; Cuban popular music, capitalising on its existing appeal, boomed most of all. Not only could members of the prestigious Ballet Nacional de Cuba work abroad, but the universal popularity of the 'Buena Vista Social Club' phenomenon and what was broadly called *salsa* saw both traditional musicians and younger rock, *reggaetón*/Cuban hiphop exponents permitted to work abroad, and saw a diet of 'Buena Vista' Cuban music served to the incoming tourists.

This all led to a shift in cultural policy, from the 1980s' concern with democratisation and *aficionados* to a new focus on the professional artists, since their status and economic importance were now unprecedentedly enhanced. In fact, as many professionals denigrated what they saw as the outmoded practices and ideas of the *instructores* in the Casas de Cultura and the poor quality of the *aficionados'* work, coupled with a shortage of funds, the movement stagnated and many Casas closed.

However, the same crisis bringing disaster and opportunity to Cuba's artists also saw a new development in the long trajectory of cultural democratisation, forced on the artistic world by the same factors which militated against any high-profile public support for artists' cultural production: namely a tendency towards a 'localisation' of activity. For, just as all Cubans sought daily practical solutions to their material needs in their immediate locality, so too did Cuba's artists and public start to seek cultural solutions locally; the former began to practise and disseminate locally and likewise the latter began to participate in culture.

This now generated a revival of the Casas de Cultura after 2000, stimulated by the *Batalla de Ideas* and seeking to develop the new *casas comunitarias* (community centres), *barrio*-level cultural institutions. That same *Batalla*, however, had also targeted a further cultural issue, surfacing as a widespread concern in the late 1990s: the apparent decline of reading as a practice, through either the impact of the internet and television (echoing similar Western concerns) or the decline of available books, time for reading and encouragement to read (Chapter 5 develops this in more detail).

In fact, even before the *Batalla*, policy shifts were already evident, with a 1995 Programa de Cultura y Desarrollo (programme for culture and development), outlining the basic principles of cultural policy; most notably these indicated as the first priority the conservation, defence and development of Cuba's cultural heritage and identity (a theme reiterated repeatedly), but also stressed support for community cultural activity, through enhanced participation, with an equal emphasis on artists and community (Casanovas Pérez Malo, 1997). Indeed, this whole strategy had generated a range of programmes focusing on the prioritised themes, all coming into greater focus after 2000.

This particular strategy, together with the priorities of the *Batalla*, highlights the remarkable continuity in the Revolution's broad cultural policy, which, regardless of ups and downs at different times, has always emphasised popular participation, the fundamental importance of culture to both 'the Revolution' and integration, and the need to constantly expand (production, dissemination and reception). In other words, the *Batalla* echoed the Literacy Campaign forty years earlier, and the emphasis on *nación* and community, equally, echoed the 1959–61 concerns. Throughout, it was also clear that, although it might be possible schematically to divide the Revolution's political and cultural trajectories into defined periods or phases, there was not necessarily an easy match between those apparently similar trajectories; either this was because culture followed its own route and momentum, or, more likely, because, just as those recognised 'periods' in the political or economic sphere hid a multitude of contradictions and complexities, so too in culture was there always more to 'cultural policy' and cultural practice than met the eye or fitted preconceived expectations.

2

Understanding literary culture in the Revolution

This chapter presents an overview of the existing scholarship on Cuban literature since 1959. The first section thus offers a critical review of the ways in which the whole question of literature and revolution in Cuba has been treated to date, underlining the very valuable work undertaken both inside and outside Cuba, but also exploring the many areas of misunderstanding, neglect or omission. This forms the foundations for a review of the theoretical models and critical currents that have informed this study and an explanation of their usefulness and function within it. The chapter ends by setting out the conceptual tools and methods that have been developed here in order to understand literary culture in the Revolution.

Many commentators have noted the teleology (based on ideological continuity, commitment and consensus) which, it is argued, has been constructed by the Revolution's political leadership to facilitate its survival and, in the cultural field, to explain the role of literature and the writer over fifty years. This teleology, they note, is almost always dependent on a minimisation of crises, ruptures and conflicts, if not a blindness towards dissent and dissidence. However, in response to this version of history, a series of alternative narratives have been constructed over this same period which are similarly exclusive, universalising or neglectful in their understanding of Cuban culture over fifty years, and which we can divide into two general tendencies: firstly, those which focus almost uniquely on moments of extreme crisis and conflict; and, secondly, a narrative focusing almost uniquely on the state as all-powerful, monolithic and largely unchanging. Both approaches are underpinned by a perspective which seeks evidence of the subjugation of art (and the individual autonomous artist) to the dictates of socialist politics and ideology.

Furthermore, a range of external factors, including the limits of technology (with the Cuban publishing structures always obliged to prioritise internal readerships over international ones), limited access to new technologies, the siege mentality and the insistence – perhaps making a virtue out of necessity – on following endogenous models, are set against a backdrop of economic instability, if not extreme economic crisis, and have contributed to the fact that scholarly work on Cuban literature published on the island, by Cuban-based intellectuals and academics, has rarely left the shores in significant enough numbers to make an impact on international debates and trends in literary criticism and theory. However, given the network of academic and cultural institutions that exist in Cuba, the scope of publishing outlets for their work (academic and cultural journals and magazines, edited collections and monographs), the reality that many individuals engage simultaneously in cultural journalism, academic writing and creative writing, and, more recently, the digital textual spaces affiliated to newspapers and cultural institutions, it is only logical that a vibrant and dynamic culture of literary criticism and theory has evolved.

Nevertheless, other than a handful of cultural theorists (e.g. Ortiz, Fernández Retamar) and a small number of literary and cultural scholars resident on the island (notably Luisa Campuzano, Nara Araújo and Fornet), all of whom have been published internationally, in Spanish or in English translation, an outsider's understanding of the state of Cuban letters is rarely influenced by these figures, with many non-Cuban scholars preferring to employ theoretical and conceptual frameworks developed outside Cuba in order to understand the island's cultural production.

The list of scholarly works on literature and Revolution published outside Cuba, however, is long and exhaustive; hence, closer attention is paid here to those published more recently. Logically, the changing approaches generally follow the thrust and direction of wider critical movements. The first phase of analyses tended to focus on the boom which the Revolution engendered, mostly through anthologies with commentary (Cohen, 1970), or offering a largely impartial survey of trends and patterns (Miranda, 1971) and literary genres (Menton, 1964 and 1975). However, with the first exodus of well-known writers and, above all, with the *caso Padilla*, the predominant approach became a focus on tensions between the socialist state (rather than 'the Revolution') and the individual writer, with particular attention to those writers who had experienced problems or chosen to leave (Coulthard, 1967 and 1975; Del Duca, 1972; Franco, 1970; Ortega,

1973). Even the most subtle commentators on the new literature tended to assume an inevitable dichotomy between the two (Casal, 1971; González Echevarría, 1985).

From 1961, this general approach dominated the overall treatment of the topic, being further reinforced by theories of cultural resistance emerging from Latin American cultural studies (Franco, 2002). In addition, and quite logically given the movement from literary to cultural studies and the prominence of a notion of diasporic Cuban identities after 1990, a focus on questions of identity (such as gender, race and sexuality) that are narrower than the notion of national identity in Cuban literature, emerged, similarly assuming an inherent tension between individual or minority groups, on the one hand, and a monolithic state, on the other (Bejel, 2001).

Since the 1990s, and under the influence of now established critical and analytical methods in cultural studies, scholars have aimed to explore the engagements of authors and texts with their social, political and historical moments. Catherine Davies's much-needed study of women's writing in the Revolution (Davies, 1997) made an important contribution to making visible an area of Cuban letters which, for some thirty years, had remained unrecognised both on and off the island. Similarly, post-2000 studies have focused on how individual authors and texts responded to wider social and political discourses, namely, the New Man (Serra, 2007), the theme of money in the literature of the Special Period (Whitfield, 2008) and the representation of the Chinese in Cuba (López Calvo, 2008).

Finally, the concept of nation and identity in literature was broadened to include the diaspora, both as a result of the emigrations of the 1990s and as part of a wider scholarly interest in diasporas, migration and transnational movements. Ariana Hernández-Reguant's 2009 edited volume examined how the force of diasporic perspectives, both political and cultural, transformed notions of *cubanidad* into '*multicubanidad*' ('multiple Cuban-ness') in the 1990s. However, although noting that the embracing of a 'deterritorialised discourse' was merely a pragmatic response to economic crisis, her essay, and many others in the volume, perhaps overplayed the importance of diaspora and transnationalism in the 1990s, discrediting as they did the weight in many quarters of a continued discourse of national sovereignty, and choosing to focus almost uniquely on those practices which articulate specific visions of identity. She stated: 'In the island, being Cuban no longer meant, necessarily, being revolutionary – in the sense of being committed to a nationalist political project. It meant, more than ever, being cosmopolitan' (Hernández-Reguant, 2009a: 10). Furthermore, the volume as a whole, although providing an often original, subtle and detailed examination of culture and ideology in the Special Period, was underpinned by a reading of the Cuban cultural state apparatus as monolithic, static and essentially unchanging.

Throughout the decades, and within the wider patterns of interest noted above, scholars have largely chosen to pay attention to one of three areas of Cuban literature. Firstly, the vast majority have preferred to study selected individual writers – mostly the 'greats', such as Carpentier or Guillén (with their literary production often decoupled from the Revolution) or, alternatively, the 'problematic' writers, such as Lezama, Cabrera Infante, Arenas or Piñera, this time creating a clear link between the writers and their milieu, often seen as repressive or intolerant. In this regard, a clear assumption evolved that, given that Cuba lost or silenced its best literary talent after 1959, those who remained on the island had no choice but to 'trade in' artistic quality for political credibility, and thus become mediocre artists. As recently as 2002, in an edited collection of articles on literature, Roberto González Echevarría noted that the canon of Cuban literature experienced a sudden *decadencia* (decline) after 1959 (González Echevarría, 2004: 28), producing no writers comparable in artistic quality to Lezama, Guillén, Carpentier, Cabrera Infante, Ortiz, or Gastón Baquero, but stating, in no uncertain terms: 'Burócratas y comisarios con abultadas obras sobran: la historia los absorberá' (2004: 29) (bureaucrats and commissars with extensive oeuvres abound: history will absorb them). González Echevarría was by no means alone in his categorical evaluation of the Cuban canon, and in the automatic assignation of Soviet influence to Cuban political and, thus, cultural life; indeed, the question of internal and external models of literature and the writer, and their respective quality, prestige or value, will form a central part of the theoretical discussions in this book.

Secondly, substantial attention has been paid to selected genres, such as prose fiction (Menton, 1964 and 1975), detective fiction (Wilkinson, 2006), poetry (James, 1996), and *testimonio* (Kumaraswami, 2006). Thirdly, there have been occasional collections of interviews with individual writers (Bejel, 1991; Bernard and Pola, 1985; Kirk and Padura Fuentes, 2001). Either way, what has characterised, but also helped shape, the trajectory of this overall treatment has been a changing, but, we argue, always rather narrow and contested, notion of the 'canon'.

This changing canon of writers and texts, for forty years subject to a variety of literary and extra-literary forces has, since 1990, been more noticeably influenced by socioeconomic and cultural phenomena particular to the Special Period. This has led to the privileging (through translation and international marketing) of a handful of Cuban writers and, additionally, to an overwhelming emphasis on internationalising the literature produced by particular identity groups, such as women writers. Indeed, the unarticulated assumption seems to exist that postmodern notions of identity are the only viable explanation for subjectivity. Hernández-Reguant, for example, drew attention to the natural, although delayed, attention to 'the possibility of queer, black, feminist and diasporic vantage points' that was heralded with critical work such as that of Margarita Mateo Palmer (Hernández-Reguant, 2009b: 12). While attention of this kind is not to be minimised, and is certainly necessary to gain a more nuanced understanding of contemporary Cuban reality, a focus on Western notions of identity without an acknowledgment that other frameworks exist, reproduces dominant expectations without first questioning their relevance and validity. Although the picture is far more complex than a simple desire outside Cuba for now-familiar narratives of individual and collective crisis and dystopia or for texts that fulfil formulaic expectations of 'dirty realism', the failed revolutionary project or fractured and multiple identities, the distorting effects of commercial activity after 1990 on the changing canon of Cuban literature, and our understanding of the changing position of the writer, are hard to ignore.

The result of these dynamic trends in literary and cultural analysis has been that, over fifty years, most commentators outside Cuba have focused their scholarly attention, with few exceptions, on specific writers and their works, following an established method in literary, and now cultural, studies that fulfils a series of expectations about literature and the writer. The very necessary detailed textual analysis of literary works of particular writers, for example, has often been further informed by an interest in those writers who are, were, or had been, explicitly in conflict with the Cuban state, either as dissidents still on the island or as political self-exiles or émigrés throughout the revolutionary period. Indeed, the successive waves of emigration from the island have provided rich textual material for the literary analysis of work by émigré writers such as Cabrera Infante, Arenas, Padilla and, more recently, Zöe Valdés. In each of these cases, the dominant question for analysis almost inevitably centred on attacks on cultural freedom by the socialist state. As Fornet described in his speech during the much-publicised *Encuentros* (conferences or seminars) of 2007:

'A veces, hablando ante públicos extranjeros sobre nuestro movimiento literario, encuentro personas – hombres por lo general – que insisten en preguntarme únicamente sobre hechos ocurridos hace treinta o cuarenta años, como si después del "caso Padilla" o la salida de Arenas por Mariel no hubiera ocurrido nada en nuestro medio. A ese tipo de curiosos los llamo Filósofos del tiempo detenido o Egiptólogos de la Revolución cubana' (*La política cultural*, 2008: 46).[1]

Secondly, the (sometimes limited) commercial success outside Cuba of these same writers, and the scholarly attention resulting, has logically been awarded to a handful of 'bestseller' or commercially visible writers living on the island (writers such as Padura Fuentes or Mirta Yáñez), whose texts are easily available through having been published abroad. Thirdly, individual writers have seen portions of their work opened to international critical attention through the internationally published anthologies based on preferred identity groups and themes, and some participation in international prize networks that were a characteristic of the 1990s.

How, then, to explain these critical tendencies that have been so influential in moulding outside visions of Cuban literature? Perhaps the most obvious explanation for these analytical and canonical decisions can be found quite simply in the disproportionate prominence, recognition and textual space awarded to writers living outside Cuba compared to those living, writing and publishing predominantly on the island. Although the attempt to unite across national borders, to 'de-territorialise' Cuba, and thus heal cultural rifts between the island and the diaspora, was entirely praiseworthy, it once again obscured imbalances in access and exposure that were less desirable. While scholars outside Cuba were increasingly focused on removing Cuban literary production from its territorial anchoring and temporal limits (before and after 1959) in order to articulate a broader notion of nation and history, thus rejecting the validity of revolutionary literary canons, by doing so they not only reproduced and supported the structural imbalances implicit in literary production systems and mechanisms in the First and Third worlds, but also assumed that Cuban cultural policy and practice had been unbending in its reproduction of national sovereignty through culture. To speak of critical methods that questioned and rejected a so-called revolutionary narrative of *dentro* and *afuera* (within and without) [sic] (Birkenmaier and González

Echevarría, 2004: 16), was to tell only one side of the story, and a rather conventional story at that.

Nevertheless, it is not only conceptual desires and methodological debates that have contributed to these imbalances. One major challenge for those working on Cuba is, simply, basic access to source materials and perspectives published exclusively in Cuba. More recently, as the interviews in this book demonstrate, the influence of new technologies and the opening up of Cuba's cultural products to new markets has gone some way to redressing this difficulty, and a number of Cuba-based writers regularly negotiate the relationship between the national and post-national or transnational to reach wider audiences. This historical imbalance in exposure, however, and the assumptions that it created about literature, politics and the writer in Cuba, has been inflected in other ways, one of the most basic but also significant being the inevitable importance given to émigré memoirs as a source of reliable information about literary and cultural life in the Revolution.

Firstly, the question of reliability of memoirs is ambiguous, arising from an imbalance between the production and dissemination of self-narratives on and off the island. Cuban-based writers do not largely engage in self-narratives, except in brief press interviews, as part of collections of essays, or, more recently, as part of public cultural debates (such as the 2007 *ciclo de conferencias* (series of conferences) on the *quinquenio gris*). There are, of course, some exceptions, one of the most interesting being that of the late Lisandro Otero. His memoirs, published in Havana in 1997 as *Llover sobre mojado: una reflexión personal sobre la historia* (Otero, 1997), and then, in a revised version in Mexico in 1999 as *Llover sobre mojado: Memorias de un intelectual cubano, 1957–1997* (Otero, 1999a), and concurrently in Spain with the original Cuban title (Otero, 1999b), hinted at the political challenges and risks of Cuban self-writing, in terms of the necessity of creating dual narratives for internal and external readerships, and the inevitable selectivity that accompanied this dual mode of self-representation. By and large, nevertheless, constructing narratives of the lives of individual writers is normally the task of colleagues and friends, most typically as a part of commemorative collections or editions to recognise a prominent individual who has been awarded, for example, the annual *Premio Nacional de Literatura* (national literature prize).

Why, then, is the memoir not favoured on the island? Inside Cuba, there are many different pressures militating against a desire to write one's individual past as a coherent narrative. Firstly, while there is plenty of public interest in the memories of leading participants in key events or periods (especially now that some difficult periods are being openly reassessed), there seems little interest in reading about a writer's past. Secondly, therefore, there is unlikely to be much publishing interest in such books, partly reflecting canon and market forces but also reflecting a wider ethos of focusing on the collective picture and the ordinary life through testimonial writing, if at all, rather than on the individual picture and on what is essentially a minority, or even an elite, group. The recalling of contested times tends to come in Cuba through the collective processes of remembering (as with the 2007 *Encuentros*) but less to recall details or recount than to reinterpret, publicise, reintegrate or rehabilitate. Lastly, Cuban-resident writers simply do not share the émigré or exiled writer's need to defend or explain.

Memoirs written by émigré and exiled writers, however, are available in abundance and share particular characteristics which, it might be argued, are common to many traditional modes of self-writing. Firstly, émigré memoirs inevitably tend to have a selective memory, eliminating any commitment to the Cuban system, and any reference to the opportunities which the Revolution brought, and inevitably focusing on the problems, restrictions and pressures – that is, everything which supposedly drove them out. As with all traditional modes of self-writing, from the classical autobiography to the contemporary celebrity autobiography, they share an inevitable tendency towards post-hoc rationalisation, to reorder from the present moment of writing. Secondly, they tend to justify their subjectivities and lives through an elaborate dialogue which combines their consciousness of broad target audiences with the expectations of the Western literary and political communities to which they now belong. Most commonly, they see the repressive hand of Fidel Castro personally in the historical narratives they recount, and even in their own individual cases. Finally, by definition and following the pattern of political defectors, these writers tend to give themselves an importance (in Cuba, in the artistic world, etc.) that they did not necessarily possess in reality; in some cases, writers emigrated precisely because they were not central to decision making, or they left as children or young people, or simply for largely economic reasons.

Memoirs of exile intensify these motivations and objectives: driven as they are by a mixture of needs and desires – to expurgate past sins, to explain their abandonment of their homeland, to heal traumatic memories and personal loss – they are especially favoured among

Understanding literary culture in the Revolution 41

publishing houses in the United States and Spain, where they fulfil a strong cultural demand for readable narratives that reinforce the horrors of the Caribbean gulag, of the realities of Stalinist restrictions and the inevitable conflict between the visionary writer and the uncomprehending, if not downright repressive, state bureaucracy. This means, curiously, that many émigré memoirs are as political as they allege writing on the island to be, although, for those cultural commentators who follow these paradigms, the extent of politicisation is usually only recognised in its island-based version, and state repression becomes for these commentators a useful shortcut for evaluating and ultimately identifying literary quality (or the lack of it) in revolutionary Cuba: *pace* González Echevarría's irony-ridden description of the Cuban literary scene: 'el hostigamiento es el premio literario más sincero en Cuba, el verdadero juicio de valor de los mediocres que ven sus prebendas y privilegios amenazados' (González Echevarría, 2004: 23) ('harassment is the most genuine literary prize in Cuba, the real value judgment exercised by those mediocre figures who see their benefits and privileges threatened').

To a great extent, then, the expectations of many scholars have been constructed – and reproduced in critical practice – by prolonged exposure to such canons, narrative modes and a priori judgments, which, along with the difficulties of access to Cuban-published texts, both literary and academic, has given rise to the easy insertion of Cuba's literary figures and texts into models taken, perhaps at times simplistically, from the Soviet experience (itself much more complex than is sometimes assumed). What all of these approaches have excluded, therefore, are a number of critical factors or dimensions allowing us to gain a more comprehensive view and thus present a more diverse and nuanced interpretation of the evolution and contemporary state of Cuban literary life. Excluded, for example, is a broadening of the notion of 'the canon' to include those writers who are less known because they do not fit the patterns indicated above; that is, excluded because (i) they are simply not published or studied outside Cuba, in Spanish or translated versions; (ii) they have not published memoirs or other self-narratives which inevitably contribute to the visibility and prestige of the author, according to Western models of canon construction; (iii) their literary authority or cultural capital – in the form of texts and public recognition – exists predominantly in Cuba rather than in the centres of international canon formation. Although subtle commentators such as Hernández-Reguant have drawn attention to the increasingly complex and often competing networks of national and international relationships sought by Cuban artists and intellectuals in the 1990s, her perspective is nevertheless rather one-sided, stressing as she does how the national (revolutionary) capital of Cuban intellectuals has been recognised and prized abroad, but neglecting both how this symbolic capital has also been vilified abroad, and how the movement between national and international capitals has been unremittingly unequal: 'Cuban intellectuals – like visual artists before them – had to negotiate diverse intellectual circles while acquiescing to revolutionary ideology and hierarchy, for it was precisely their official status within the island that endowed them with a cultural capital abroad' (Hernandez-Reguant, 2009b: 6).

These inequalities and the assumptions that have both underpinned them and been regenerated by them, although for many decades the subject of scholars in postcolonial and subaltern studies, have only recently begun to be explored in relation to literature. Pascale Casanova's groundbreaking work *The World Republic of Letters*, published in English translation in 2004, although touching only briefly on the Latin American context, uncovered many of the mechanisms and strategies by which entrance to the autonomous world of literature is achieved by peripheral nations and their literatures and by which a global literary geography is constructed over time, obscuring inequalities in trade and competition between nations. Through the interventions of cosmopolitan and polyglot intermediaries (Casanova, 2004: 21), themselves 'naively committed to a pure, de-historicized, denationalized, and depoliticized conception of literature' (Casanova, 2004: 23), literary recognition – literariness – is conferred upon individual writers and, by extension, their nations. Through processes of repetition and recitation, these national literatures, or those texts which fulfil the centre's conditions of literariness – pure and autonomous – are granted access and integrated into the global literary system. The resulting canon, then, merely reflects the central articulation of literature as 'a kingdom of pure creation, the best of all possible worlds where universality reigns through liberty and equality' (Casanova, 2004: 12), but is in reality enabled by a complex network of mechanisms designed to confer literary status. While an understanding of the mechanisms that 'make' literature outside Cuba would make an important contribution to challenging dominant external paradigms of literature and the writer in Cuba, our concern here is with how literature comes into being on the island.

Here too, another key dimension largely excluded from the corpus of work on Cuban literature in the Revolution is an awareness of the mechanisms through which literature is produced in Cuba. Pamela Smorkaloff's studies of the world of Cuban publishing (1987, 1997) made an invaluable contribution to an understanding of the processes; however, given her focus on institutions and quantitative data, the studies inevitably ignored the question of writers as a whole. While the myth of individual (and, paradoxically, universal) genius is, nevertheless, very pervasive, a tradition of context-focused approaches to literature also exists. Robert Escarpit's seminal sociology of literature, first published in the 1950s, recognised that any attempt to uncover the mechanisms by which the written text became literature was both indispensable and controversial, posing as it did a challenge, according to the authors of the Introduction, to 'the classical framework of the man and his work' (Escarpit, 1971: 6). As will become clear in subsequent chapters, the autonomy of the literary work, the purity and unique originality of the artist, the hierarchy which values aesthetic worth over other kinds of worth (and literary discourse over other sociocultural discourses), are all constructions which reproduce the key theme of individuality in literary production in Cuba and elsewhere and which resist attempts to uncover the processes, structures and mechanisms which underpin the cultural practices that make up literary production. Escarpit's early championing of this necessary sociology of literature evolved in many directions in more recent decades.

The disciplinary area of book history, in particular, has made huge contributions to our understanding of how literature comes into being, how the values associated with it are established through the interactions of a range of elements which are ideological, practical, social and economic. John Brewer located the origins of individual literary value in the eighteenth century when, as a result of the emerging debate between money and art – new notions of intellectual property (the early commodification of literature) versus liberal notions of art (art as the ability to amuse and educate) – the literary text became associated with the individual author. Originality and novelty as indicators of the true author 'underscored the special relationship that the writer bore to his text. If a work was original, it was also unique, the distinctive consequence of a writer's imagination' (Brewer, 2002: 246).

Following Escarpit and others, then, it is possible to develop an approach that 'runs no risk of destroying the internal validity of works of art by distorting them, namely that of the study of the entire environment of literary creation, distribution and consumption' (Escarpit, 1971: 7). Such an approach – one that recognises the extra-textual context for literary production but does not assume that all texts are strictly determined by it – would necessitate examining a number of factors: firstly, all the processes which make up the literary 'circuit', what Robert Darnton refers to as the 'communications circuit that runs from the author to the publisher (if the bookseller does not assume that role), the printer, the shipper, the bookseller, and the reader' (Darnton, 2002: 11); secondly, all the institutions which are responsible for making that circuit flow – institutions that enable the writing, publishing, promoting and reading of literature; thirdly, all the pressures that are operating – social, economic, ethical and not just political.

Lastly, and here lies perhaps the most complex element, this approach would require us to examine the book both as an object but also as an activity or event enabled by each act of reading, in the journey from author to reader. As D.F. McKenzie expressed it: 'The book as physical object put together by craftsmen – as we all know – is in fact alive with the human judgements of its makers. It is not even in any sense 'finished' until it is read. And since it is re-creatively read in different ways by different people at different times, its so-called objectivity, its simple physicality, is really an illusion' (McKenzie, 2002: 190).

These dimensions necessarily mean stressing the wider context within which literary activity has operated. While the assumption, as seen in many of the studies listed above, is that the wider context consists of a particular notion of 'the state', the actual experience of the Revolution for most writers is not only 'the state' but also the provision of new opportunities, the impact of social change (both of course involving both promotion and regulation) and experiences such as the Literacy Campaign of 1961 and subsequent reading and education programmes. Indeed, one of the major areas of neglect in the treatment of literature and the Revolution is precisely related to the implications for literary activity of the Literacy Campaign, although it is clear from Castro's *Palabras a los intelectuales*, delivered while the one-year Campaign was in full swing, that the two were already clearly linked in theory and practice, and would thus be related in cultural policy making. This early articulation of policy and logic – the fact that a mass readership was quickly being constructed via the Campaign – suggests that the Campaign must have been fundamental to the future activity of literature, whether in the form of writers' expectations,

Understanding literary culture in the Revolution

the authorities' attitudes, readers' abilities and attitudes, publishing policies, and so on. Moreover, many of the conventional interpretations outlined above have not only been based on the de facto canons that have emerged through the imbalances of consecration and commodification between centre and periphery, but have also preferred to assess Cuban literature according to external paradigms of both art and politics, thus obscuring or ignoring the uniqueness of the Cuban experience. Even the most subtle recent commentators have tended to follow models of resistance that may be applicable to elements of the Cuban context, but are certainly not universally true. They thus assume an inherent opposition between state and citizen, between collective and individual, which is not always relevant. By applying those paradigms – such as notions of the 'captive mind', cultural resistance against political repression, globalisation, transnational commonalities – they often ignore what is obvious in Cuba, namely that the Revolution's trajectory, roots, nationalism, survival and participation all point to the uniqueness of literary activity on the island.

Here we come across an oddity: while Cuban 'exceptionalism' is often now accepted by political science, social studies or history (Hoffmann and Whitehead, 2007), cultural studies approaches to revolutionary Cuba have tended not to share that view, preferring instead to apply models of cultural expression and individual and collective organisation that emphasise the weight and impact of the state as the principal actor in regulating literary activity through reward and punishment. Thus, cultural activity in general, and literary activity in particular, has emerged as a field seen to be most in danger of undemocratic, if not downright repressive, state intervention. While external commentators have been keen to expose the ideological foundations of literature in the socialist system, however, the natural opposition in this model – the literary texts as a commodity under capitalism – has emerged magically free of ideology. Likewise, although usefully employing the work of Stuart Hall, Pierre Bourdieu and others in their exploration of cultural production as a social activity capable of generating individual and group agency (especially when applied to the complex terrain which emerged in the Special Period), many external commentators have been unable to recognise individual and group agency and autonomy unless it is associated with enterprise and commerce. Hernández-Reguant, for example, states that her edited volume on Cuba in the Special Period would 'track the agency of various social actors faced both with the constraints of the socialist bureaucracy and the possibilities opened by both new commercial stakeholders and foreign constituencies' (Hernández-Reguant, 2009b: 13).

We argue, however, that, while the interaction of external concepts – of literature, the writer, the state – may rightly guard against the risks of seeing Cuban literary life under the Revolution as a self-contained utopian sociocultural experiment, these must not be the only interpretations that circulate. It is thus important to uncover and assess the various functions of literature within the Cuban context itself, an exploration which soon reveals literature in the Revolution to be an aesthetic practice, but also with ideological, political, social, economic and symbolic levels of operation or interpretation, and which functions at both individual and collective, or social, levels. Thus, what is also often missed in external appraisals is a more complex view of the relationships between the individual and the collective in a revolutionary Cuban environment where the individual neither enjoys complete agency nor suffers complete subjugation to institutional or ideological forces, but, rather, experiences a dynamic negotiation with the collective. Here, one should remember the wider context and discourses in which this individual/collective relationship must be located, namely both the processes of nation-building – which at one level is what the Revolution has been about (Kapcia, 2000) – and postcolonial dichotomies and tensions regarding the adoption of either endogenous or exogenous models. In other words, incorporating all the above observations of neglect, assumption or imbalance, this book advocates a focus on literary activity as *literary culture*, a term which encompasses the wider context of policies, practices and discourses on literature, spans the whole revolutionary period, includes both the national and the international – identifying elements of coherence, continuity and contradiction over fifty years of revolution – and explores the vast range and complexity of all the mechanisms that have shaped literary activity since 1959.

Our understanding of 'literary culture' is thus informed by a wide range of approaches in cultural studies. Firstly, it takes a perspective which sees it not only as the product of individual or elite artistic practice (Eagleton, 2000; Williams, 1981) or the cultural economy (Du Gay and Pryke, 2002), but also as everyday sociocultural practice (De Certeau, 1984). Furthermore, our understanding also incorporates the newly emerging focus on cultural policy studies (Bennett, 2008; Lewis and Miller, 2003) as well as currents in contemporary cultural studies which examine mass and popular cultures (Du Gay, 1997; Hall, 1997). Paul Du Gay's formulation of the 'circuit of culture', in particular, although based on largely profit-oriented mechanisms within a capitalist context, can help to develop an initial theoretical framework for the Cuban case. His circuit involves six aspects: production, regulation, consumption, identity, values and representation. However, given that two of these elements – identity and values – are largely immeasurable, and already have an established literature focusing on them (not least in studies of ideology), the first step is to focus on those elements that can already be seen, naturally and without bending definitions or imposing a priori assumptions, as *processes*.

Given the relevance of the circuit model now common in cultural studies, a second step is to question how these cultural processes integral to literary activity can be measured; in other words, how does one evaluate the judgments made in order to take a text from author to reader? To return to McKenzie, the book is not an inert object but, rather, 'each and every one shared in a creative act, an expressive decision, within a definable historical context, to serve an author's intention, a bookseller's pocket, or an implied reader's comprehension of the "text"' (McKenzie, 2002: 190). In terms of theoretical work which has attempted to account for where and how (and by whom) cultural activity is assessed, the work of Bourdieu has been particularly valuable in both theoretical and methodological ways (Bourdieu, 1984, 1986, 1990). Bourdieu's contribution to the humanities and social sciences, and to a socialised understanding of culture, is too vast and exhaustive to explore in great detail here. Hence, what follows is a brief review of the relevance of his *oeuvre* to our object of study.

Given the conventional perspective of literature as a sacred or 'enchanted' field of activity, possessing an ineffable and indefinable essence, itself resting on notions of the uniqueness, originality and the autonomy of the writer and his work, Bourdieu's central contribution has been to reveal the mechanisms and strategies by which the collective – whether society at large, social class, dominant social group, or smaller sub-group – produce and reproduce the conditions of their existence: in other words, to explore artistic practice as a social construction which employs classificatory mechanisms in order to award acceptability, status, prestige (or 'distinction', in Bourdieu's terms). In particular, his work on *habitus*, or the internalised relationship with objective structures which allows the individual or group to 'get along' practically in the social world, has gone a long way towards explaining how individual and social groups interact productively (although, for Bourdieu, often largely self-interestedly) with the wider context in which they function. In particular, for the Cuban case, it allows for a more nuanced – and realistic – approach which privileges neither the individual nor the collective, neither individual free choice nor coercion by the collective. Given the often simplistic external assessment of Cuban writers and cultural actors who remained within the system – as being co-opted, coerced, socially engineered or simply opportunistic – it provides a means to understand how consensus and continuity have existed alongside crisis, conflict and rupture. Put simply, it allows us to understand these individuals both as individuals but also as social subjects engaged in a social activity.

Thus, the articulation of a relational model – which binds individuals, groups and entire societies in mostly consensual contracts with objective structures – helps to build a more subtle understanding of social and cultural activity which goes beyond the extremes of idealism (subjective individual motivation) and materialism (objective determining structures). For Bourdieu, then, the micro/voluntarist, and macro/determinist are all part of one single conceptual movement, and social existence encompasses the social, the cultural and the economic. However, his work on capital has also provided other insights: through relationality, once again, his work has served to explain how the legitimacy of a cultural practice (cultural, political, social) is always conferred in relation, or even opposition, to other practices, that is, via symbolic binarisms such as high/low, aesthetic/political. The types of capital (for Bourdieu, these are economic, social, cultural and symbolic) that build up over generations, and the mechanisms developed to award these (whether in the form of the awarding of educational credentials, admission to professional organisations, acquisition of specialised skills or the creation of objects that require specialised skills or knowledge in order to be interpreted or enjoyed) are all strategies to confer a new autonomy from traditional forms of dependency. The Cuban Literacy Campaign and massification of education, the provision of a publishing infrastructure, the creation of cultural institutions, then, could all be seen under this perspective as mechanisms for acquiring capital and, simultaneously, moving out of underdevelopment.

To return to the Cuban case, however, it is logical that perspectives developed from contexts external to the Cuban experience of revolution have not always explained successfully the exceptional nature of that

Understanding literary culture in the Revolution

reality: in general, they have neglected literature as cultural practice, preferring to see it as an elite or minority activity, or focusing on popular or mass cultural forms such as television, film and music; they have focused on ideological and social contexts which bear little resemblance to the Cuban case; they have often taken a broadly Marxist approach to cultural production and reception, specifically with the concept of culture industries developed by Adorno and the Frankfurt school. In short, they have dealt universally with cultural practices and cultural commodities under capitalism, especially those produced through processes of globalisation and transnational movement.

A more sophisticated analysis of literary culture in the Revolution thus requires the significant adaptation of existing cultural theories, and the incorporation of the work of Cuban cultural theorists, in order to explain in a more complex way its exceptional nature, and, of course, to go beyond externally grounded assumptions, imbalances and expectations which are only partially relevant to our object of study. This is because literary activity under the Revolution has meant, firstly, both the massification and the democratisation of a previously elite or 'high' cultural form, in a society not necessarily geared to capitalist ideas, and in a largely self-contained environment which, for thirty years and for a variety of reasons (both domestic and external), did not experience sustained exposure to outside influences; and then, since 1989, the fact that Cuban society and economy has experienced the effects of globalisation, but only in limited ways.

In recognition of these exceptional conditions for the development and evolution of a literary culture, it is essential to rethink our perspectives on a variety of elements that make up this culture, in order to understand better how individuals, groups, institutions, practices and policies interacted and informed one another over the revolutionary period. The book's method, therefore, is to use three conceptual tools to enable us to go beyond the normal approaches: the notions of spaces and agents; the notion of a continuum of the individual and collective, and the national and international; and the notion of value.

Spaces and agents

The concept of space has been theorised extensively (Massey, 1994, 2005; Lefevbre, 1991; Harvey, 1990). However, rather than embark on a theoretical discussion about the relevance of these theories to this case, we introduce the notion of space here as a methodological instrument which allows us to sidestep potentially misleading assumptions about literary culture and participation. Space here is therefore a comprehensive concept, encompassing physical space (the physical infrastructure for literary activity), discursive and textual spaces (magazines, conceptual groupings that recur in discourse on literary life), symbolic spaces (the sense of belonging or identification – or not – that such spaces provide), but also, lastly, the wider 'social' spaces – perhaps the most important being 'the Revolution' as space which excludes and regulates, but, at the same time, includes and enables.

Another aim is to go beyond conventional approaches to culture, which stress the weight of state power and the institution (the 'official') over the individual (the 'unofficial'), and instead to assume a relationship which is based on negotiation and broad consensus, and on a different model from that of 'state and civil society'. In most non-Cuban perspectives of Cuba, 'institutions' are usually taken to refer to the 'problem' of 'the state', seen invariably as a monolithic structure of necessarily restrictive and bureaucratic institutions – such as the CNC or UNEAC – all of them ultimately regulating (and thus also preventing) cultural expression. While it would be tempting to apply a Foucauldian approach of this kind, identifying the gatekeepers – both individual and institutional – who are the mediating mechanisms between the individual citizen and the ultimate power (the state), this model is not suitable for two reasons: firstly, its focus on the prohibitive and regulatory thrust of these mechanisms is overly negative; and, secondly, it assumes that the element that joins the individual and the state is inevitably working exclusively on behalf of the state, to implement top-down policies.

Another more suitable model, then, is to see the relationship between individual and state along a continuum, so that the mechanisms joining the two, and, indeed, the extremes of that same axis, are themselves dynamic and mobile, not just in conflict but negotiating a range of relationships, depending on the positioning of each in the wider context. Under this schema, the mediating mechanism – conventionally the notion of the state-sponsored formal institution, working on behalf of the state – can be replaced by the idea of space, a permissive and changing context in which cultural or literary activity is not only regulated and prohibited, but also allowed, even encouraged and protected.

Thus, the use of space as a conceptual tool both takes us beyond potentially simplistic assumptions about power structures and their ability to determine sociocultural life (or the state and civil society), even in a highly collectivist and politicised context. Furthermore, the concept recognises and addresses a basic reality: that, for long periods in the Revolution's trajectory, state structures were actually inchoate, evolving and undefined. In the 1960s this was partly through the very process of revolution (by definition constantly changing everything that it touched) and partly through deliberate policies, such as a so-called 'anti-institutionalism'. In the 1990s, that same state came under damaging attack following the debilitating economic crisis; the result was a state that was considerably weakened, leading to the development of many new spaces below the national state level.

Thirdly, 'space' allows us to recognise that, after 1959, what actually happened, empirically, was the gradual and incremental emergence of an inverted pyramid of spaces inside 'the Revolution', consisting of several cultural spaces below the national level. For example, the CNC was not the only mediating mechanism, as is often assumed. Within a few months, other entities emerged rapidly alongside the early MINED Dirección de Cultura, such as the BNJM, the Escuela de Artes y Letras, ICAIC, the Imprenta Nacional, the Editorial (or Editora) Nacional, Casa de las Américas, newspapers such as *Revolución* and its cultural supplement *Lunes de Revolución* and the cultural pages of the PSP's *Noticias de Hoy*, and publishing ventures such as El Puente.

However, these physical and symbolic spaces were not merely conduits for the effective cascading of top-down cultural policy; they also functioned as agents in their own right. The use of the term 'agent' here works in two ways that are especially appropriate. Firstly, it articulates the cultural studies idea of active engagement as an actor and subject (the institution as such, or under the direction and influence of an individual), thus invalidating the notion of a monolithic state, where each institution is a passive dependency of 'the state' or 'the Party', with no autonomy and allowing no leeway or room for negotiation and manoeuvre. Secondly, and more interestingly, it offers the opportunity of invoking the term in its everyday sense, as a broker, something (or someone) which mediates between actors or between actors and state. In other words, each of the defined 'spaces' is, or has been, not only a gatekeeper, moulding what is politically, socially, culturally acceptable (although this certainly has been an important role at specific moments), but, more generally has had the capacity to act both on behalf of the emerging 'Revolution' and on behalf of the writers, editors, promoters and readers on the ground.

Hence, following this dual use of 'agent', we can see the emergence of a structure, or set of networks, whereby each space has created, in turn, a series of other spaces below, and whereby the real focus of interest is neither the macro (collective, institutional, objective, state-led, determinist) nor the micro (individual, subjective, voluntarist), but the complex and heterogeneous relationships between the two ends of the spectrum.

The ideological continuum

Conventional approaches to the question of the individual and the collective in Cuba have largely focused on instances of opposition or conflict between the two, stressing the extremes of this relationship: either the individual crushed by the weight of collective, state-determined, decisions and discourses, or, alternatively, finding their singular voice and subjectivity in spite of a monolithic and inflexible state. The notion of a continuum, however, allows for the individual to be positioned simultaneously – including the potential for contradiction – at various points on the axis, a model which is especially apposite in a number of ways and for a number of social agents. For example, most writers in Cuba do not make a living solely from their literary production but combine this with roles within the cultural infrastructure – as *asesores* (cultural advisors), *promotores* (specialists in promoting cultural activity), editors, *investigadores* attached to specific institutions – where they exercise individual autonomy but also participate in group decision making and consensus. Equally, reading policies and programmes have been designed to encourage both solitary and collective enjoyment of literature; hence, since reading in all cultures is an activity that is both individually and socially constructed, a conceptual model that allows for dynamism, contradiction and multiplicity between the individual and social elements of subjectivity seems most suited to the revolutionary Cuban context. This model, then, is not relevant only for literary activity. Indeed, it could be argued that this was, and still is, essentially the matrix along which all ideological positioning has worked in Cuba since 1959, and thus actively allows one to build into the conceptual framework for an understanding of literary culture a recognition of the wider ideological context in which all culture has emerged, been negotiated and been realised.

The advantage of this continuum lies in three areas. Firstly, it underlines the continual need to recognise the importance of ideology in post-1959 Cuba (and thus not just thinking of ideology as emerging after the 1961 formal recognition of socialism, and then communism and Marxism-Leninism), growing out of pre-1959 traditions and the collectively empowering experience of revolution in 1959–61. Secondly, it emphasises the wider social context in which all cultural activity after 1959 developed – its collective imperative, purpose and motivations – which is a context that, as argued above, is usually ignored by conventional approaches to 'the writer' or to 'the reader' seen as a solitary individual. Thirdly, it reminds us that there has always been an element of individualism in all social activity in revolutionary Cuba (including in literature), with the individual seeking to negotiate space, a sense of belonging and an identity inside an environment that has always stressed the collective. One sub-category of this continuum, of continuing significance throughout the Revolution's trajectory, is also the tendency for writers to identify with small groups, often gathered around 'spaces' or agents (such as a given locale, a magazine or an individual mentor), or even with historical generations.

The point here is that, since 1959, individuals have always positioned themselves along this continuum, that position changing according to time, motivation, pressure or activity, and according to the prevailing emphasis on, or climate of, collectivism. For example, in 1961, *Lunes* and ICAIC acted at different points of that continuum, but ICAIC also encouraged individualism in some areas, at certain moments. Hence, ICAIC (often seen as the more 'militant' and politicised or 'heteronomous' of the early cultural institutions) was not simply collectivist in the sense of creating a climate to restrict individualism, while *Lunes* (usually associated with notions of creative freedom and autonomy) was not simply individualist, since the aim of the group behind the supplement was to improve the cultural levels of the collective, seeing their revolutionary duty as lying in that task.

What, though, does 'the collective' actually mean here? At one level, it can be equated to 'society', both the organised, regulated structures and processes of governance (theoretically created and operated on behalf of society) and the associative structures and processes of social patterns, responsibilities, duties and rights (often going by the loose term 'civil society'). The critical issue, however, is how collective is such an entity? The answer in part lies in how far it is perceived as legitimate by its members; but it may also lie in its evolution.

This brings us directly to Cuba, where one might convincingly argue that the system and 'society' are especially collective because of a very particular historical evolution. Certainly, the social and political patterns after January 1959 were actively collectivist (and directed towards collectivism), militantly so after late 1960, more defiantly so after April 1961 and, after the 'siege' was imposed, more relentlessly and restrictively so. This exceptional experience (of transformation, mobilisation, emigration and isolation) thereafter challenged what had been considered the normal patterns of the individual–collective negotiation before 1959; then, the individual's location on the continuum had depended on social status and economic capacity (the poor being more likely to be 'collectivised' in their poverty or apart residential patterns), and the collective had been more a matter of social mores (what was acceptable and 'normal') and a state apparatus which regulated through coercion or patronage. From 1961, however, the negotiations on the continuum became ever more conflictive, between the individual and a constantly changing collective.

At one level, this changing pattern was no different to those of any society and polity; in reality, it was very different indeed. This difference lay in Cuba's unusual combination of characteristics. These were, essentially: its history of late and postponed postcolonialism, followed by the special dilemmas, traumas and tensions created by a neocolonialism more legally defined than most other Latin American societies and then ensured through economic patterns; the resulting delays in the processes of nation-building and, after 1959, nation-rebuilding, made especially frantic and distorted by Cuba's unique geopolitical position within the Cold War; the whole process of social transformation within an essentially underdeveloped economy, with all the challenges, instabilities, tensions, and crises of identity which this created; the particularities of an identifiably socialist direction, always defined and redefined according to external pressures and influences and internal debates and needs; the whole experience of 'siege' and all that this implied for debate, group identity and belonging; and the steady loss of hundreds of thousands of people, depriving the remaining collective of much-needed expertise, intellectual leadership and social support, leading to a constant redefinition of the remaining collective, and what has been described as a 'conciencia de exilio' (Espinosa Domínguez, 2008: 32) (consciousness of exile). All of this can be argued to have created the idea of a collective as a shared state of mind (belonging to those who remain behind on the besieged island), as a unifying weapon (of defence and redefinition) and as a perceived solution (to the loss of expertise and the enforced isolation). Here, another element can be added to the idea of the Revolution as a matrix of *continua*: while the first continuum connects the individual and the collective, a second connects the national and international.

Although many conventional approaches to Cuban literature have stressed either the isolated, self-contained, stridently nationalistic nature of literary production under the repressive socialist state (one of the central bases for the depiction of literary life as impoverished, mediocre, heavily politicised), or the opposite of that – namely, Cuba's dependence initially on the Soviet bloc and, after 1990, on international allies or trading partners –, the reality is surely more complex. Notably, Cuba's cultural and geographical positioning, along with its necessary political and economic affiliation with other nations and continents, its programme of internationalism and the ideological and cultural exchanges of ideas and personnel which resulted from these initiatives, points to a complex relationship between the nation and the outside world.

Especially after 1990, when the need for joint ventures with international partners became an urgent necessity to ensure the survival of the Revolution (although the terms of these transnational alliances were not always clear or favourable to Cuba), and when the notion of a Cuban diaspora became a more common currency in cultural and intellectual circles, a model of Cuban cultural life which continued to follow the (always erroneous) pattern of *dentro-fuera* (rather than the correct *dentro-contra* relationship) could reveal only part of the picture. Indeed, one feature of post-1990 reassessment inside Cuba was a belated recognition of the need to include diasporic literature within the accepted canon (Espinosa Domínguez, 2008: 32). Equally, however, and as Jacqueline Loss has noted, a model which reduces the impact of international currents of thought and culture merely to Soviet imposition on its docile satellite in the Caribbean fails to take into account the transcultural and transnational sociocultural practices that emerged and continued to be transformed over generations in a postcolonial context (Loss, 2009: 107).

What, then, is the particular relevance of this axis of the matrix to literary culture? The identification of an axis connecting the national and international allows us to examine not only the conflicts between the two at a structural or institutional level, but also the agreements and negotiations between the two: a publishing infrastructure largely oriented towards an internal readership, which has been obliged, since 1990, to seek agreements with non-Cuban publishers and printers; the impact (although not exerting a mass influence) of new technologies, allowing Cubans to write for, and read, texts from abroad. Perhaps most crucially, given the Revolution's postcolonial and anti-imperialist underpinnings, this axis allows us to examine how individuals and institutions have attempted to negotiate a delicate balance between economic dependency, receptivity to international currents, the pervasive force of globalising tendencies, and an ideology of Revolution built on national sovereignty. Thus there emerges a picture of how Cuban literary culture has operated domestically and abroad, with periods of greater or lesser dialogue with a range of sociocultural, economic, political and ideological communities: the Soviet Bloc, the Caribbean, Latin America, the Third World, and, most recently, the Cuban diaspora and the Alternativa Bolivariana para las Américas (Bolivarian Alternative for the Americas) (ALBA).

Value

To return to the discussion of Bourdieu's notion of capital (Bourdieu 1986), what are the advantages and shortcomings of using a vocabulary of economic life, 'the *bourse* of literary values' (Casanova, 2004: 13) in a study of literary activity in a socialist nation in Revolution? Where Bourdieu's work on capital is less useful to the case of revolutionary Cuba is in the notion of capital itself, and the types of capital: for, in a socialist society, where economic profit is not a principal objective of most state-sponsored cultural activities (at least until 1989 and perhaps even to the present day), the significance of social, cultural and symbolic capital must surely take precedence over economic capital in the processes of decision making. In fact, economists might argue that the political leadership's lack of attention to economic capital was precisely the reason for both the 1990 crisis and the current reforms under Raúl Castro. In addition, the notion of self-interest and competition inherent in the idea of capital or profit is equally unsuitable for a society where effort towards a collective project has been encouraged and valued over individual gain, and where moral and political validity and social benefit have often been more highly valued than material benefits, although developments after 1990 reordered and reorganised many of these elements, giving economic benefit a greater prominence.

Despite these few limitations for the purposes of our study, Bourdieu's immense contribution as a conceptual foundation for this study is unquestionable. The development of Bourdieu's ideas by more recent scholars has been equally central, such as the work of Arjun Appadurai (1986), with his formulation of the concept of 'domains of value' and John Frow (1995), with his sustained development of the notion of 'cultural value' as a theoretical and methodological framework by which cultural practice can be assessed at the multiple and various points where it is received and interpreted. Importantly, the idea of a hierarchy of fields or domains of value can nuance Bourdieu's initial categorisation of capital by highlighting the simultaneous engagement of several types of value, either by one or a range of actors or social groups, as well as emphasising the constructedness, rather than the essence, of social categories such as class.

However, Frow's attention was clearly focused on postmodern, pluralist, capitalist and industrialised societies, societies where 'it is no longer either possible or useful to understand cultural production in terms of a general economy of value. What may in some sense always have been the case has become self-evidently so now: that different social groups employ criteria of value which may well be incompatible and irreconcilable' (Frow, 1995: 130). For Frow, one possible strategy for dealing with this transformed economy would be through a move that seems to go beyond the problem of valuation. 'The move involves deciding that, rather than engaging *in* a discourse of value, calculating the relative worth of this text against that text according to some impossible criterion of value, the job of the critic is rather to analyse the social relations of value themselves: to analyse the discourses of value, the socially situated frameworks of valuation from which value judgments are generated by readers' (Frow, 1995: 134). However, any attempt to explain the infinite number of interpretive moments and the value judgments which they entail, and to do so in such a way that internal contradictions within one valuing agent, or between members of the same valuing group, are recognised, is a complex and perhaps unachievable task. Frow suggested, instead, that a focus on institutional mediating mechanisms, categorised according to regimes of value, could account both for the diversity of value and for the absence of any simple or necessary coincidence between social groups and the structure of valuation.

Drawing on Appadurai's understanding of 'regimes of value' as 'a broad set of agreements concerning what is desirable, what a reasonable "exchange of sacrifices" comprises, and who is permitted to exercise what kind of effective demand in what circumstances' (Appadurai, 1986: 4), Frow further characterised these regimes as spaces or domains that permit the construction and regulation of value-equivalence, and, indeed, permit cross-cultural mediation. Thus, again in the words of Appadurai, the concept

> does *not* imply that every act of commodity exchange presupposes a complete cultural sharing of assumptions, but rather that the degree of value coherence may be highly variable from situation to situation, and from commodity to commodity. A regime of value, in this sense, is consistent with both very high and very low sharing of standards by the parties to a particular commodity exchange. Such regimes of value account for the constant transcendence of cultural boundaries by the flow of commodities, where culture is understood as a bounded and localized system of meanings. (Appadurai, 1986: 15)

How, then, does the theoretical and methodological discussion detailed above assist us with our object of study? The notion of 'regimes of value' has particular advantages. Firstly, and crucially, it allows us to get away from the essentially commercial implications of the term 'capital', as discussed above. By using the notion of value, itself taken from economics but applicable to a wide range of human activity, there is greater scope to explore in a more subtle and complex way the worth awarded to literary practices and products without being beset by the simplistic 'art vs. money' or 'art vs. politics' oppositions that have featured so strongly in conventional perspectives. Just as the *continua* described above enable us to identify tensions, contradictions and consensus across the network of processes that make up literary culture, the inclusive and comprehensive framework of regimes of value allows us to measure the worth of a literary activity or object from the perspective of the range of actors involved in the process, or, even according to the various perspectives that one agent, individual or institution, may hold, and in such a way that the relationships between the aesthetic, social, political, ideological and economic are included. After all, if literary culture takes us beyond the text and author to an examination of mechanisms, networks, spaces and agents, it is not just the writer who attaches worth to their work but also the many individuals and institutions that thereafter intervene in that work and give it physical presence, meaning and value. It allows us, in short, to examine literary activity in terms of objects, events and processes, and in relation to the physical, symbolic and discursive spaces of the wider context that they inhabit.

As Frow himself indicated, it allows us to examine discourses *of* value, the ways in which literary activities and objects can simultaneously hold the same or different kinds of worth for agents (both individual and institutional) involved in seemingly incommensurate fields of activity. Rather than assume that the commercial interests of the publisher or bookseller are at odds with the aesthetic interests of the artist or the editor, we can explore in greater detail what kinds of value each of these agents might assign to a literary text or activity. In other words, we can explore the points where these apparently incommensurate fields negotiate and cooperate via agreements between several parties (agreeing on publishing plans, agreeing on the design of a novel, setting the price of a novel, establishing its physical features), but also where these same agents have the potential to disagree. As Frow expressed it, '[t]he concept of regime expresses one of the fundamental theses of work in cultural studies: that no object, no text, no cultural practice has an intrinsic or necessary meaning or value or function; and that meaning, value, and function are always the effect of specific (and changing, changeable) social relations and mechanisms of signification' (Frow, 1995: 145).

Specifically, in the case of literary culture in revolutionary Cuba, this transactional, non-essentialist and inclusive focus of the concept of regimes of value enables us to evaluate why literary activity has remained a constant of the revolutionary process, being supported, prioritised or maintained even at times of economic or political crisis; equally, it provides a framework within which to understand periods of cultural crisis (as times of incommensurate types of value in the political and aesthetic domains, or in the economic and aesthetic domains) without resorting to simplistic notions of freedom of expression versus censorship, or pure art versus commercial art. In addition, and incorporating Frow's further development of the idea of value to include 'scenes of value' (Frow, 1995: 148), it allows for both consensus and disagreement: 'Judgements of value are always choices made within a particular regime. This is not to say that the regime determines which judgement will be made, but that it specifies a specific range of possible judgements, and a particular set of appropriate criteria; in setting an agenda, it also excludes certain criteria and certain judgements as inappropriate or unthinkable. Regimes therefore allow for disagreement, specifying the terms within which it can be enacted. Disagreement may also take place in the space of overlap of regimes, or between discrepant and non-intersecting regimes; but in a sense disagreement is only ever really possible where *some* agreement on the rules of engagement can be held in common' (Frow, 1995: 150).

Literary culture: precise focus and methods

Finally, why the term 'literary culture'? Why not refer to 'print culture' as it relates to literature (incorporating literary journalism), or, in even broader terms, 'textual culture' (thus incorporating non-printed published texts such as the handmade editions made by Ediciones Vigía in Matanzas, or the infamous *plaquettes* of the early Special Period)? Why not, indeed, 'book culture'?

Firstly, the focus here is resolutely on the processes, mechanisms and functions of literary activity (such as presentations, prizes and book festivals), many of which do not generate concrete physical texts, although they may well contribute to their production. Given that conventional perspectives on literature in revolutionary Cuba have predominantly centred on the individual author and/or his or her corpus or individual text, our use of the term 'literary culture' deliberately excludes the text, at least in terms of the conventional approach of literary analysis. However, an exploration of the book as the physical focus for these processes and functions forms the centre of Chapter 7.

We thus explore literary culture as interlinked processes of production, distribution, promotion/regulation and reception, within the wider processes of cultural democratisation since 1959. Also central to these processes of democratisation and massification is the question of the social context in which literary culture takes place. While book historians such as Walter Ong drew attention to the three revolutions in the history of the book – the movement from orality to literacy, the invention of the printing press and mass production/consumption, and recent new technologies to turn consumers into creators (and their ability to change psyches and practices at individual and collective levels) (Ong, 2002) – other scholars in the field, such as Roger Chartier (1989) countered that there is no fixed logic of print culture, that texts must be interpreted in cultural spaces whose character helps to decide what counts as a proper reading. In other words, literacy and writing/reading are not fixed practices with fixed types of value, but embedded in ever-changing contexts. As regards Cuba, the most recent textual revolution – the internet – has further unsettled the credibility of those fixed values, and press reporting on the social and political problems associated with the internet in Cuba are frequent. However, this book pays similar attention to less-publicised technological phenomena relating to literary culture which have, if only for the inhabitants of a small, previously underdeveloped island in the Caribbean, changed both psyches and practices, such as the abolition of copyright, the idea of *piratería* (pirating), the creation of *talleres literarios*, or, more recently, the RISO effect (see Chapter 5) and the explosion of provincial publishing spaces.

As Brewer has noted, the essential question underpinning literary production since the eighteenth century has been how can the writer be paid but at the same time be respectable? The long-standing writer's equation of financial independence with good writing, and, conversely, of financial dependence on the marketplace with low quality 'compromised' art, coupled with the parallel phenomenon that has ensured that for booksellers who know the market best, originality and innovation brought prestige but also meant financial risks, means that, for several centuries, both author and booksellers have walked a tightrope between financial reward and intellectual interest. In Cuba, this tightrope is even more complicated since, from 1959, financial considerations were replaced by expectations and judgments based on political and social values. One potential solution in Cuba – the double existence of writers as cultural workers – meant that, at least from the late 1970s to the late 1980s, writers could be financially solvent and politically/socially responsible and respectable, freeing themselves, in principle, from having to hawk their literary works for a living. However, in the absence of significant financial rewards symbolising prestige and recognition, this came in the form of peer approval, itself leading to tight-knit authorising communities of fellow writers, critics, academics, which had the ability to mobilise resources, endorse texts and writers and act as valuing agents. In this sense, returning to the dry characterisation by González Echevarría of cultural figures as *burócratas* and *comisarios*, in the revolutionary Cuban case, the balancing act between art and money has been interrupted and inflected by a more powerful set of political and social judgments, and the structures developed to harness their participation have made them as much agents and policymakers as 'pen-pushers'.

Many of the conflicts, tensions and multiple roles undertaken by cultural figures are reflected in the data that forms the principal source for the subsequent chapters. Our data and methods – around 130 semi-structured interviews with these agents, spanning the entire period of the Revolution and, in many cases, articulating their experience and position in a variety of roles – thus offer a counterpoint to published memoirs and textual analysis as both source and method. Similarly, as many of these individuals have, in their public roles, been central to policymaking around literature, their comments are used both to corroborate documented evidence and to add texture and detail to published policy documents, allowing us to examine more fully the effects (or perceived effects) of policies such as the massification of printing or the abolition of copyright.

We thus examine policy through conventional routes (theses and resolutions, public declarations of, and reports commissioned by, the major cultural institutions) and consider many of the published 'position pieces' on literary life by intellectuals, ranging from the 1961 *Palabras* to short articles in Cuban cultural magazines, introductions to anthologies and monographs, as not only central to the theorisation of culture over fifty years but also instrumental in the reassessment and reorientation of cultural policy regarding literature. Lastly, given that our focus here is on the processes enabling literary activity to develop on the island since 1959, we have not included the myriad and diverse perspectives which are articulated from the Cuban diaspora. Although we fully recognise the cultural, social and political importance for many scholars of creating wider and more inclusive conceptual frameworks, of achieving a 'disentanglement of nation from territory' (Hernández-Reguant, 2009a: 72), our motivation and objectives here are to explore how processes, spaces, agents and types of value have been understood, constructed and have evolved *on the island*.

Notes

1 'At times, when speaking to foreign audiences about our literary movement, I come across people – generally men – who insist on asking me exclusively about events which took place thirty or forty years ago, as if nothing had happened on our island once the "Padilla affair" had taken place and Arenas had left with Mariel. I call that strange kind of people Philosophers of a land where time stood still or Egyptologists of the Cuban Revolution'.

3
1959–61: The first flush of revolution

It was therefore against this backdrop, together with the wider context of an emerging but inchoate cultural policy, that the Revolution's approach to literature now emerged, partly consciously and partly empirically. Here, one of the most important points to make is that, whether following deliberate policy or feeling its way, it was not so much 'the state' which determined the direction for the new literature, because such a state was slow to emerge and in constant flux, being shaped and reshaped by all the pressures of rapid and deep social and political change, together with the relative paucity of trained cadres to enact decrees, enforce conformity and shape a new revolutionary state.

If there was no conscious strategy, however, there were some parameters already evident: in part these were set by the pre-1959 context (especially the importance of literature in the national psyche and in any project of nation-building, and also the traditional drive to popularise culture), and in part they were evident in the rebels' earlier declarations. Hence, as with all other aspects of the Revolution, the shape of 'a revolutionary literature' was by no means a matter of a 'Revolution without blueprint' (Zeitlin, 1970: 117), except in its details. However, it was in those details that the arguments began, since the literary world of 1959 reflected all the uncertainties, tensions and fluidity of the whole revolutionary process; if the shape of a new society, political system and economy was open to debate within defined parameters, then that was equally true of a new culture and, within that, a new literature. Given the fragmented nature of Cuba's pre-1959 literary culture, and the absence of a whole literary generation until 1959, that was not surprising. Moreover, the momentum of change and redefinition which the revolutionary victory unleashed – which made any attempt to define the whole process at any one time doomed to failure – then went on to create its own logic and dynamic in this sphere, as in others, and therefore to establish (often empirically) its own emerging criteria, thereby increasing the uncertainties, the tensions and the potential for fragmentation, but also – dangerously for some – making those early debates very quickly either less relevant or much sharper.

What, then, were the parameters? Essentially, the most important was the rebels' decision, even while in the Sierra, to prioritise education and literacy, a policy which could not help but affect literature more directly than any other cultural genre, by prioritising the written word. Hence, Guevara's position as the Ejército Rebelde's Director de Cultura (thus being the Revolution's first) was especially significant, since, having been largely responsible for the rebels' attempts to spread literacy among the Sierra peasants, it could be assumed that he shared that tacit prioritisation.

This, therefore, was the context for the largely spontaneous explosion of literary activity which visibly emerged immediately after the victory, mostly engendered by the enthusiasm felt by writers hitherto either unable to publish in Cuba – and who now rushed to produce what had been pent up before – or who had been living and writing abroad and had now returned to Cuba, to contribute to, and benefit from, the new Revolution [AAM; CL; PAF; LO].

What emerged in terms of both a revolutionary strategy for the new literature and a new literary culture was thus a mixture of both the organised and the spontaneous. The former soon came in the shape of the decisions emanating from the new MINED, under Hart from 23 January 1959 and allocated 20 per cent of the national budget from June 1959 (Cantón Navarro and Duarte Hurtado, 2006a: 36); as seen in Chapter 1, these included the creation of new cultural institutions, designed to provide the infrastructure or the encouragement for a cultural renaissance; two of these (ICAIC and Casa de las Américas) were visibly active, autonomous and politically significant from the start.

ICAIC, of course, had relatively little impact on literature (except, in 1961, in the notorious *PM* episode); Casa, however, had greater relevance, since its establishment came partly in response to the literary 'boom' already beginning in Latin America, and also in the prestige accorded to its literary prizes from October 1959. Hence, its strategy (from July 1959, when it began operations) of making Cuba and Latin America more culturally aware of each other had an initial basis in the literary. However, it soon became clear that Casa, as an institution, and then its rapidly successful eponymous magazine, had significance far beyond literature, developing into an institutional and intellectual space across several genres and cultural forms. Moreover, as its focus was eventually, and decidedly, on Latin America, perhaps more than Cuba, it never offered Cuban writers the same opportunities as did other, internally focused, outlets; indeed, some complained that, because *Casa* tended to invite specific contributions, the magazine only ever reflected the more established among the existing writers. Nonetheless, as Pogolotti has observed, as part of the extent to which the Revolution brought Cuba's intellectuals into the heart of many debates and intellectual and political developments (about definitions of art, cultural decolonisation, new artistic movements, the question of popular culture) and face to face with the sustained strategy by the United States to challenge via its own publications the intellectual hegemony of the Latin American Left, Casa made those Cuban intellectuals into continental protagonists of all of this ferment (Pogolotti, 2006: xx); indeed, it was fundamentally this role which gave Casa such primacy within Cuba, giving Cuba's emerging artists and intellectuals a much wider significance than in Cuba alone.

However, MINED's early decisions also included the creation of one institution of more direct relevance to literature – the Imprenta Nacional (founded as early as March 1959, coinciding with ICAIC) – and a drive to resurrect and develop the BNJM (and, with it, a network of public libraries). Initially, however, both institutions were more a case of unresourced good intentions (led by well-established figures, most notably Lezama in the Imprenta), rather than entities which made an immediate difference.

Given the responsibility for printing all school texts and all MINED books 'contributing to the education and culture of the people' (Smorkaloff, 1997: 84), the Imprenta nonetheless initially lacked the equipment and infrastructure to be anything other than a theoretical organisation; hence, through the CNC's emerging Departamento de Literatura y Publicaciones, Lezama was obliged to select books to be farmed out to private presses for runs of around 1,000–2,000 copies, to be distributed free (Smorkaloff, 1997: 85). These were mostly the small pre-1959 presses, such as Lex or La Tertulia. However, it was the Imprenta which launched the characteristically ambitious publication of *Don Quijote* (see below).

By March 1960, it had acquired the necessary print shops in the form of the idle rotary presses of the closed *El Excelsior* and *El País* newspapers (Smorkaloff, 1997: 85; Rodríguez, 2001: 67), and then began its crusade to become 'the cornerstone of Cuban publishing' (Smorkaloff, 1997: 78). Soon, the rudimentary nature of its operations led to it being subsumed into the Editorial Nacional, as an autonomous organisation directly responsible to the Council of Ministers. Since it was slow to develop, however, its place was, to some limited extent, filled by the existing and new small presses which took advantage of the new context and sought to respond to the sudden enthusiasm for both writing and reading; hence, though 'the organised' seemed to lead, it was actually 'the spontaneous' which, for a while, was the protagonist of the new literature.

The BNJM was a little more fortunate in that it did at least possess newly opened purpose-built premises in the newly renamed Plaza de la Revolución, to which it had already recently moved from the Real Castillo de la Fuerza in Habana Vieja and from which it could launch a coherent strategy. The fact that it was coherent was ultimately down to the energy and vision of one person: on 5 January 1959, the 26 July Movement took over the Library, naming Maruja Iglesias as *interventora* (interim director), but shortly afterwards María Teresa Freyre de Andrade became the Revolution's first Director (Fernández Robaina, 2001: 63). Under her, a major reorganisation was enacted and a completely new strategy developed. That strategy, however, had historical roots in a 1940 lecture by Freyre (at the Havana Ateneo) on 'Hacia la biblioteca popular' (towards a people's library), which made her appointment logical and the strategy inevitable (Acosta, 1998: 5).

There were several aims to the strategy. The first was to reverse the deterioration of stocks of the previous years (which had suffered from the diversion of funds towards the new building), by 'rescuing' Cuban resources which had been lost; this aim (interestingly, reflecting a constant theme of discussions about culture in the early years and later) meant appropriating for the Library the books of those Cubans who left (Acosta, 1998: 64), but also (under Pogolotti and using a new special tax on sugar for the purpose) systematically buying up books from Cuban bookshops to restock the shelves [GP], and persuading the government to require all publishers to deposit copies of every book produced thereafter. The second aim meant opening Cuba up to world literature and a greater awareness of the world outside by acquiring as many non-Cuban resources as possible (with the same sugar tax) [GP]. The third aim was to convert the BNJM into a leading space for all cultural activity, beyond literature; indeed, that began what became a constant characteristic of the institution: the use of space inside the building to sponsor lectures, art exhibitions, music concerts, and the like (Acosta, 1998: 67; Medina, 2001: 10). Finally, taking up a major part of Freyre's 1940 vision, moves began to generate a network of public borrowing libraries, to extend access, and including for a while a part of the BNJM itself, as the Biblioteca Circulante de Adultos (adults' lending library) (Acosta, 1998: 65). In this way, the whole institution confirmed two basic facts about the emerging cultural strategy: that libraries were fundamental to all culture and that reading was not yet necessarily prioritised to the extent it would later be. The effects of this whole effort were initially impressive, with a massive increase in public usage of the Biblioteca from 24,598 visits in 1959 to 156,768 in 1960 (Acosta, 1998: 69); however, almost certainly reflecting the steady loss of a major proportion of the traditional reading public in the form of the departing middle class, numbers then fell, until a new drive in 1964 was undertaken to encourage the new readers into the institution (Acosta, 1998: 69). All of this effort highlighted one important question: while reading evidently figured prominently in Freyre's view of Cuba's libraries, it was still not clearly outlined as a priority by the Revolution's leaders.

However impressive and well intentioned these two literature-focused enterprises may have been, though, the fact was that they were both slow to affect literary culture on a massive scale, reflecting three factors: the dearth of resources, the scale of the task to be undertaken to correct the effects of the previous neglect, and the inchoate state of the whole infrastructure of culture beyond the few prestigious early institutions. This, therefore, left the field open for other actors to fill the void in the meantime, again in a characteristic mixture of the organised and the spontaneous.

The latter took the form of an immediate burst of enthusiasm among authors and cultural activists, eager to seize the sense of opportunity and freedom created by the end of the old regime and the euphoria of the revolutionary victory. Not only did many writers return from self-exile, but those who had remained in Cuba also sensed a new atmosphere that allowed them to express themselves, and cultural life in Cuba 'adquirió una vitalidad, un dinamismo, una energía que no tenía' [AAM] ('acquired a vitality, dynamism and energy which it had not previously had'). As Lezama himself, the supposedly apolitical grand old man of Cuban letters, expressed it in *La cantidad hechizada* of 1970:

> La Revolución Cubana significa que todos los conjuros negativos han sido decapitados. El anillo caído en el estanque, como en las antiguas

mitologías, ha sido reencontrado. Comenzamos a vivir nuestros hechizos y el reinado de la imagen se entreabre en un tiempo absoluto. Cuando el pueblo está habitado por una imagen viviente, el estado alcanza su figura. (Abreu Arcia 2007: 31)[1]

Reflecting this euphoria and expectation, the appropriate state bodies made efforts to respond with ambitious publishing drives. The best known was the production and distribution in 1960, by the newly equipped Imprenta Nacional, of *Don Quijote*, which, in 100,000 copies each composed of four volumes, on cheap paper and rotary presses (Smorkaloff, 1997: 102; Rodríguez, 2001: 67), was distributed to be sold, in kiosks, alongside newspapers, at twenty-five centavos for each volume (Fornet, 1997: 29). This was in great part intended to make a bold statement about the Revolution's cultural ambitions and the central place of culture in the Revolution, reportedly reflecting Fidel Castro's own choice of iconic text. This was, however, followed by other initiatives, such as the newspaper serialisation of Stendhal's *Le Rouge et le Noir* in 1960, which reflected an unplanned imperative in several magazines to spread culture of all sorts to the Cuban people [FMH].

Although these initiatives were formally enacted through state agencies, they in fact reflected the dynamism and imagination of individuals, who, keen to take advantage of the freedom to educate Cubans culturally, were able to carve a space in the many gaps in the emerging infrastructure. Thus, for example, a combination of *Lunes de Revolución* and the more directly state-owned agencies created in 1960 a small publishing house, Ediciones R, which, instead of bringing world literature to Cubans' attention, focused on producing new, or unpublished, work by Cuban writers, especially those recently returned and already beginning to constitute the first *promoción* of the Revolution. Characteristically, the first book from this press was *Cuba ZDA*, a *testimonio* on the recent agrarian reform, from the journalist and novelist, Lisandro Otero, closely followed by another, *Huracán sobre el azúcar*; the third book in 1960, of poetry, however, began the pattern for which Ediciones R was best remembered: introducing the Cuban readership to Cuba's new literature [FMH].

In a similar vein, new magazines began to spring up and old ones resurfaced, all filling the gap and becoming publishing outlets for much of the pent-up creativity, promising to revive the former tradition of a literary culture based on a lively magazine activity: 'esa dinámica siempre abierta hacia la pluralidad de receptores donde el libro … no suele llegar con la prontitud e impacto del periódico o la revista'

(Zurbano, 1997: 5) ('that dynamic of always being open to a plurality of readers, whereby the book ... does not reach the reader with the same promptness or impact as the newspaper or magazine'). One such was the Dirección de Cultura's *Pueblo y Cultura*, with an explicit remit to popularise art [LC], but the major contributor to this emerging magazine culture was unquestionably *Lunes de Revolución*.

As already seen, this arose from the initiative of two former members of *Nuestro Tiempo*: Franqui (a former radical who, leaving the PSP in the 1940s, had since trodden a more liberal, and even anti-communist, path, becoming the editor of *Revolución* in the Sierra from 1957) and Cabrera Infante, film critic and editor of *Carteles*. With a political position committed to the principle of revolution, from somewhere left of centre, these two conceived of a journal as the cultural parallel to the 26 July Movement. The idea was to use the gap created by *Revolución*'s absence on Mondays (in keeping with all Cuban newspaper practice) to produce a supplement – hence the *lunes* (Monday) of the title – representing the cultural counterpart to the rapidly emerging political revolution.

The composition and character of the *Lunes* group, albeit fluid over its two years, soon became clear. Fundamentally based on the sentiments and tenor of *Ciclón*, it consisted of several of the younger artists now becoming active. Pablo Armando Fernández was initially approached in New York (Luis, 2003: 22) and then, after a spell in Oriente, moved to Havana to become deputy director, supporting Cabrera Infante who, in the prolonged absences of Franqui (on other duties during the period), effectively became the magazine's editor. Others included Tony Evora (Cabrera Infante, 2003: 141), Pogolotti, Roberto Branly, Piñera and Rine Leal (Luis, 2003: 155–6). In short, it was a gathering of the brightest talents of the generation below *Orígenes*, fusing *Nuestro Tiempo*, *Ciclón* and many of the self-exiled writers, especially when one adds to this list the many artists and writers who, although not running the magazine, tended to gather around it regularly to help form a definable grouping, especially including Arrufat, Fausto Canel, Humberto Arenal, Luis Agüero, José Baragaño, Severo Sarduy, Jaime Sarusky, Fornet and Desnoes (Padilla, 1989: 239).

Although this group never shared a clear political position (other than enthusiastic support for the new Revolution), the magazine did have clear aims, always as much artistic as political. Most evidently, one of these was to copy the 1920s' *Revista de Occidente* or *L'Express* (Luis, 2003: 22–3), by bringing Cubans up to date with the latest in outside artistic developments and making Cuba part of the aesthetic mainstream (Luis, 2003: 10), and to do so by being as open and eclectic as possible. The magazine's inaugural edition (23 March 1959) made that all clear in four paragraphs that stated its purpose as seeking to create a 'Revolución en el Arte y la Literatura' (the original idea for the magazine's title), as expressing the 'hora de nuestra generación' ('our generation's moment'), which, untrammelled by figures who had passed into history, could now come back from the margins and become part of national life again, explicitly in their work (Luis, 2003: 23). With this emphasis on their generational identity there was, therefore, another implicit purpose: namely to distinguish themselves clearly, and even vehemently, from *Orígenes*. Indeed, *Orígenes* and all that it represented became as much a target for *Lunes* as any other of the pre-1959 ills; rejecting its perceived hermeticism, escapism and even their Catholicism, *Lunes* sought commitment (Luis, 2003: 169).

The success and importance of the magazine were unquestionable. As William Luis put it: 'El boom latinoamericano no se hubiera dado cuenta sin la Revolución Cubana y el impacto de Lunes' (Luis, 2003: 11) ('The boom of Latin American literature would not have occurred had it not been for the Cuban Revolution and the impact of Lunes'). Running weekly for thirty-two months (with additional special issues), and growing from the original twelve pages to forty-eight, it eventually had a circulation of between 200,000 and 250,000 (Cabrera Infante, 2003: 142), larger than either the *New York Review of Books* or any other cultural magazine in Latin America (Luis, 2003: 21). Moreover, given the nature of circulation in Cuba, these figures almost certainly meant that it actually reached at least half a million Cubans regularly [AAM] and dwarfed all rivals, such as the PSP's *Hoy Domingo*, directed by Manuel Díaz Martínez and Jamís (Luis, 2003: 160), or the short-lived *Diario Libre*'s 'Arte y Literatura' section.

The magazine's and group's ambitions were also seemingly boundless: their imaginative and deliberately avant-garde art work reflected the wider scope of their whole strategy (to modernise culturally across the gamut of artistic endeavour), and at the end of 1960, taking advantage of *Revolución*'s control of Cuban television, they began their own television programme, *Lunes en Televisión*, under Rodríguez Peña, Sergio Nicolás, Humberto Arenal (Cabrera Infante, 2003: 143) and Pablo Armando Fernández (Luis, 2003: 161). Lasting thirty minutes every Monday evening, it tended to be somewhat ad hoc in its content, responding to the magazine's issues of the same morning, and hoping to shape the

1959–61: The first flush of revolution

Cuban public's cultural tastes and awareness of artistic developments. Beyond this, *Lunes* people also influenced televised culture by putting on plays by Tennessee Williams, Chekhov, Piñera and Ionescu (Luis, 2003: 27). In addition, there was also a recording company, Sonido Erre, and, of course, the Ediciones R publishing house.

It was from the television team that the notorious *Lunes* film experiment also began. At Christmas 1960, Orlando Jiménez Leal (the *Lunes en Televisión* cameraman) and Saba Cabrera Infante filmed *PM*, a short documentary-style film of black Cubans celebrating, with strong themes of alcohol, drugs and sensuality. Deliberately challenging the increasingly neo-realist hegemonic style of ICAIC (and most specifically Tomás Gutiérrez Alea's *Cuba baila*) and also the tendency to produce earnest and somewhat propagandistic historical documentaries (Cabrera Infante, 2003: 150), the *Lunes*-funded film tended to follow a free-camera approach, recording as it watched, without explicit judgment or comment. Shown on *Lunes en Televisión*, it was an immediate success among the *Lunes* group, who then endeavoured to distribute it nationally, firstly via the remaining private cinema, the Rex. By then, however, film distribution was monitored by the ICAIC-linked Comisión Revisora de Películas (film monitoring board, also termed the Comisión de Estudio y Clasificación de Películas, or Film Classification Board) led by Mario Rodríguez Alemán (Luis, 2003: 50) – which refused permission for the film to be shown. *Lunes* promptly organised a protest letter by some 200 intellectuals (including the already politically influential Fernández Retamar and Otero), calling for a meeting with Fidel Castro to discuss what they feared was open censorship. Meanwhile, the media began to discuss and review the film; the director Néstor Almendros and the writer Luis Agüero, especially, both praised it in *Bohemia* in June 1961.

It was in June, though, that the requested meeting took place; not, however, as seemingly intended – namely a small-group meeting with Castro alone (Luis, 2003: 190) – but rather in the form of three successive large gatherings in the BNJM on 16, 23 and 30 June, to which scores of concerned writers and artists were invited and which were also attended by Castro, President Osvaldo Dorticós, Hart, the Foreign Minister Raúl Roa, the leading PSP member Carlos Rafael Rodríguez, Guillén, Carpentier, and prominent PSP members, notably the geographer Antonio Núñez Jiménez (Otero, 1999a: 80), Alfredo Guevara, García Buchaca and Vicentina Antuña (the latter now president of the newly formed CNC) (Padilla, 1989: 60). At the first meeting (from which

Franqui absented himself), Piñera was the first to speak, expressing his fears about a 'cultura dirigida' (Otero, 1999a: 81) ('controlled culture'); he was answered by Castro himself, after which others contributed, including Ricardo Porro, Baragaño, Padilla, Violeta Casals, Natalio Galán, Hugo Consuegra, Mario Parajón, César Leante, Carlos Rafael Rodríguez and Gutiérrez Alea (Otero 1999a: 81). The pattern continued into the second and third meetings, the series ending with Castro's summing-up speech, *Palabras*, with its defining words and repeated reassurances, within the clear parameters now seen to be operating for all cultural expression. For *Lunes* what followed was its eventual closure, although some months afterwards, after the 6 November issue; officially, *Lunes* and the PSP's *Hoy Domingo* (the latter usually forgotten by the commentaries on the whole affair) were replaced by the newly created UNEAC's *Gaceta de Cuba*. Hence, the usual judgment made on the affair is that *Lunes* was a case of free expression closed by censorship and replaced by a state-run controlled organ.

What, however, did really lie behind the affair and its outcome? The main protagonists among the 'victims', especially those who subsequently chose self-exile, have always been clear enough. For Franqui, Cabrera Infante and Padilla (who, although not directly involved in the running of the magazine, was later directly affected by what he saw as the fallout from the affair), the '*Lunes* affair' arose from ideological differences, political machinations and personal animosities. Franqui and Cabrera certainly read it all as the latter, dating from the time when they both, having founded *Nuestro Tiempo* (Luis, 2003: 176), left the group because of its perceived takeover by communists (2003: 48); hence, according to them, this enmity and opposition to Franqui's subsequent anti-communism led Alfredo Guevara and ICAIC, supposedly also controlled by PSP people (2003: 49), to vent their spleen when *PM* gave them their chance. Certainly, Guevara turns out to be the villain of the piece according to this reading (Padilla, 1989: 58), especially as – it is argued – he resented *Lunes* trespassing on territory (film-making) which he had marked out as his own. Behind Guevara, however, (so goes this interpretation) there were several members of the PSP, or others close to it, who served the PSP's purpose to close *Lunes*: notably, Antuña, dismissed by Cabrera Infante as a 'títere comunista' (Cabrera Infante, 2003: 148) ('communist puppet'), and Otero (Cabrera Infante, 2003: 146–9).

Inevitably, the matter turns out to be somewhat more complex than these explanations. That is not to say that personal animosities did not play a part: they clearly did, and would continue to do so inside all debates within the very small, and often narrow, world of the Cuban intellectual community. Nor is it to say that the PSP were not suspicious of what *Lunes* represented: the typical position adopted by those most vociferous on culture within the Party (such as García Buchaca or Portuondo) were explicit in their preference for what one might call orthodox definitions of realism, popular culture or politically committed art, and viewed with disdain what they perceived to be, among some intellectuals, either an irresponsible attitude towards their cultural duties or anti-Soviet positions.

However, rather than see the affair in terms of communist definitions and free cultural expression, it is actually more helpful to identify deeper patterns and trends that made the whole episode almost inevitable. The first was that Cuban politics and the direction of the Revolution – both among the leaders and also the population at large – had shifted radically between the first edition of *Lunes* and the last, to the extent that the heterodox, unstructured and free-ranging radicalism which characterised the magazine in March 1959 (so representative of the moment) was simply both less acceptable and less relevant by June 1961. Thus, when Luis defined the magazine as 'una revista liberal con un amplio contenido cultural, pero antiimperialista y comprometida con la Revolución' (Luis, 2003: 36) ('a liberal magazine with a broad cultural content, but anti-imperialist and committed to the Revolution'), he admitted that its vision of revolution remained essentially the same between 1959 and 1961, while that of the political leadership and many Cubans had shifted fundamentally. Equally, the attitudes towards the role of intellectuals had shifted: from the early mix of agnosticism on the subject and tolerance towards a class that was traditionally respected, those attitudes had, by 1961, become much more demanding of serious and more responsible commitment. While Franqui might argue that the *Lunes* people fought for the Revolution (itself a somewhat exaggerated definition of their actions in 1957–58 or 1961), the fact was that the revolution for which they 'fought' was different from the one which had emerged by mid-1961. Not least, the defining moment of Playa Girón (a real watershed in terms of political clarity about the Revolution's purpose and nature, and about the opposition) had happened, and the equally defining process of the Literacy Campaign was in full swing; in those circumstances, to continue with the same attitudes towards culture and the intellectuals' role in the new process was anachronistic. *Lunes* was thus a manifestation of a particular interpretation at a particular time, a magazine of the moment; by mid-1961 that moment had passed. As Che Guevara put it in 1960 in his otherwise laudatory contribution to the first anniversary edition: 'Otras veces padece unos intelectualismos fuera de la realidad cubana' (Luis, 2003: 36) ('at other times it suffers from a intellectualism which lies outside Cuban reality'). The time for defining politics had come for everyone, and the intellectual elite was no exception, as Pablo Armando Fernández later admitted: 'Era el momento propicio para definirse políticamente (Luis, 2003: 169) ('it was the favourable moment for defining oneself politically'). Indeed, one of the group's leaders' mistakes was to assume that the magazine's politics could be defined by intellectuals and artists alone, excluding non-artistic politicians from that task (Luis, 2003: 166).

In a clear sense, therefore, one might argue that the group had, by 1961, lost direction and coherence. In 1959 little united the group other than their age (and many were explicit about the whole experiment being a generational manifestation, distinguishing them from the *Orígenes* generation in this way, as in others); by 1961, that was insufficient to provide a cement for an always politically disparate group. Once the attacks on *Orígenes* began, and even became personal in one case (Cabrera Infante, 2003: 147), even that unifying factor disappeared, not least because some of the early group (Fernández Retamar, Jamís, Pedro de Oráa and Fernández) had been the embryonic younger generation of that earlier grouping (Luis, 2003: 167;[RFR]).

A further reason for the affair may well have been the fact that the content and tenor of *PM* was not simply a pretext for ICAIC's criticism but, rather, something that was seriously out of touch with the evolving attitudes of the revolutionary process. For it may well be that the *Lunes* group's whiteness had a bearing on their collective approach to culture and revolution, which made *PM* an anachronism by 1961; the film illustrated a traditional, 1920s' exotic view of black Cubans (as an erotic, sensual underbelly of society), out of kilter with the reality of social liberation being experienced by most blacks by then and echoing the much earlier Parisian-based Cuban artists' discovery of Cuba as 'other', as exotic, as though they were Europeans and not Cubans (Kapcia, 2005: 80). Indeed, this may also have been part of their generally shared interest in European models of culture; in 'exile' (as most of them had been), they may well have been solitary but were always essentially capable of being assimilated, as whites, in ways that black Cubans would never have been, and, just like the Cuban artists and intellectuals of the early Republic and their penchant for a cultural *hispanismo*, perceived themselves as belonging to a European-led cultural community. Therefore, their failure to realise the scale and import of the wider cultural revolution going on outside *Lunes* was partly because the majority of the beneficiaries of educational revolution and cultural democratisation (as with every social change), because they were poor, were more likely to be black.

Indeed, that was yet another underlying reason for the affair: namely that, while the *Lunes* group were continuing to define 'cultural revolution' in the same aesthetic terms as in 1959, the processes of cultural democratisation had begun, changing attitudes to the role and purpose of culture. In fact, the other major emphasis of Castro's *Palabras* (usually overlooked by commentators) was on this process and the new ideas of *instructores de arte*. Hence there was an element of the ivory tower about the *Lunes* position; inside, all manner of debate about art was going on, while, outside, a real social revolution was under way in culture, which was described by one outside observer as 'wholly admirable' (Foreign Office, 1961: 11).

In fact, the whole *Lunes* episode was actually as much about the magazine being at the crux of wider debates as it was about political battles. In narrow terms, one such debate was about the desired nature and purpose of film in revolutionary Cuba, a debate which went beyond the personality and possible ambitions of ICAIC's Guevara and embraced the several radical film-makers who had already begun to debate inside *Nuestro Tiempo*. While Luis (following Franqui and Cabrera Infante) saw the film debates as a proxy for underlying political battles (Luis, 2003: 46–8), it is also possible that it was the other way round: that seemingly political battles were in fact the manifestation or form of a deeper set of differences about what film should be doing in the new Cuba and how it should be doing it. The fact that those debates continued into the later 1960s, and were essentially between ICAIC and what might be called the PSP position somewhat undermines the notion that the *Lunes* affair was a case of ICAIC carrying out the PSP's programme.

Beyond this debate, however, by 1961 a wider debate was emerging about the whole role of culture and, within that, of the artist and intellectual. This debate would crystallise dramatically in the 1968 and 1971 cultural congresses, but the ground was already being laid in the early years. Hence, the *Lunes* position (essentially arguing for a Sartrean definition – of the intellectual as the critical conscience of society – and for a liberal view of artistic freedom) soon found itself being outflanked by other arguments which saw a more formative role for art and a more responsible role for artists; as Fernández admitted (Luis, 2003: 171) and as Fornet put it, the first thing the intellectuals noticed was their own ignorance (Fornet, 1971: 35).

This all, of course, focused attention on the wider cultural revolution, and the question of democratisation and popularisation. This drive – an ambition shared in principle by the emerging state, *Lunes* and the PSP, however much these entities differed over what it meant and how to achieve it – took several forms. Sometimes it took the shape of activities, such as *cine móvil* (travelling cinema), theatre workshops or *talleres literarios*, organised by enthusiasts within the cultural apparatus, with official blessing but little active official support or infrastructure; at other times, they were grassroots-based enterprises arising from the initiative of local groups or communities. What they all shared, however, was a desire to take up one of the underlying principles of *cubanía* (belief in, or ideology of, *cubanidad*) – the fundamental role of education in any project of national construction – and therefore to spread the benefits of education as widely and as rapidly as possible. As well as building or opening new schools (Jolly, 1964: 222), in July 1959 the price of textbooks was lowered by 25 per cent (Cantón Navarro and Duarte Hurtado, 2006a: 38), this figure being later changed to a 35 per cent price decrease.

This drive soon also extended to higher education; in 1959–60 those who had participated in the insurrection and hundreds of workers were given the opportunity to enter university through a new system of government grants [SA], and in 1960 it was announced that the Universidad de la Habana would accept an additional 3,500 students, with 15,000 being given pre-university education to enable them to follow them (Foreign Office, 1961: 10; Rodríguez, 1984: 35). In March 1960, a new Universidad Popular began on television and radio to back this initiative up and include more Cubans.

Then, in 1961, came the Literacy Campaign, the initiative which most changed the conditions, opportunities – and also responsibilities – attached to literature. The political and social impact of the Campaign was, as we have seen, enormous; equally it could not help but have a profound impact on the emerging literary culture: not only did it create a potential massive readership overnight for whatever writing Cuba's established and emerging literary talent could create [RFR], with all sorts of implications for the already strained productive capacity of Cuba's publishing industry, but it also fundamentally challenged the

1959–61: The first flush of revolution

assumptions on which much in the first two years' experimental or evolving cultural strategies had been based. On the former point, the *Don Quijote* experiment had already shown the possibilities of cheap mass publication and distribution to the existing readership; now publishers had to address the particular needs of thousands of new readers, and also the demands which would inevitably grow as the virtues of reading were continually emphasised. On the latter point, the existing debates which had spelled the end of entities such as *Lunes* were now radicalised further, as different interpretations of cultural democratisation now faced a real and challenging new public.

However, one of the fundamental points about all of these cultural phenomena in the first two years was that they had all been created within the context of an inchoate state negotiating with, or represented by, diverse individuals, groups or new institutions, all of which necessarily enjoyed an unusual autonomy while the new state found its feet, built its structures of functionaries, and determined its agreed policies. Indeed, neither of the two types of cultural activity – either the more spontaneous enterprises (such as *Lunes*) or the more organised (such as the structures and initiatives for cultural democratisation) – was necessarily directed or planned coherently by something called 'the state'; indeed, the former was largely realised through individual or small-group initiative (filling the vacuum left by the weakness of the new state), while the latter came about through a range of initiatives, some locally generated, some encouraged by political leaders or activists.

One curious effect of this fluid context was to either exaggerate the power of key individuals or to genuinely endow them with more influence and even autonomy than one might normally have expected. What made them 'key' could be any number of circumstances or talents: privileged access to critical institutions or members of the political vanguard, usually through pre-1959 friendships (the case of Alfredo Guevara, for example); particular dynamism and energy (notably people like Franqui or Cabrera Infante); a degree of trust and influence endowed on those who had remained in Cuba (rather than seek solutions outside Cuba) – such as the *Nuestro Tiempo* group – and especially those who had actually contributed to the insurrection in some way [RFR; LO]. Thus the list of these individuals told its own story about commitment, accident or existing relationships: Aguirre (a PSP member but evidently significant within the Escuela de Letras); Arrufat (editor in chief of *Casa* for 1960–65); Branly (ex-*Nuestro Tiempo* and a key organiser of the Primer Encuentro Nacional de Poetas and Primer Congreso Nacional de Escritores y Artistas of 1960); Carpentier (Vice-President of the CNC and later head of the new Editorial Nacional); Guillén (appointed to the Consejo Nacional de Educación, national educational council, and then president of UNEAC after 1961) and Otero (editor in chief of *Revolución* for 1960–61). One might add the rather neglected but representative writer Arenal: returning to Cuba in August 1959, he worked in ICAIC as a *documentalista* (documentary film-maker) and writer on Gutiérrez Alea's monumental *Historias de la Revolución*, then worked on a weekly television programme about theatre, with Padilla, then moved on to theatre for seven years, while writing stories, but meantime founded the first *escuela de instructores de arte* (cultural teachers' training school) – a personal trajectory that mirrored the whole early cultural explosion [HA].

Equally, that same context created the ideal circumstances for key groups to develop a considerable autonomy. The most obvious was *Lunes*, but the ex-*Nuestro Tiempo* gathering of film-makers which formed ICAIC was essentially another similar group, with El Puente a few years later going on to perform a similar role.

The essential point, then, about these early years is that it was the *lack*, and not the presence or weight, of any central authority and of any mechanisms for ensuring conformity which allowed these different 'spaces' and agents (whether institutional or group-based, whether directly state-run or responding to individual initiatives) considerable freedom to operate, define, take the lead and therefore fill the gap being left by the emerging state. In this very significant respect, therefore, the Revolution's early experience of cultural development was precisely the opposite of what was either expected (by those whose previous paradigm of state–culture relations under socialism was based on the Soviet Union or post-1948 Eastern Europe, and by those who feared such a system) or of what has often been argued to be the case in Cuba during those first few years: that it was not the existence of a centralising state which determined cultural development but the very absence of such an entity.

However, by 1961 the signs were becoming clearer that both a stronger state and a greater pressure towards centralisation might well be in the offing, with the move towards socialism and a Socialist Bloc model of political operation, but also with the siege mentality beginning to set in (given the embargo and the invasion) and with the familiar pressures and tendencies of decolonising nation-building beginning to become

1959–61: The first flush of revolution

apparent. Hence, in the cultural world it was no surprise that the CNC had emerged by 1960 (replacing the MINED's Dirección de Cultura) and had begun to seek to impose a pattern on all cultural manifestations (especially given the influential political leadership within that body), nor that UNEAC was created in 1961. As far as literature was concerned, the nature of the CNC was relevant, since, as we have seen, until the new Imprenta Nacional began to operate fully, with proper resources, it was the CNC's Departamento de Literatura y Publicaciones which took responsibility for publishing.

Equally, the signs were already emerging that accepted notions of the value of literature might also be changing or at least be under greater pressure to change. For, while those whose ideas of the aesthetic role of literature had been developed in Europe or North America (especially the *Lunes* group and some of the older writers) continued to see its value in terms of international prestige and according to conventional norms, others (especially those associated with ICAIC, the PSP and the 26 July Movement) were increasingly drawn to the idea that its value might lie elsewhere: namely in social, cultural and educational democratisation and massification, and in the socialisation of culture. This meant that notions of the artist and the intellectual were also changing, sometimes by design but also through the momentum of events and developments; for example, the Literacy Campaign was, de facto, about to force Cuban writers to face up to a public with uncharted expectations, for which many in the literary world were not necessarily ready (Benedetti, 1971: 8–9). Hence, while some argued about rights and freedoms, others recognised that this also meant new responsibilities (Fornet, 1971: 35; Luis, 2003: 171); while some focused on the creation of literature, others focused on the benefits of distributing free or cheap books and on the fundamental importance of making literature accessible to all [FMH].

Therefore, all of the debates which characterised those years – about the nature and purpose of art, the rights and wrongs of socialist realism, and so on – were essentially debates about the value of literature, with aesthetic value in one corner and social and political value in the other. Even the discussions about the need for good-quality critics was based on the idea that the social value of literature needed to be protected, pursued and explained. In other words, everything was now focused on self-definition in individual or collective terms. For, in one sense, what distinguished *Lunes* from the *Nuestro Tiempo*-ICAIC axis was that they located themselves differently along a spectrum that was already beginning to develop within the evolving process, namely the individual–collective (or individualist–collectivist) continuum. For many within *Lunes*, and in spite of whatever shared ideas the *Lunes* group displayed, they essentially represented an argument for the individual artist, supportive of and even participating in, but separate from, the political process; hence, while not towards the individualist end of the continuum (since they welcomed the Revolution, supported most if not all of its initiatives and certainly believed in spreading culture to 'the masses'), they nonetheless continued to think in terms of the artist rather than the public. On the other hand, ICAIC's perspective was essentially one of focusing on those 'masses' and of shaping film (and also music and art) to serve the Revolution's desire to integrate and educate them.

What this all means is that the so-called '*Lunes* affair' should not necessarily be seen as demonstrating the impossibility of cultural freedom in an increasingly communist state, but rather that, within what was essentially an impatient and radicalised nation-building process, 1959–61 saw, in the world of literature especially (and particularly in the pages of *Lunes*), the playing-out of pre-1959 attitudes, cultural approaches and aesthetic tastes. Hence, while a genuine cultural revolution was already under way in terms of cultural democratisation, the Literacy Campaign and the cinema, in literature such a revolution really only began *after* 1961 and not, as the *Lunes* people argued or hoped, *before* that year. In that sense, therefore, literature essentially caught up with film in its understanding of what actually was meant – or ought to be meant – by a cultural revolution realised inside a constantly evolving social and political revolution, and only then after it became clear what the implications of the Literacy Campaign actually were or might be. From that point of view, the *Lunes* claim to be the cultural parallel of the political vanguard, and their unwritten assumption that they were the arbiters of the cultural revolution, were always debatable and soon anachronistic positions, their claim and posture being left behind not so much by the machinations of politicians and communists, but rather by the social changes taking place within, reflected by and as a result of, culture. Therefore, 1961 was clearly the end of one phase and the start of another, but not, as is usually suggested, because *Lunes* was closed and UNEAC became the arbiter, but rather because the first phase – of uncertainty and unfocused enthusiasm – was closed by the ending of the Literacy Campaign. Since that also coincided with the total ending of relations with the United States and the start of isolation, and the shock and elation of Playa Girón, the Campaign gained a significance which few anticipated, but which would shape Cuban thinking on literature for the coming decades.

Notes

1 'The Cuban Revolution means that all the evil spells have been exorcised. Like the ancient myths, the ring waiting in the depths of the lake has been found again. We are beginning to live our own spells and the kingdom of the image half opens in absolute time. When the pueblo is inhabited by a living image, the state gains its form'.

4
1961–89: The years of radicalisation and consolidation

As already argued in Chapter 3, most historians of culture within the Cuban Revolution see 1961 as a turning point, because of the *PM* affair, *Lunes* and the CNC, and they therefore focus on regulation and Castro's *Palabras*. Yet, whatever importance we may attribute to the pre-*Palabras* meetings, most Cubans remained unaware, the contemporary media giving no indication of the prolonged highest-level talks over the future of cultural expression in Cuba; the only clue came in the unexplained postponement (to 18 August) of the planned Primer Congreso de Escritores y Artistas Cubanos, due on 26 June in the Centro Gallego.

The reason is that, in the scale of priorities, they were less relevant than other cultural issues, most obviously the post-Playa Girón sense of siege and defensiveness; revealingly *Revolución*'s 12 June headline explicitly linked the broader cultural revolution to the destructive counter-revolutionary actions at, and after, Girón: 'La Revolución alfabetiza: el imperialismo destruye' ('the Revolution spreads literacy: imperialism destroys'), with the sub-heading, 'La batalla de la cultura' (*Revolución*, 1961c: 1) ('the battle of culture'), and the Primer Congreso's slogan was proclaimed as 'Defender la Revolución es defender la cultura' (*Revolución*, 1961d: 2) ('to defend the Revolution is to defend culture'); the syntax was interesting, suggesting that, instead of culture defending the Revolution, the duty was the other way round.

A second major issue was what 'culture' now meant. For, with the Literacy Campaign under way, 'culture' clearly now referred less to the minority concerns of intellectuals than to the wider cultural and educational revolution. Moreover, the nationalisation of all private schools made education part of the *patrimonio nacional cultural* (national cultural heritage), to be defended for universal benefit; for the Campaign was part of a wider educational revolution and democratisation, demonstrated by study bursaries for literacy workers. However, shortages (of funds and personnel) and the Campaign's demands meant that only by 1967 did school enrolments reach 1956 levels [FMH], and the shortage of teachers in schools and universities (caused by emigration) meant years of ad hoc adaptations, using volunteers or half-trained junior staff [RV; MDO].

Hence, as seen in the preceding chapter, the conventional 'watershed' of 1961 (supposedly between freedom and state control) might better be seen as ending an individualist definition of cultural revolution and beginning a collectivist one, already emerging empirically and legitimised by the Campaign, shifting literary and priority focus from writers to readers. This change paralleled the emerging democratisation of culture: between March and September 1961, the new Escuela de Instructores produced a thousand graduates (*Revolución*, 1961f: 6), with other initiatives, such as the *brigadas de cine* [GRR], well under way.

As already seen, the Campaign profoundly affected those participating, making them the Revolution's most ardent followers. However, it also implied a veneration of education and the written word, inextricably linking *cultura*, education and social liberation. The most immediate change for literature, however, was the dramatic increase in potential readership, transforming the context for reading and writing [GRR], and implying both opportunities and responsibilities. For these were not just more consumers in a market economy but a reading public in an underdeveloped society in revolution and under siege (with growing shortages), which all meant a new urgency about quantity and availability, priorities, guidance and also a clear consensus on whether this meant raising levels towards a predetermined notion of 'good literature' or a massification of production. Many were acutely aware of this new responsibility [JLM1], but others were slower to come to terms with it; indeed, the *Lunes* question was less one of censorship than an anachronistic adherence to increasingly meaningless approaches. While making literate, handling arms or cutting cane (like all other Cubans), writers now had a special duty to mediate between their work and the public, as 'maestro, divulgador y funcionario cultural' (Fornet, 1971:34) ('teacher, disseminator and cultural bureaucrat').

This combination of uncertainty and enthusiasm characterised initial approaches to that duty; revealingly, pragmatism created the first official, albeit ad hoc, strategy of *piratería*. This began in 1965, responding to a growing demand for university texts; in 1959–61 Cuba still imported necessary textbooks, especially through a Spanish publisher selling translated US-produced books to MINED. However, from 1962, US pressure ended that trade and, with massively increased enrolments and a post-reform university curriculum, a major shortfall loomed, encouraging student complaints (Rodríguez, 2001: 68); on 7 December 1965, Fidel Castro himself approached the Universidad de la Habana's Departamento de Filosofía – possibly attracted by their unorthodox arguments against Soviet 'manuals' of philosophy and discussions with President Dorticós about Marxism [RRG] – and asked the director, Rolando Rodríguez, and his deputy, Fernando Martínez Heredia, to identify textbook needs [FMH]. They soon identified 200 books (Rodríguez, 2001: 69), only for Castro to suggest 500 [RRG].

Two people then went to Spain, with thousands of dollars, to buy two copies of each book; these were then sent on Cuban ships to the department [FMH], and reproduced systematically, with the collaboration of Joel Domenech, Minister of Light Industry, through the Empresa Consolidada de Artes Gráficas, under Gustavo Arango [RRG; FMH], in a characteristically ad hoc way and with a typically militant flourish, calling it *fusilamiento* ('copying illegally', but also meaning 'shooting', thus obliquely making it *guerrillerista*). Effectively Cuba had abolished copyright laws inside Cuba (although this was not formalised until 1967) [AF], a decision arising from necessity – to break an embargo which, in Castro's words, killed Cubans through hunger and ignorance [RRG] – and principle: Cuba's right to challenge imperialism's monopoly of knowledge. Each book was then distributed free, as an *edición revolucionaria* (revolutionary edition), proclaimed in an inserted leaflet saying:

> Este libro tiene un gran valor. Por eso se te entrega gratuitamente. Vale por el trabajo acumulado que significan los conocimientos que encierra; por las horas de esfuerzos invertidas en confeccionarlo; porque sintetiza un paso de avance en la lucha del hombre por ser tal. Su mayor valor estará dado, sin embargo, por el uso que tú hagas de él. Porque estamos seguros de ese uso, y por su gran valor, se te entrega gratuitamente' (Rodríguez 2001: 70).[1]

This characteristic defiance of capitalism also asserted the new value of the book: in its use and not necessarily quality. The whole operation now had its title: *Ediciones Revolucionarias*.

The strategy continued with passive external collaboration. Firstly Madrid allowed low-interest credits (up to US$2 million) to buy the books, cementing a long-standing Cuban respect for an otherwise politically alien Spain. Then, when the International Book Association

1961–89: Radicalisation and consolidation

in Geneva demanded an end to illegal reproduction of the Larousse encyclopaedia, Rodríguez wrote to Larousse, and the Association thereafter turned a blind eye [RRG].

The *piratería* idea was then taken up by the literary world, notably Fornet, Desnoes and Herminio Almendros. In 1962, Almendros, the Editorial Nacional's Director de Publicaciones, brought Fornet and Desnoes from MINED's Editorial (where they had published literature from 1961) specifically to reproduce the best literature. Carpentier and Luis Suardíaz, the CNC Director General de Literatura (Codina, 2003: 98–102) were amenable: the Editorial had, from 1963, produced Martí's *Obras Completas* in twenty-eight volumes and its *Biblioteca del Pueblo* initiative had opened up literature to a whole new generation [NC]. Hence it now allowed ample space for Fornet and Desnoes to choose their own 'canon', their choice (including Proust, Joyce and Kafka) challenging the press's previous staid canon of largely nineteenth-century classics. After *Ediciones Revolucionarias*, they now had *carte blanche* to follow suit with literary texts, and literary *piratería* began in earnest; travelling abroad, they collected what they considered the best literature and, translating where necessary, reproduced and sold them cheaply, in print-runs of 10,000 (compared to the norm of 50,000–100,000 [AF]). Once again, in flagrant breach of international copyright and aware of their responsibility to the nation and all new readers – Almendros termed the initiative 'patrimonio de todos los niños y jóvenes de Cuba' (Espinosa, 2008: 22–9) ('the heritage belonging to all Cuban children and young people'), they printed what they thought Cuban readers needed [AF].

Meanwhile, this drive to educate Cuban readers also implied a responsibility on the authorities to provide writers with facilities, opportunities and protection. For, while 1959–61 had seen a largely individualistic focus on production, this now shifted towards more collective responsibilities: towards the individual and the smaller collective of the literary community. This imperative led to UNEAC, the formal vehicle for intellectuals' collective protection and shared space (Codina, 2003: 78–87). Of course, while protection could also mean restraint, it had benefits, especially a new economic security for writers, now free of worries about economic survival, since the collective (the state) employed them within the emerging apparatus. Hence, although the copyright abolition extended to royalties, this affected few.

Furthermore, writers now enjoyed encouragement through the many literary prizes created, the collective's legitimising of their contribution.

Hence, the prizes guaranteeing publication also promoted a greater publishing infrastructure beyond the Editorial Nacional. The first (October 1959) was the Casa de las Américas prize, followed in 1961 by several CNC prizes; in 1965, UNEAC prizes began (with categories for novel, short story, theatre, poetry, essay and biography), adding the David prize in 1967 for young writers and (1978) prizes for children's literature and *testimonio* (testimonial writing). Meanwhile, in 1969, the Revolutionary Armed Forces' Dirección Política added their *Premio 26 de Julio*, with categories across all genres (novel, story, theatre, poetry, *testimonio*, research, essay, biography, music and plastic arts), stipulating that all works submitted must 'reflejar en su contenido un estímulo a la conciencia y actitud revolucionaria de nuestro pueblo' (ILL, 1980: 226) ('reflect in their content a stimulus for the revolutionary consciousness and attitude of our people'), while, in the 1980s, the Ministry of the Interior created a prize for detective fiction (ILL, 1980: 227). Finally, more specific prizes were awarded by universities (especially Havana's *Premio 13 de Marzo*), including one inter-university prize, and by all mass organisations, UJC, and the Unión de Periodistas de Cuba. Thus, even before the 1990s' 'prize inflation', Cuban writers enjoyed ever more stimuli to write, publish and be recompensed, some prizes earning 1,000 pesos [JTS].

These prizes therefore created more spaces for writers; however, as the state apparatus grew, slowly and haphazardly, it too created a growing range of spaces, often limited in scope but usually permissive and protective. As already seen, ICAIC and Casa always offered such protection and patronage, for all genres [FR], the latter especially within its research centres, the Centro de Estudios del Caribe and Centro de Investigaciones Literarias [AAT]. Even UNEAC offered spaces through its constituent associations, physical spaces, publications and the small groups forming around key individuals [RLA; MSM; JLM1]. Another supportive and influential space (in terms of skills) was the Havana-based post-1962 Escuela de Artes y Letras; while the FEU ran its own Frente de Cultura, organising *talleres* by 1966 [RRC], the Escuela's staff and atmosphere, by general consensus, particularly influenced writers' development, sometimes through the curriculum (with its increasing focus on Hispanic and Cuban literature), sometimes through the impact of the staff, including younger teachers like Fernández Retamar and Adelaida de Juan [MSM; GRR; RRC], and sometimes through small-scale publications (such as *Alma Mater*) or prizes [JLM1].

Key individuals also offered further space through their tutelage, their prestige or authority giving them a similar autonomy to ICAIC and Casa, and continuing the long Cuban tradition of literary mentors (Kapcia, 2005: 43). In addition to those cited, these included Camila Henríquez Ureña and Ezequiel Vieta, with César López and Juan Arcocha also providing guidance [MY], and with figures such as Pogolotti being important to others; but their role often came from their positions – as editors (such as Carpentier [SC]) or as CNC officials (such as Carlos Lechuga, replacing Antuña in 1965, or Otero, Vice-President from early on). Spaces certainly abounded, inside and alongside the new structures, as the emerging state remained in flux, with groups tussling for authority. Hence, protection, support and identification could also be found in less formal institutions. Indeed, this was the context for the role of self-defined 'generations', post-1961 literary culture being as characterised by the need for generational distinctiveness as any previous manifestation, albeit now with less material urgency. Now, this need came from two different impulses: the perception of the Revolution as by, and for, the young (allowing young writers to emphasise their youth, as the first revolutionary generation) [MSM; GRR] and younger writers' fears about the new cultural vanguard's composition by older established writers and the *primera promoción* (Simo, 2006: 377; Abreu Arcia, 2007: 70). In 1967, that sense of difference encouraged one university group to issue a manifesto, 'Nos pronunciamos' ('we declare our position').

However, such self-definition was not unproblematic, with increasing pressure to emphasise collectivity and not difference; Portuondo, for example, dismissed talk of generations as irrelevant (Portuondo, 1979: 22). Hence, as slightly younger writers emerged, they were termed a *segunda promoción* (i.e. 'within the Revolution'), stressing belonging rather than discrete identity. This became more problematic with one new group which met separately (echoing the *tertulia* tradition of the small literary gathering), published separately, and followed explicitly different ideas: the El Puente group and publishing initiative. Its appearance after *Lunes* only increased nervousness, especially as they contradicted the arguments of one side of those earlier debates.

Ediciones El Puente was founded in 1961 by the poets José Mario and Gerardo Fulleda León, and by the story-writer Ana María Simo, the latter two remaining co-editors until 1963 and 1964, respectively, Simo finally falling out with Mario; the group shared no clear aesthetic ideas or ideological positions, simply seeing themselves as their generation's first literary expression (Simo, 2006: 370). This heterogeneity helped them survive but prevented cohesion, their heterogeneity drawing criticism from the usually maverick Piñera:

> Uno se levanta todas las mañanas diciéndose que ya no puede más con esos artistas, con esas pláticas, con esas exclamaciones, con uno mismo; que basta ya de Arte, de Belleza, de Rigor, de Seriedad; que no hay tal predestinación, tal éxtasis, tal destino....que somos francmasones del arte, ¡que horror!: yo te muestro y tú me muestras, y todos se muestran; que la meta está próxima, que llegaremos, ¡cómo no!, ¡no faltaba más! (Abreu Arcia, 2007: 71)[2]

Finally, differences arose over Mario's role and the issue of a collective or single-individual leadership (Simo, 2006: 371; [GRR]); this produced resignations and a new editorial board, under Mario, whose sexuality also attracted criticism, leading some to label the group dissolute (Simo, 2006: 373). The group's deliberately apolitical position was also deemed inappropriate. Nonetheless, El Puente always remained under UNEAC's protection [FMH], including its publications (printed on old machinery, with randomly gathered materials, in runs of 2,000, distributed initially by volunteers (Abreu Arcia, 2007: 69) but eventually by the Ministry of Internal Trade (Simo, 2006: 374); in 1964, it came under the wing of the Editorial Nacional (Simo, 2006: 375). The UNEAC link also led to them being asked to create the proposed cultural organisation for young people, the Brigadas Hermanos Saíz (named after 'martyrs' of the insurrection, the Saíz brothers); although refusing, they drafted statutes and the first edition of the Brigadas newspaper proposed a Brigada *taller literario* (based on Lorca's travelling theatre) (Abreu Arcia, 2007: 374–5). Therefore, for all its problems, El Puente was no ivory-tower group, and clearly part of the formal structures.

Ultimately, El Puente was condemned by its internal dissension, immaturity and lack of responsibility, its delay in formalising its position more clearly (as a space for young writers with shared stylistic positions), and finally with the furore of the January 1965 visit of the US beat poet, Allen Ginsburg, whose behaviour and overt sexuality became a pretext for those seeing El Puente as a threat. In 1965, when UNEAC withdrew protection, the Editorial Nacional ceased printing its work (Abreu Arcia, 2007: 373–6). However, the gap which they had identified (space for younger writers) was immediately addressed by the UJC's *Juventud Rebelde*, with a new cultural supplement, *El Caimán Barbudo* (hereafter *Caimán* or *Caimán Barbudo*), in 1966. This opened with a manifesto condemning El Puente for neglecting the wider context, unleashing a bitter political and personal debate between Jesús Díaz and Simo (Pogolotti, 2006: 367–90; Abreu Arcia, 2007: 81–2), although *Caimán* proved to be as generationally focused as its predecessor. *Caimán*'s strident tone soon harmonised with other emerging patterns. The first was the process of literary democratisation, in the *talleres literarios*, parallel to the movement of *instructores de arte* and *aficionados*, which had excluded literature in its remit, implying that the art of writing could not be taught, presumably because of some special quality. Hence, the unplanned emergence of *talleres* now implicitly ended that exclusion, given the growing logic of collectivism, shifting from a collective environment for reading towards a collective environment for creating writers. However, the *talleres* still focused less on writing than on an environment to appreciate literature, through 'un ambiente de diálogo en torno a la literatura y también de promoción de la lectura' [RRC] ('an atmosphere of dialogue around literature and one conducive to the promotion of reading'); only the University boasted a writer-focused *taller* in 1962–65 [MY]. Perhaps one obstacle to such early writer-focused *talleres* was a perception that the likely beneficiaries would be from the middle class.

A second discernible process was the steady broadening of that collective emphasis, extending into a wider community, of which Cuba was now a leading part and to which Cuban writers had responsibilities; not the socialist world but the Third World. As has been seen, Casa had already signalled that Cuba belonged to Latin America, leading Cuba's intellectuals to consider themselves part of Rama's *ciudad letrada* (lettered city):

> La dinámica entre lo nacional y lo latinoamericano, para quién se escribe, América como comunidad imaginada por los sujetos letrados, la inquietud sobre el valor social de la obra literaria, las tensiones entre las representaciones autónomas y heterónomas, entre realismo y antirrealismo, son los dilemas y las disyuntivas que enfrentan los productores de ambos campos a la hora de asumir el reto de escribir tanto la *novela de la Revolución Cubana*, como *la Gran anhelada novela latinoamericana*.
> (Abreu Arcia, 2007: 90, italics in original)[3]

Now, writers were encouraged to look to the wider Third World, battling alongside its intellectuals against imperialism and for cultural decolonisation:

> La descolonización cultural es un producto inevitable de esa toma de conciencia. Al descubrir nuestra realidad y con ella la ineficacia de los

instrumentos teóricos que habíamos incorporado precipitadamente en el curso de lecturas y viajes, comprendemos lo que *no* somos, lo que ya *no* compartimos con los intelectuales del mundo industrializado. (Fornet, 1971: 36)[4]

Curiously, however, this internationalism bore traces of cultural nationalism; in 1961, the pre-UNEAC Congress had stressed the rescue and conservation of cultural traditions and folklore (*Revolución*, 1961e: 5), and even the PSP cultural authorities advocated returning to popular (often rural) traditions, García Buchaca talking of rehabilitating the cultural past and folklore (*Revolución*, 1961f: 6). Hence, all the early debates reflected these concerns with 'the authentic'.

A third visible process arose directly from this collectivism and cultural nationalism: the awareness that, if writers were encouraged to think of collective needs and readers were encouraged to read more, the onus was on the collective to ensure some regulation of the hitherto ad hoc production, recognising that siege, shortages and the importance of reading demanded rationalisation, ensuring enough copies of the 'right' books for the new readership, rather than relying on the vagaries of the 'market' or personal whim.

Certainly, the early years had seen an unplanned proliferation of publishing [FMH], reflecting uncertainty about what should be produced. For the initial consensus was to catch up, confirmed by Fornet:

simple y sencillamente, de "ponernos al día". Creíamos que la Revolucion representaba – en el aspecto editorial, también – el impulso necesario para salir del atraso y proyectarnos al futuro, así que llegamos a la arrogante e ingenua conclusión de que bastaba leer a los autores de la vanguardia del siglo XX para ser cultos y, sobre todo, "modernos"' (Espinosa, 2008: 26).[5]

Nevertheless, as shortages increased, there was an inevitable re-prioritisation and centralisation, already attempted by the CNC – a failure which demonstrated their weakness rather than their strength [FMH]. However, by 1966, Fidel Castro himself had demanded centralisation essential (Rodríguez, 2001: 71), and the first steps towards a single Instituto del Libro (hereafter IL) were taken.[6]

This was especially important as attention shifted to the reader: 'Yo creo que eso fue una época formadora de lectores, no de escritores, los escritores, yo creo que se forman en su soledad, y en sus lecturas' [RRC] ('I think that this was an era for creating readers, not writers; writers, I think, are created in solitude, and in their reading'). Certainly a series

1961–89: Radicalisation and consolidation

of programmes now enhanced the Campaign's effects, raising levels and sharpening tastes of the newly literate, creating more active revolutionary readers [FMH].

Rationalisation also extended to roles within publishing, such as that of editor, a role hardly existing before 1959, with largely private or business-oriented presses [DGS]. Booksellers also came into focus, struggling with a vastly increased supply and demand but also confusing admonitions about their responsibilities to readers and the collective. The number and range of bookshops increased, some specialist and others more general [RM; AF; FMH]. Meanwhile, price subsidies were imposed to ensure access to books, and, in 1966, all bookshops came under state control, to ensure coordination [RRG], since low prices had driven more commercially minded booksellers out of business, leaving a few state-owned shops selling new books and a range of mostly private second-hand bookshops [RRG].

This new focus had other curious effects, such as a new emphasis on journalism, which, as a prime means of educating the newly literate, now had a special role within the emerging literary culture. In 1959–60, journalism enjoyed considerable prestige, a pre-1959 inheritance, since journalists were critical to spreading information about the insurrection and more literate exponents had perpetuated Hispanic traditions of erudite commentary, recognised by the prestigious *Premio Justo de Lara* [IMR]. Now, however, prestige came from journalists' place in a newly literate society, as a vocational didactic instrument for explaining the world and the bewildering changes [IMR]. Hence, many future writers honed their skills through journalism [GRR; MY], and, before becoming a separate Facultad de Periodismo – first located in Ciencias Políticas, then in Comunicación Social – journalism studies belonged to the prestigious Escuela de Artes y Letras [ASC].

Another important factor was the consolidation of library provision, with the BNJM playing a leading role after its reorientation from 1967, when, under Otero as CNC Vice-President, the inexperienced twenty-seven year old Aurelio Alonso became Director, at a time of significant staff upheaval. Alonso continued its programme of expansion and diversification: setting up Radio Biblioteca Nacional (Fernández Robaina, 2001: 72), reactivating provincial libraries (Fernández Robaina, 2001: 75), and completing the construction of the Marianao library (Fernández Robaina, 2001: 77–8) – later recognised as the site of Arrufat's marginalisation [AAM] and Alberto Guerra's self-motivated reading [AGN].

Sidroc Ramos (1967–73) then continued the development of a national library network (Fernández Robaina, 2001: 82); formerly education director of the Ejército Rebelde and then Rector of the Universidad Central, his equal lack of specialist experience suggested that the subordination of cultural policy to education after 1971 actually began some years earlier, in April 1967 when the CNC came under MINED (Fernández Robaina, 2001: 83). However, although Ramos later recalled it bearing the hallmarks of Martí (Fernández Robaina, 2001: 81–3), rather than Soviet influence, only after 1971 did the CNC take a firmer grip on the BNJM, leading to Ramos's resignation (Fernández Robaina, 2001: 84).

However, even during the *quinquenio gris*, under Suardíaz (1973–76), the BNJM was firmly oriented towards making books accessible within the libraries system. Again, Suardíaz's background is telling: formerly provincial director of culture in Camagüey, he had become CNC Director de Publicaciones, where, with a commission to stimulate *círculos de lectura* and *círculos de literatura*, he sought to distribute 500–1,000 copies of every book published to all libraries. Now, he sought to convert every public library into a *biblioteca escuela* (Fernández Robaina, 2001: 90), emphasising the need for proper training of staff.

In other words, throughout the 'greyest' years, the BNJM aimed to socialise literature via the space of the public library, and the resulting insitutionalisation was motivated more by the need to expand beyond Havana than the need to centralise or homogenise.

A further effect was a special role for criticism, now given a gatekeeping role, less for censorship than to ensure quality. However, this was underpinned by a new ethic: whereas, before 1959, the term *crítico* included book reviewers and learned essayists, it now had a more precise purpose of guidance, to ensure the availability of the best material for the new readership. Guidance came in many forms, for example an explanatory prologue [RRC] or through the essay tradition, moving away from specific texts to more general perorations [RFR]. Of course, this meant a need for writers to have adequate aesthetic and political knowledge, worrying outsiders and insiders alike; in 1968, Benedettii observed that essay-writing was comparatively weak in Cuba (Benedetti, 1971: 26). The question of political awareness was, however, fundamental, and Portuondo, unsurprisingly, stressed the duties and rigour demanded of the 'new critic', starting with the perennial need for self-criticism:

Mantener, sin perjuicio de esta absoluta libertad de ensayo y de búsqueda, de creación, y precisamente como acicate a la misma, una constante actitud criticista, favoreciendo la labor de los críticos y sometiendo esta misma al crisol de la más severa autocrítica,...... en las que pueda y deba participar el verdadero protagonista de la Revolución y sujeto, en definitiva, de la nueva expresión estética: el pueblo. (Portuondo, 1963: 60)[7]

Of course, the perceived weaknesses of criticism partly reflected the speed of social changes. As one critic admitted [SC], his generation knew little of literary theory or Cuban literature, past or present; hence, a new drive began to raise the appreciation of good Cuban literature, now studied in educational establishments, research centres and the media. One significant development here was, undoubtedly, the 1965 creation of the Instituto de Literatura y Lingüística (ILL), under Portuondo, specifically to conserve and study Cuban literature (and Cuban Spanish).

This steady increase in well-intentioned regulation had a negative side: the possibility of greater pressures to conform. For some, that meant a sense of marginalisation, as new hierarchies of writers emerged. Some who had lived abroad, either before 1959 or afterwards (albeit as cultural attachés or journalists) felt particularly singled out for suspicion, because of fears of possible contact with dangerous ideas, examples and models, or because they had not shared the collective struggles of Playa Girón, October 1962 and the siege. Many of these remained loyal, although aware of the dangers and of the possibility of being used; in the words of García Márquez: 'Los intelectuales no sirven para nada excepto cuando sirven para algo' [CL] ('intellectuals are good for nothing except for when they are good for something'). But all felt some disorientation and even marginality on returning in the mid-1960s: 'Una de las dificultades en cualquier sociedad son los obstáculos que a diario enfrentamos que se llaman envidia, celos, resentimientos, competencia, y algo terrible que es la falsedad' [PAF] ('one of the difficulties in any society are the daily obstacles that we face, such as envy, jealousy, resentment, competition, and something terrible called falseness'). Most suspicion, however, was felt by those educated before 1959, for their relatively privileged background, something which, by definition, included most writers active before 1959 or soon after [RMR; CL; AAM; HA]. Youth was not yet the issue it would later become (with concerns about rock music and hippie lifestyles); instead, youth alone (accompanying political commitment) was no bar to important roles: 'Nuestra adolescencia, nuestra juventud fue muy diferente de otros muchachos de otras partes del mundo [RGZ] ('our adolescence and our youth were very different from those of kids in other parts of the world').

Such fears about a hierarchy of generations extended to a possible hierarchy of literary forms, through prizes or publishing decisions. Older writers inevitably felt pressure towards socialist realism [EDL; PAF], but younger writers felt attracted in that direction [VLL], especially if it offered them opportunities to express the immediacy of their experiences [SC]. While this transmogrified into 'la literatura de la violencia' [JTS] ('the literature of violence'), it owed something to orthodoxy. Meanwhile, some older writers or those of the *primera promoción* were clearly seen by some in authority as guilty of a fusion of homosexuality and artistic irresponsibility; while the former was not per se a cause of harassment (Arrufat remained Director of Casa de las América for six years), despite the prejudices among some ex-guerrillas [GRR], the combination gave sufficient cause to exert pressure or withhold publication, although this became a greater problem after 1971 [AAM].

Besides any authorised ideological preferences for style or content, the whole question of hierarchies arose from the double reality of siege and shortages, leading to a necessary revision of priorities. For, by the mid-1960s, the consensual value ascribed to literature (within a revolutionary society, an underdeveloped economy, and under siege) changed subtly: now literature was seen as contributing to cultural knowledge and to 'crear a un ser humano, lograr valores en un ser humano, abrir los horizontes de un ser humano, y a la formación misma del individuo' [RRC] ('creating a human being, creating values in a human being, opening up the horizons of a human being, and the very creation of the individual'). Hence, literary culture should be focused on the collective duty to mould the New Man and new society, changing all previous criteria for judging the value of a text, writer, or style, and for assessing the effectiveness and economic value of book-related infrastructure: the opportunities for creation, facilities for production, scope and manner of dissemination, and guidance for its reception. By 1967, the pattern of the future literary culture was already evident, foundations having been laid for the sustained (if rarely coherent or consistent) consolidation of a new value for literature.

Equally, many of the characteristic spaces (physical, textual, imagined, or generational) constituting the new literary culture had been created, some authoritative and inclusive (UNEAC, ICAIC, Casa), others more fleeting but influential (El Puente); the spatial infrastructure for writers to belong and readers to gain access to their products was also under way. Moreover, with the state still in the process of formation (helped by the 'anti-institutionalism' of 1963–68 and the siege), these spaces often remained fluid and ambiguous; El Puente might enjoy UNEAC protection, but the CNC was already demonstrating a desire to confine certain aspects of expression, although still lacking comprehensive power. Hence spaces were occasionally antagonistic and divergent – termed 'un espacio de luchas' (Abreu Arcia, 2007: 70) ('a site of struggle') – lacking an overall strategy to ensure conformity. While CNC-controlled spaces enforced some conformity, other spaces could be permissive, allowing individuals and groups to be dynamic and influence each other.

Nonetheless, by 1967, the underlying continuum of the individual– collective, developing apace since 1959, was tilted decisively in favour of the collective, changing ideas of the aceptable and normal. Spaces had now become more collective than individual. Given the diversity, complexity and proliferation of spaces, the hierarchies determining their level of acceptance, and an increasing institutionalisation, the conventional focus on the individual writer misses much, demanding that we see writing as part of the wider mechanisms and patterns of literary culture. This section thus examines the significant actors, events and processes of a turbulent and vexed period for Cuban literary culture, because of – but not entirely centred on – what is consensually the *quinquenio gris* of 1971–76 (although debate still rages inside Cuba about whether it was only five years and whether it was merely *gris*, César López, for one, arguing for the term *decenio negro* (Castellanos, 1998: 29) (black decade).

The IL was established on 25 April 1967 (the day of the CNC's move to MINED), taking shape two days later (Rodríguez, 2001: 71), under Rolando Rodríguez for 1967–81, with the aim of centralising all publishing (except UNEAC and Casa) and establishing a nationwide network of distribution, through state-run bookshops. Hence, like the BNJM, its impetus came not from a desire to standardise literary culture, or control political content, but, conversely, from a desire to improve the processes of textual culture, for educational and cultural ends. Indeed, Rodríguez later described it being firmly focused on the parallel and interdependent processes of writing and reading, within the context of postcolonialism and national development: '[P]romoción de un lector, libros para desarrollar una cultura elevada en sus más diversos terrenos y muy accesibles en su precio, tiradas abundantes, puerta ancha para la edición de las obras de los escritores cubanos de antes y ahora, y una política descolonizadora en la literatura' (Rodríguez, 2001: 71) ('the promotion of the reader and of books, in order to develop a high level of culture in the most diverse areas at an accesible price, abundant print-runs, a wide remit to publish the work of Cuban authors from the past and present, and of a policy of decolonising literature').

Rodríguez's apparent autonomy is perhaps best understood not as politicisation, but rather as the consonance of the vision shared by key political and cultural actors, and the commensurability of value between the domains of politics and culture, social development unifying the (now revolutionary) nation's educational, cultural and political aims. The IL received wide ministerial support, under Llanusa as Minister of Education (1967–77), almost certainly because it was Castro's personal initiative – as Rodriguez expressed it: 'porque donde está Fidel metido no se mete nadie. Muy importante. Yo tenía una sombra verde detrás que me protegía y no era fácil meterse conmigo (risa). No tenía a nadie en contra' [RRG] ('because where Fidel is involved no one else gets involved. That's very important. I had a green shadow behind me which protected me and it wasn't easy to have a go at me (laughs). No-one was working against me'). However, it was also because, in publishing, the commonality of vision between cultural, social, educational and political sectors was easier to achieve than elsewhere in literary culture.

The rapid and sustained expansion of the IL's scope during Rodríguez's term was remarkable, publishing 15.9 million copies in 1967–68 alone. By 1968, the process was in full swing, represented especially by the unusual decision to produce 20,000 copies of Wilkie Collins's *The Moonstone* – seemingly chosen because it was more accessible than *Don Quijote*, and sold out in a week (Benedetti, 1971: 8) – and the legendary *Colección Huracán*, the ambitious series of world classics reproduced in huge runs of 50,000–70,000, in rudimentary form (often newsprint) and sold for between twenty-five and forty centavos each. The availability of paper – often identified as a central obstacle to publishing after 1990 – was prone to the vagaries of supply routes: Rodríguez described procuring paper from various sources, including Algeria and Finland, but also of times when availability exceeded the printing facilities' capacity. However, the emphasis was clearly on making books available, regardless of paper quality, responding to the massively increased demand and the lack of a coherent canon of foreign or Cuban works.

There was therefore little attempt to gauge readers' needs or desires, as all texts were deemed necessary, and in this context, specific series and collections played a vital role, practically and symbolically [RRG].

Huracán arose from a visit to El Crisol printing press (on Carlos III) which, though fully equipped and staffed, was inactive. Learning from the *Quijote* episode of the almost limitless demand for texts, *Huracán* began by re-printing books sold out in other editions, such as *Biblioteca del Pueblo*; it soon began publishing a wide range of unavailable works, including 100,000 copies of the *Diario de Maximo Gómez*, all quickly sold out. Despite its ambitious remit and popularity, *Huracán* typically mixed pragmatism and resourcefulness: with insufficient typists, the Crisol linotypists copied text directly from previous editions [RRG]. This versatility ensured a wide range of titles, print-runs averaging 50,000 (sold for around twenty *centavos*), but some runs reaching 250,000 (García Márquez's *Cien años de soledad*) and even 400,000 (a translation of Malraux's *La condition humaine*) (Rodríguez, 2001: 75). By 1967, Cuba was producing some sixteen million books annually, almost three books for every Cuban; in 1967–74, the average print-run doubled from 20,000 to 40,000, again suggesting that textual space for literary culture boomed then, benefitting from this institutionalisation (Mas Zabala 2000: 49).

Fornet adds another dimension to this experience, positioning *Huracán* as a radical large-scale response to the demand for literary texts, with quantity overriding any concern for the physical quality of the book as object: '*Huracán* eran libros pésimamente editados, en un papel espantoso que se te deshacía en las manos pero que te tiraban cincuenta, sesenta mil ejemplares y valían veinticinco centavos, treinta centavos, cuarenta centavos en la calle' [AF] ('*Huracán* books were really badly made books, with awful paper which came apart in your hands, but they would do print-runs of fifty or sixty thousand copies and sell them at twenty-five, thirty, forty cents in the street'). *Huracán*'s remit also allowed space for more specialist literary publishing aspirations to be addressed:

'A nosotros *Huracán* nos daba un gran, una gran tranquilidad. ¿Por qué? Porque no teníamos que tener la preocupación de estar publicando al Galdós, ni de estar publicando al Dickens. ¿Tú sabes? Ya nosotros queríamos otra cosa…ir más allá, entonces eso lo podíamos hacer porque digamos, el consumo masivo de literatura estaba garantizado por *Huracán*'. [AF][8]

Indeed, Smorkaloff's analysis of the Instituto's remit emphasised that the sustained attempt to 'organize into one more or less organic system all the diverse components of the publishing industry' in order to address and accommodate growth was accompanied by a parallel attempt to structure a new range of 'series' or 'groups' organised by genre, content or discipline, 'responsible for the editing, production and distribution of literary, scientific and educational texts', including Arte y Literatura (Cuban and foreign literature), Ciencia y Técnica, Ciencias Sociales, Orbe, Gente Nueva, Pueblo y Educación (text books), Ambito and Ediciones de Arte, all precursors of the specialised structures created by MINCULT in 1976 (Smorkaloff, 1997: 116–17). According to Smorkaloff, the IL also addressed distribution, proposing a bookshop in every province (1997: 116); in fact, the more ambitious aim was for a bookshop in every *municipio* (municipality, or township). Indeed, the whole expansion, diversification and specialisation since 1959 boosted bookshop infrastructure, in terms of quantity and diversity, with more specialist booksellers running bookshops such as that on Reina or the *Centenario* in Vedado.

This growth in overall infrastructure enabled the expansion and evolution of literary production and reception, but implied a degree of regulation. The CNC, through its prizes and departments, actively encouraged production and circulation of literature, but also sought to establish norms and parameters. Once again, therefore, the question of regulation and promotion was experienced in diverse, complex and sometimes contradictory ways by writers whose introduction to literary culture occurred around then, experiencing the effects of the early 1960s' projects and the ways that rupture and continuity co-existed. The continuing debate between visions of revolutionary literary culture, set against changing national and international contexts, thus provides a revealing backdrop for the whole 'crisis' of 1968–76.

The recollections of individuals coming of age as students, writers, cultural participants and cultural workers in the late 1960s offer fresh perspectives on the period [NAG; AAL]. One writer who came to prominence only in the 1990s, but experienced literary culture at the Universidad de la Habana, albeit informally, in the late 1960s, was Nancy Alonso, who identified 1967 (when she enrolled), as a moment when the focus on development, progress and modernity had significant implications for aspiring writers, eliciting, as in her case, a response of individual intellectual and professional self-sacrifice for the collective good:

1961–89: Radicalisation and consolidation 99

A pesar de mis inclinaciones literarias, nunca se me ocurrió escribir y cuando llegó el momento de escoger una carrera [...] yo me decidí por las ciencias biológicas por un sentido de... digamos del deber en ese momento. Es decir, había un llamado que el futuro era de las ciencias y que había que desarrollar el país, y toda esa historia, ¿no?, y yo tenía ese sentido del deber y lo volvería a tener – el de contribuir y desarrollar el país. [NAG]⁹

Despite her response to this 'call', however, Alonso was able to participate in the more informal literary culture characterising student life then, such early experiences shaping her subsequent self-definition, although it was many decades before she fulfilled her literary aspirations.

The atmosphere of debate, exploration, experimentation, rupture and constant reinvention was, likewise, crucial to the later development of many who, through youth or lack of access, were new to literary culture. The co-existence of a wide range of youth cultures, incorporating and fusing national and international trends, and liberal and more radical ideologies, is evident from the recollections of writers of that time, the key concept being that of *discusiones* (Codina, 2003: 70–1) (debate). Marilyn Bobes, for instance, talked of the more restrictive aspects of regulation of youth culture at that time, locating them within wider practices of radical questioning and reinvention: 'Entonces todo era proyecto, ruptura, borrón y cuenta nueva. Teníamos una despiadada facilidad para el olvido y una candorosa energía para las ilusiones' (Codina, 2003: 145–51) ('and so everything was a matter of starting a project, then breaking it off and making a fresh start. We had a ruthless ability to forget about things and an innocent energy for dreaming').

Nevertheless, a more militant strand of daily life, including literary culture, was clearly gaining strength in the 'siege'. Similarly, the consonance of those discourses and value systems with radical movements in Europe and Latin America is aptly described by the Argentinian-born writer and critic Basilia Papastamatíu; through meeting Julio Cortázar and Cuban writers (including Sarduy and Fernández Retamar) in Paris in the mid-1960s, and motivated by events there and in Buenos Aires, she was encouraged by Cortázar to visit Cuba, initially as part of a Casa de las Américas jury. Her arrival in 1968 concided with the start of the *caso Padilla*, her reaction demonstrating that prior frames of experience, in space or time, were vital in evaluating such moments of cultural and political tension: '¿Pero qué pasa? Yo que había vivido tantas coyunturas en Francia y en Argentina, uno sabe que las cosas van, vienen, se desarrollan, no puedes cambiar de lugar y de país porque pasa tal fenómeno tal. En mi país estaba peor porque había una dictadura militar (risa)' [BP]. ('but what happened? I, who had lived so many crisis moments in France and in Argentina? One knows that things come and go, develop, that you can't change place and move country just because such and such happens. In my own country things were much worse because there was a military dictatorship [laughs]'). Although she herself suffered some effects of the *caso* (moving from experimental writing to *periodismo cultural* during the *quinquenio*), she described the *caso* not as a moment of crisis, but as a series of 'coyunturas que pasan' ('passing moments'), which eventually dissipated; however, she echoed many Cuban scholars' observations that such passing moments have tended, among outside commentators, to be frozen in time, seen as representative of the entire Revolution [BP].

Despite the controversies and tensions which surfaced with the *caso*, another understanding of national development through culture (seeing literary culture as central to social integration) continued to thrive in the late 1960s, along with more Havana-based ideas and values. Emilio Comas Paret's recollections offer an illuminating counterpoint to a Havana-dominated view of literary culture; from a humble fishing family in Caibarién, Villa Clara, Comas Paret did not start writing until 1969, having studied electrical engineering, and worked in petroleum engineering, and then (1963–68) as a *técnico medio* (technician). He began his university career teaching in the Facultad de Pedagogía at the Universidad Central, while studying for a degree in history, subsequently becoming a *dirigente* (leading activist) in the Party and the CTC. He clearly defined himself not as a student of *letras* (literature), but a self-taught writer learning his craft through mentors (including Rodríguez Feo) and reading:

> Lo que he hecho es leer mucho. Cuando yo me decidí a escribir.... Primero yo me puse a leer ... y después, cuando empecé a escribir, me puse a leer a todos los grandes narradores que me caían por delante, es decir, a Quiroga, a Onelio Jorge Cardoso, a Guy de Maupassant, después como sí, a los grandes americanos, a Faulkner, a Salinger, a Hemingway que me influyó muchísimo en mí. [ECP][10]

He then went on to read Russian realist classics, all of which broadened his literary vision, as did the *talleres literarios* movement, which he joined in 1975, winning first prize for a short story at the first Encuentro Nacional [ECP].

Clearly, then, far from a steady process of restriction, leading inexorably to the monolithic *gris* 1970s, this period saw a continuing proliferation of spaces that also, however, partly created the conditions for the later atmosphere of suspicion. UNEAC, for example, saw the organic proliferation of sub-groups around 1969 (including those soon to become Brigada Hermanos Saíz) being motivated by an individual/ personal and collective/social need for a group identity, as had an earlier project, where a group of young people formed their own impromptu version of *Caimán Barbudo* [NC].

Hence, we should question our understanding of 'institutionalisation' during this period: rather than ICAIC, UNEAC, Casa, the CNC, and the IL being created to prescribe cultural practice, these formal institutional spaces validated the emergence of parallel groups and spaces – often uniting the traditionally separate spheres of culture and politics – which allowed individuals to develop their contribution. Perhaps the key to understanding how these two phenomena could co-exist – and, thus perhaps, to understanding that the *quinquenio* was not experienced by everyone uniformly – lies in the value attributed to literary activities, and the fact that literary culture could embrace a number of types of value. For those accustomed to pre-1959 Havana cultural life, however, social transformation created conflicts and tensions; Fornet explained how one's sense of the Revolution depended as much on location (physical space, and the symbolic qualities attributed to it) as on other factors; echoing the disorientation of the urban middle-class protagonist Sergio, in Gutiérrez Alea's *Memorias del Subdesarrollo* (1968), Fornet described 1968 in Havana as a year when the 'normal' reference points were lost: 'con la prematura desaparición de de los pequeños negocios privados, perdió los puntos de referencia que le daban a ciertos barrios sus señas de identidad' (Espinosa, 2008: 25) ('with the premature disappearance of small private businesses, the points of reference which gave certain neighbourhoods their distinctive identity were lost').

With these radical developments in the goals and scale of literary publishing, the importance of the question of copyright should not be underestimated, its formal abolition being declared during the 1966 Tricontinental (Rodríguez, 2001: 77), but most explicitly being reiterated at the Seminario Preparatorio (25 October to 2 November 1967) for the January 1968 Congreso Cultural de La Habana. That Congress – bringing together over 400 participants and 100 journalists in the Habana Libre Hotel (Cantón Navarro and Duarte Hurtado,

2006a: 185) – came in the chaotic and conflictive context of debates and jostling for position, between individuals, spaces and forces united only in their agreement with the nation-building project and the project's need for a complex notion of culture. Its slogan – 'Colonialismo y neocolonialismo en el desarrollo cultural de los pueblos' ('colonialism and neocolonialism in the cultural development of peoples') – made explicit the centrality of the themes to be debated; the question of how to achieve this, however, remained vexed. Portuondo later described emerging Cuban intellectuals being 'seduced' by the number of foreign guests, who, while sometimes truly revolutionary, were often still tainted with neocolonialism and tried to teach the Cubans 'cómo había que conducir la Revolución en el terreno estético y en el terreno cultural' (Portuondo, 1979: 45) ('how to lead the Revolution in its aesthetic and cultural fields'), turning younger Cubans' heads towards hypercriticism (of Cuba) and exogenous cultural models. While one might see this reading as a justification of the *caso Padilla*, especially since he then talked of the 1971 Congress, quoting its final declaration at length and extolling its virtues, the evidence suggests a complex set of forces at play.

One particularly active group, clustered around *Caimán* – which, in 1967, had become autonomous from *Juventud Rebelde* (*Granma* 1967: 4) – found an immediate platform in the Congress, seeing the project as legitimising their generational claim, putting them on the Latin American literary stage and differentiating them from the previous 'contaminated' generation, through their closer contact with literacy and growing (young) readerships. The confidence engendered by that sense of generational entitlement found its first public stage at the Congress, which crystallised a moment of political instability and radicalism, when the incommensurability of the domains of value within literary culture – existing since 1959 but now more noticeable through internal evolution and external circumstances – came to the fore.

Abreu Arcia considered the core members of the *Caimán* group to have been central to the debates of 1968, the natural consequence of the earlier radicalisation of aesthetics, writing practices, and sociopolitical and intellectual projects. However, he interpreted the period as 'Un segmento de tiempo en el que las pugnas y escaramuzas entre autónomos y heterónomos por el usufructo del capital simbólico estimulan nuevas ambiciones, voluntad de protagonismo, resentimientos, ajustes de cuenta' (Abreu Arcia, 2007: 102) ('a segment of time when the fights and skirmishes between autonomous and heteronomous groups over the permanent entitlement to symbolic capital stimulates new ambitions, desires for protagonism, resentments, and the settling of scores'). Moreover, he noted how these groups authorised their legitimacy by prioritising action and politics over the written word and representation, and, more specifically (in the sphere of literary culture) by privileging the social and political utility of art over its aesthetics qualities, and coercing the 'sujeto letrado' (educated subject) into becoming an 'ideólogo' (ideologue) first and foremost (Abreu Arcia, 2007: 107).

Abreu Arcia drew attention to new ideological discussions, reflecting a continental dimension of the siege mentality that would influence Cuban literary and intellectual life. When Angel Rama, writing in *Casa de las Américas* in November–December 1967, warned of an imperialist plot by the US government (focusing on Casa) to undermine the intellectual movement in Latin America (Abreu Arcia, 2007: 122), *Caimán*'s political concerns and frustrations seemed less indicative of a local and provincial focus, and wider in nature than was imagined.

However, with the collectivist focus established, their position might simply have reflected the *segunda generación*'s experiencing a new reality, having been socialised to engage with it as agents, a process complicated by an ever-accumulating series of domains of value, each with their own spaces and actors. Hence, rather than seeing the tensions leading to the *quinquenio* as a duel between literature and politics, we could see them as the inevitable by-product of the proliferation and natural evolution of groups, ideas, generations and spaces, set against an increasingly defensive backdrop. Portuondo specifically categorised *Caimán* as an example of the false generationalism that he had previously criticised: 'El problema nuestro no es medir las diferencias generacionales por razones cronológicas sino por razones de tipo ideológico' (Portuondo, 1979: 39–40) ('our problem lies in measuring generational differences not as chronology but as ideology'). In addition, bearing in mind the notion of the individual/collective continuum, could the sometimes contradictory shifting of positions of individuals and groups be seen not primarily as opportunism or strategic self-interest on a national stage (and on the part of *heterónomos* (heteronomous) or *autónomos* (autonomous), as Abreu Arcia put it), but rather as the dynamic operationalisation of positions along that continuum, at both national and international or continental levels? The evidence might suggest, as Arturo Arango noted in his response to Abreu's work, that the more recent generations of writers and intellectuals were the natural products of the urge to participate actively in the Revolution, which had characterised the euphoric and chaotic early 1960s (Arango, 2009: 56–9). Indeed, by the late 1960s, there was ample evidence of the potential for 'new' cohorts to contribute to literary culture, precisely through being educated and socialised by that culture. This suggests that the debates of 1968 articulated not just internal power struggles, but also the 'ambiente creativo' (creative environment) and need for participation on local, national and continental stages that was central to the self-definition of emerging writers [AAB].

This trajectory now takes us to the most sensitive period of Cuban literary culture, starting with the 1971 Congreso de Educación y Cultura and ending with the 1976 creation of MINCULT. This *quinquenio* is usually seen as the point where the fields of culture and politics came into direct conflict, with particular effect on some genres (literature, theatre, popular music). Although we argue for a more complex approach, our aim is not to minimise the gravity of the period, individually and collectively, nor to imply that the excessive control of cultural production was either justifiable or necessary. Indeed, as became abundantly clear in recent reassessments of the period, during the several *Encuentros* of 2007, the personal and intellectual consequences for many, though far-reaching and highly damaging, had been hidden from view, remaining unknown to younger Cubans (Kumaraswami, 2009b). The initial *Encuentro* and subsequent iterations in 2007, the space created by the television broadcast of a programme (*Impronta*) apparently favourable towards the highly controversial figure of Luis Pavón Tamayo, Director of the CNC from 1971 to 1976, and the subsequent *guerra de los correos* (email war), all allowed for many narratives of political and personal marginalisation to be aired publicly for the first time in over thirty years. While the period was reassessed, it also became clear that sensitivity towards those who had suffered was rightly paramount in any such process of self-examination and reassessment: indeed, a recent debate in the *Gaceta de Cuba* between Arango and Abreu Arcia (Arango, 2009: 59) underlined the fact that, with many of the protagonists still alive, respect towards those who had been affected was the primary concern.

It is important to stress, however, that, as much as it meant insuperable challenges and anguish for some, it also brought opportunities and freedoms for others. Even more significantly, it continued and developed many collectivist projects and policies of the preceding decade, and, hence, can largely be seen as a consolidation of structures, spaces and mechanisms to further national development and cultural decolonisation. Likewise, although it would be difficult to argue that the most marginalised figures exercised significant agency during the *quinquenio*, there is ample evidence from the interviews conducted for this study that there was a range of responses to 'la mala hora' (Abreu Arcia, 2007: 155) ('the bad times'). Perhaps as a gesture of defiance against the more public repressive spaces, private local spaces became important sites of agency, collaboration and literary practice. Importantly, however, spaces for literary culture to be practised are also discernible within the institutional structure (the Universidad de la Habana, the *talleres* network, the Brigada Hermanos Saíz, the workplace).

Nevertheless, nothing represents more dramatically the moment where two regimes of value – political value and aesthetic value – came into direct confrontation than the notorious and much commented Primer Congreso de Educación y Cultura; significantly, 'culture' was added at the last minute to what had been intended as an educational event, possibly in response to the previous day's letter, signed by various European and Latin American intellectuals, protesting at Padilla's arrest (Abreu Arcia, 2007: 138). It took place on 23–30 April 1971, the full declaration being published on 1 May and the *Memorias* being published by MINED. The late change of title made explicit the conceptual juxtaposition of culture and education, reflected clearly in the opening speech, where the former 26 July Movement veteran and Minister, Belarmino Castillo, spoke of education as rejecting 'las expresiones de reblandecimiento y corrupción' ('expressions of softening and corruption') presumably to be found in cultural expression, and seeing education and culture as forming 'un todo homogéneo' (Abreu Arcia, 2007: 140) ('a homogeneous whole').

The Organising Commission was created on 14 December 1970, followed by regional congresses (4–7 March) and provincial congresses (15–19 March); the final Congreso, at the Teatro Radiocentro (later the Cine Yara), was attended by some 1,700 delegates, chaired by Fidel Castro. Several organisations sent representatives: MINED, the CDRs, UJC, CTC, ANAP and even the Foreign Ministry. However, ominously, 'las instituciones y organizaciones culturales constituyen una minoría, apenas visible' (Abreu Arcia, 2007: 138) ('the cultural institutions and organisations constitute a barely visible minority'). The best represented was ICAIC, who sent several important figures and screened two cycles of films alongside the Congreso, at Cine La Rampa. Pavón attended, representing *Verde Olivo*, but, despite the presence of individual intellectuals representing their institutions (including Casa), there was no formal presence from *Unión*, *Gaceta de Cuba* or, crucially, *Caimán*, let alone from UNEAC (Abreu Arcia, 2007: 139). The one discussion group on culture (*Comisión 6-B*) had its troubled plenary session on 27 March, attended by Castro and coinciding with Padilla's *autocrítica* in UNEAC (Abreu Arcia, 2007: 140).

The content of the Congress's formal declaration has been discussed at length, with special emphasis rightly paid to the discourse of clearing out corrupt and pernicious elements on the basis of sexuality, class, religious belief, participation, contamination by residence abroad, and so on [MY; CL; AAM; PAF; RGZ]. Likewise, ample attention has been paid to the Congress's effects and consequences for cultural life: the insularisation of Cuban culture; an acritical dependence on Soviet models, including socialist realism; and the opposition between the individual writer or artist and the monolithic and all-poweful state. Nevertheless, some aspects of the Declaration's timing and tone defy easy explanations, inviting parallel or supplementary readings: notably the continued commitment to national sovereignty and cultural massification. Perhaps most importantly, the bringing together of culture and education, and the seemingly *guerrillerista* assertion that 'El arte es un arma de la revolución' ('Los intelectuales extranjeros' 1971: 150) can be read as evidence of a particularly anti-colonial response to cultural and political developments of the time, already articulated by the *Caimán* group at the 1968 Congress and gaining strength amongst Latin American intellectuals by 1971.

In this context, the vexed question of how to define the revolutionary intellectual, eloquently argued in Fernández Retamar's essay *Calibán* (Fernández Retamar, 1980; Abreu Arcia, 2007: 143–54), became especially important. Published just months after the Congress, in Issue 68 of *Casa de las Américas* (September–October 1971), it shed different light on the *caso*, outlining the temptation (under the considerable influence of the newly emerging 'boom') for Latin American intellectuals to be 'seduced' by European paradigms of the intellectual, the risks of that paradigm to the project of cultural decolonisation, and the powerful ideological and market forces at play which, having created the Latin American 'boom', now threatened to characterise as underdeveloped those writers refusing to follow the paradigm. In this sense, the oppositions in play in 1961 in reformulating the notion of the intellectual (and, by extension, literary culture) were overlaid in 1968–71 by an emerging continentalist agenda with development at its core. In spite of the marginalisation and regulation of individual writers during this period, an overarching element of community and legitimacy was provided by the postcolonial position generally adopted.

However, 1971 did represent sharp ruptures with the previous revolutionary past: the Pavón-led forces emerged from the Congress leading a transformed CNC, largely bereft of the cultural vanguard of the 1960s (no longer deemed politically trustworthy), the only exceptions being certain prestigious figures in Casa de las Amércias and ICAIC.

Analysis of the recollections of those experiencing firsthand the worst effects of the *quinquenio* supports the view of the phenomenon as a complex and contradictory period, showing that, even within the context of prescription and marginalisation, spaces outside, or peripheral to, the CNC remit became increasingly important. As Alejandro Alvarez expressed it: 'Pero fue un momento que se puede llamar hasta tenebroso en la cultura cubana, a partir del Consejo Nacional de Cultura y las barbaridades que hizo, por una parte y las cosas buenas que se hicieron, por otra' [AAB] ('but it was moment in Cuban culture that we might even describe as sinister, with the National Council for Culture and the awful things it did, on the one hand, and the good things that happened, on the other').

The main instrument of marginalisation of those considered *conflictivos* ('difficult') was non-publication [MY; AAM; PAF; GRR, RGZ; EHL], sometimes for up to ten or fifteen years. In Reynaldo González's view, these decisions were often abrupt and unexpected: 'Yo caí en la redada de muchísimos escritores cubanos que estuvieron sin publicar. Yo fui el primero que publicó de los marginados … O sea yo estuve desde el año 68 hasta el 78 sin publicar' [RGZ] ('I fell in the raid on many Cuban writers who weren't published. I was the first of those marginalised to publish … In other words, I wasn't published between 1968 and 1978'). Others were prevented from cultural participation [CL; AAM; EHL], had their passports removed, were 'purged' from UNEAC or were 'punished' by being sidelined in manual labour or out of sight of the public [EHL; AAM]. Some found spaces as translators, printers and junior researchers, where they could at least maintain some level of participation in intellectual and cultural life [CL; AAM], while others continued to be paid their salary: 'No me publicaban, pero me pagaban un sueldo. De modo que yo podía ir, y me daban unos cheques e iba a un banco y cobraba el dinero que correspondía a mi sueldo. Lo cual te hace pensar que tú eres un mantenido, y te crea más soberbia' [RGZ] ('they didn't publish me, but they paid me a salary. So I could go along, and they'd give me some cheques, and I'd go to the bank and cash the money that was my salary. All of that makes you feel like you're a kept man, and increases your arrogance').

A frequent theme of all those interviewed was their unshaken commitment to the revolutionary project, a continued sense of belonging and an ability to distinguish that it was, in Alfredo Prieto's words, a period of 'luces y sombras' [AP] ('light and shadow'), which, despite the suffering endured by many, still achieved much at a collective level. As González expressed it: 'Y yo decidí quedarme en Cuba, y bueno, que se vayan ellos. Este es mi país, no voy a ir. Y no es por convicciones políticas ni mucho menos, no me da la gana, es mi país.... Entonces, cada cual respondió a eso como pudo y supo. Todo el mundo tuvo un poco de razón, como pasa en las tragedias, ¿no?' [RGZ] ('I decided to stay in Cuba, and there you have it, let *them* leave. This is my country and I'm not going to leave. And not out of any political conviction or anything, I don't want to leave, it's my country ... And so, every individual responded as best they could. Everyone was just a little bit right, just like what happens in tragedies, right?') Crucial in this continued belief was the support offered by small communities of intellectuals and networks outside Cuba offering some, more prestigious, individuals the possibility of publication') [CL; PAF]. Mostly, however, it was left to Cuba-based cultural figures to offer support and encouragement [CL; MY; PAF; GRR]; indeed, marginalisation unwittingly became a means of agglutination among writers and intellectuals, especially younger ones drawn more naturally to 'underground' culture. Even more interestingly, those figures who remained institutionally prominent after 1971 still offered their support; as López expressed it:

> Ahora bien, si oficialmente dejamos de existir, y muchos ni siquiera venían a la casa, otros – de los grandes señores de la cultura cubana – siempre no se alejaron, siempre se mantuvieron cerca de nosotros, a veces telefónicamente. Eso es importante para entender qué es lo que está pasando en Cuba. Que aunque hubo actitudes miserables por parte de algunos dirigentes culturales, políticos – entre lo cultural está lo político – hubo también personas que nos respetaron... Toda esa gente nos alentaron explícita o implícitamente a seguir trabajando por la cultura, por nuestro país, por la patria. [CL][11]

Especially revealing was the way that physical and symbolic spaces were created and utilised in the process of 're-educating' supposedly wayward or decadent individuals. Two of the most moving and detailed accounts of the process of *parametración* (the term used to describe the imposition of strict limits or controls) were provided by Heras León and Arrufat, recounting their removal from public intellectual life to the private and hidden spaces of, respectively, a steel factory and the basement of the Marianao municipal library. Not only was the menial and routine nature of their work revealing, but also the way in which this space assumed multiple functions for many. For those seeking to *parametrar*, the library basement or the noise of the steel factory surely created the physical conditions for marginalisation and silencing. However, both Arrufat and Heras León responded to the moments of privacy and isolation which marginalisation afforded by continuing to write or, in the case of Heras León (expelled from his university post), by 'educating' the steel workers. Ultimately, the complex and multilayered nature of this period was seen, by Arrufat, as also a foundation for sustained and powerful debate, 'una lucha impresionante entre personas dogmáticas y personas que no lo son, personas flexibles, inteligentes y personas que realmente no lo eran' [AAM] ('an incredible struggle between people who were dogmatic and others who were not, between flexible, intelligent people and others who really were not') and his resignation to his fate was partly born of the expectation that writers were supposed to criticise and question the state, which in turn would inevitably exert a level of control:

> Siempre tuve la idea de que a los escritores le ocurren esas cosas y que los escritores siempre tienen una especie de diferendo con el Estado aunque puedan participar, como en mi caso, de los principios generales del Estado en el cual viven, pero al mismo tiempo tienen una serie de diferencias con la ejecución y la puesta en práctica de esos principios. [AAM][12]

Herás León, however, considered himself and his emerging generation to be worst affected by *parametración*, truncating irreparably their literary contribution at the point they might have been compared with the celebrated young Latin American writers of the 'boom': 'Nosotros somos una generación frustrada. Yo tengo seis, siete, ocho libros publicados, y debería tener seis, siete novelas publicadas' [EHL] ('we are a frustrated generation. I have six, seven, eight books published, and I should have six, seven, novels published').

Equally revealing of a more complex relationship between the state, individuals and groups was the way that spaces could be experienced simultaneously as dogmatic or permissive, depending on the political or cultural arena at any given time, and on the status of the individuals in positions of leadership. Aurelio Alonso, talking of *Pensamiento Crítico*, described the survival and increasing importance of spaces from 1971 onwards:

> Yo creo que en Cuba nunca se pudo implantar un realismo socialista completo, porque hubo espacios en que esa visión nunca tuvo alcance ¿no? Nunca pudo apoderarse, por ejemplo del ICAIC, del cine. Nunca pudo apoderarse porque había un intelectual de una, de mucho peso ahí dentro, conduciendo eso, con criterios muy propios y distantes del realismo socialista, que era Alfredo Guevara. [AAT][13]

More revealingly, he described the way that *Pensamiento Crítico* itself 'regulated' orthodox Soviet material, to be loyal to a more radical and heterogeneous national, or even continental, tradition, while explaining the 'problems' that this caused for the members of the editorial team:

> Bueno, *Pensamiento Crítico* fue hija de esa apertura y disgustó mucho a los soviéticos en aquella época…. Nosotros nunca… y, además, nos mandaban siempre las… los boletines del *Novosti*, para que publicáramos algo. Nosotros nunca publicamos… nunca… hay que decir que nos esforzamos porque queríamos publicar algo, pero nunca sentimos que había algo que valiera la pena (risa), que pudiéramos aceptarlo en el marco teórico y ejercimos la censura nosotros ahí dentro. [AAT][14]

In that sense, contemporaneous and post hoc accusations of individual opportunism and strategic self-positioning were just as likely to be efforts toward contributing in diverse ways towards the national project. As Alejandro Alvarez recounted his recollections of the still bitter debates resulting from the 2007 *Encuentros*:

> como bien dijo Víctor Fowler, en la última reunión, hablando de Pavón, nada más y nada menos, ustedes saben el nombre. Esto … se paró Fowler y dijo, "habrá sido lo que sea pero hay que pensar que es un compañero nuestro". Recuerdo que después Sacha le comenta afuera, le dice a Fowler, "ese no es mi compañero". Y Fowler, con su ojo virado y su cara socarrona, le dice, "No, el día que haya que estar en una trinchera, yo voy a ver quién es el que va a estar a lado tuyo; ¿no va a ser Pavón?". [AAB][15]

Fowler's military metaphor likewise suggested the polyvalent nature of many of the institutional and informal spaces that regulated or enabled literary culture during this period. Revealingly, some of those interviewed saw it as inevitable that the model of institutionalisation characterising Cuban public life from the early 1960s should also be extended to literary culture. Alvarez's explanation of the permeating

1961–89: Radicalisation and consolidation

influence of the institutional model allows us to see the porosity – and hierarchies of value – between social, cultural and political institutions:

> Ahora la institucionalización se metía en todo lo que no tenía que meterse, aquello era mucho, eran unas normativas; los propios reglamentos de la UNEAC, hay que revisarlos, están en eso; que eran muy específicos y hay una realidad, o sea, hay una verdad en la realidad cubana que hay siempre una especie de transposición hacia las instituciones culturales, se convierten en una especie de trasunto de las organizaciones sociales políticas, que es lógico porque es parte del mecanismo social cubano. [AAB][16]

Nevertheless, there were 'breathing spaces' within the institutional structures of state-sponsored cultural organisations, more successful at promoting a less dogmatic or monolithic vision, or, at least, at avoiding scrutiny. Many commented on the multi-dimensional nature of the cultural projects in which practitioners were involved, indicating that the porosity between cultural institutions offers several benefits: Alvarez, for example, referring to literary culture since 1990, indicated that the precarious financial recognition awarded to writers publishing in Cuba is offset or mitigated by the ability to work across a variety of cultural forms: 'Por tanto, los escritores siempre participan activamente en el tejido social del país, vía sus propios modus vivendi, y además, porque hay una interrelación con otras manifestaciones … Siempre ha habido una interrelación muy intensa en todas las manifestaciones [AAB] ('and so, writers always participate actively in the social fabric of the country, via their own modus vivendi, and besides, all the cultural forms are inter-related … all the cultural forms have always been profoundly interrelated').

The importance of some of these interrelated spaces during the *quinquenio* has not been fully explored. Although it is well known that ICAIC maintained an unusual level of self-sufficiency – surprisingly, given the Revolution's early awareness of the potential of cinema, as a mass cultural form, to influence minds (Chanan, 1985, 2004) – less studied is the case of the Escuela de Letras. Many interviewees considered that the Escuela replaced the 'problematic' Departmento de Filosofía as a space where ideas could be studied and discussed freely. As Prieto expressed it:

> Para decirles de alguna manera, la filosofía que yo quería estudiar no era exactamente la filosofía que se enseñaba oficialmente en la universidad. Porque yo conocía ciertas polémicas que había habido en Cuba en los

años 60, estaba informado de la existencia de una cosa que se llamaba en los 60 el Departamento de Filosofía, los estudios que hicieron en ese momento, un marxismo humanista, diferente al burocratizado oficial soviético. [AP][17]

Indeed, for his cohort, it was precisely during the *quinquenio* that the Escuela, through the study of literature, provided a training in philosophy and the history of ideas unavailable in other institutional spaces.

However, the Escuela did experience periods of scrutiny [MY, MSM]. Indeed, increasing restrictions on staff and students in the early 1970s reflected the 1971 Congress's more dogmatic understanding of education. As the most talented graduates were kept on as teachers, the potential provided by individual mentors began to be replaced with a more standardised – and mass-oriented – vision of teaching: 'la docencia que me asfixiaba porque la universidad donde estudié y donde hice mi carrera fue cambiando, fue "normativizándose" de una manera donde se fue perdiendo mucho la creatividad y la libertad expresiva' [MSM] ('the teaching which suffocated me, because the university where I studied and got my degree began to change, began to be strictly regulated in such a way that it lost much of its creativity and freedom of expression'). Santos Moray also noted that journalism allowed a measure of freedom, compared with the elitist Escuela:

> Yo soy periodista porque fue el lugar que me dejaron libre, por el menosprecio que ellos sentían hacia el periodismo, lo subestimaban y por eso pude ser periodista, pero me cerraron muchas puertas con Marinello, con Guillén, con Fabio Grobar, con la propia Mirta (Aguirre), me decían que era un capricho mío'. [MSM][18]

For her, education was increasingly both a prime revolutionary duty and an inescapable obligation, measuring the moral, social and ideological worth of the revolutionary individual; she describes the reaction of a colleague at the Escuela, when she asked to leave: 'Tuve que acudir al certificado psiquiátrico para poderme ir de la docencia universitaria porque aquello era "la cárcel del pueblo a la que se entraba y no se salía", esas fueron las palabras exactas de esa mujer' [MSM] ('I had to resort to a psychiatric assessment in order to be able to leave my teaching duties at the university because it was "the people's prison which you could enter but never leave", those were the exact words that woman used'). For other *conflictivas*, such as Yánez, however, the situation was contradictory in the extreme, university teaching providing a space for self-expression: despite being marginalised for her sexuality, she continued to teach at the Escuela for several decades, an incomprehensible tolerance which she describes thus: 'me dejaron la paradoja de profesora de la universidad. Yo era muy conflictiva, sin embargo, podía ser profesora de la universidad y allí era muy querida, respetada, hasta que me cansé de ser profesora y me fui a escribir a mi casa [MY] ('they left me the paradoxical situation of my university teaching post. I was very controversial, but still I could be a university teacher and I was well loved and respected there, until the day that I got tired of being a teacher and stayed at home to write').

Other interviewees pointed to the availability of alternative spaces and mechanisms within the university structures for developing and representing their ideas. The Escuela de Periodismo emerges as another key prestigious institution facilitating cross-fertilisation and collaboration: one prominent journalist alluded to the competitive entry requirements to study journalism – not only sufficient grade points, but also a *prueba de aptitud* (proficiency test) consisting of a submitted essay [IMR]; while others identified a training in journalism (even through the informal *movimiento de corresponsales* (correspondents' movement)) as a route into writing literature: 'En fin, sin darme cuenta, fui como preparando un camino – mi voz de locutor siempre me ayudaba en eso – fui como preparando el camino hasta que un día me dijeron "oye, si quieres, ven a trabajar como periodista"' [PJG] ('well, without even realising it, I sort of prepared the ground – my presenter's voice always helped me in that – I sort of prepared the ground until one day they said to me "listen, come and work as a journalist if you want"'). Indeed, especially for those individuals whose social and educational background had not prepared them for higher education or literary culture, the Escuela de Periodismo provided an entrance into these environments by allowing them a cultural and textual space for using life experience as a basis for their writing.

Once they had graduated, aspiring intellectuals also had other institutional spaces enabling them to pursue their literary interests during the worst years: the ILL became an important base for literary researchers [EDL], for the typology and historiography of Cuban literature [SA], but, importantly, as a valuable place to employ writers and researchers [SC]. Perhaps more than most, Casa de las Américas also provided protection for marginalised writers such as Pablo Armando Fernández, describing himself as having been 'amparado por la poesía' [PAF] ('sheltered by poetry').

What, however, of the spaces outside the capital, or 'under the radar' of the more prominent individuals and institutions in Havana? Were the writers emerging through these mechanisms subject to the same regimes of value and expectations as those emerging through more traditional or prestigious routes? One particularly controversial phenomenon, now receiving attention, was the *talleres literarios* movement. Originating as a nationwide project in 1970, it was really the institutionalisation of existing spaces for the circulation of literary culture at a mass level.

The exploration of the national *talleres* movement in the 1970s invites us to formulate a more complex and dynamic understanding of the *quinquenio*, and of what exactly was understood by 'literary culture' during this period. The multiplicity of experiences and perspectives of the *talleres* is reflected in many of the interviews undertaken, most interviewees depicting the movement as bringing mixed blessings, although recognising that it certainly promoted new writers and new writing, allowed Havana's dominance to be challenged, or at least mitigated, by aspiring provincial writers, through the mechanism of the Encuentros Nacionales, and, finally and more generally, created an awareness of modes of literary expression, through the act of reading or writing. Interestingly, several writers reflected on some contradictions in their valuation of the movement: the complex interpretation by the literary scholar Salvador Arias is a case in point. Talking of the movement in the 1970s, he stated:

> Hubo muchos autores que ahora son reconocidos que salieron de los talleres literarios. ¿Qué es lo que pasa? Que eso tendía a estancarse un poco. ... Yo siempre pienso, él que llegó a ser escritor, los talleres literarios lo podían ayudar pero él que lo iba a ser lo iba a ser. Lo mismo lo iba a ser por muchos talleres que tuviera (risas). Pero fue muy importante, sobre todo porque el tallerista, si no salió un escritor de allí, por lo menos salió un lector. [SA][19]

The role and value of the *talleres* in creating readers (rather than writers) can be seen within the same trajectory of cultural and educational policy as the Literacy Campaign and the Casas de Cultura movement: an initiative not to standardise expression (although that undoubtedly happened), but, via a variety of agents and spaces and to a mass population, to realise the potential to interact with literary texts and culture, within a collective but local environment where the influence and guidance of individuals (whether *asesores literarios*, other *talleristas* or invited established writers) was at least as powerful as any notion of top-down monolithic policy directives. Two individuals at the centre of this drive to accelerate the development of an increasingly 'literary', rather than merely literate, culture – what Fornet has described as 'madurar con carburo' (the process by which bananas are artificially ripened) (*La política cultural*, 2008: 18) – are María Dolores Ortiz and Marta Terry. Ortiz described the creation (and unexpected instant success) of the television programme *Lea y Escriba*, first broadcast in 1969 to introduce an appreciation of texts, movements and individuals to mass audiences, specialist and non-specialist:

> Porque el programa empezó en el 69, o sea en un país recién alfabetizado, y nosotros pensábamos que era un programa que no le iba a interesar a nadie – a las grandes mayorías porque no sabían nada de nada, o estaban empezando a dar los primeros pasos; y él que sabía, ¿pues para qué iba a ver el programa si de lo que se pregunta allí, lo que se habla allí, se supone que una persona cultura lo sabe, ¿no? ... Para sorpresa nuestra, el programa se sostuvo – nosotros le dimos un cálculo de dos años – llevamos treinta y nueve casi (risa). O sea, como yo digo, me he puesto vieja en la televisión. [MDO][20]

Terry, on the other hand, described a short-lived *taller de lectura*, in the early 1970s, at Casa de las Américas, which allowed for the circulation and socialisation of literature across a range of levels of expertise, with a wide range of functions:

> Y entonces seleccionamos los libros que menos se leían. Eso los bibliotecarios lo seleccionaron a partir de estas estadísticas de lo que se lee y lo que no se lee. Era eso que se llama "mover la colección".... Y como era Casa de las Américas, entonces (risa), los mejores escritores de Cuba, los que estaban de paso, todo el mundo iba allí, y hablaba del libro'. [MTG][21]

What both of these visions described was an attempt to square the circle of bringing specialist and non-specialist readers and writers together to share the same spaces, each contributing their own understanding of the value of literature. Indeed, Doribal Enríquez indicated that the *talleres* movement and other initiatives had more in common with the *movimiento de aficionados* than with any Soviet-style imposition of literary and political norms [DE].

The *talleres*' nationwide dimension merits attention. For aspiring or established writers outside Havana, they provided a collective space, to incentivise literary appreciation and production and bring a visible measure of local recognition and prestige; but, through the Encuentros

Nacionales, they were also a mechanism for that currency to permeate the capital. Many provincial writers indicated that, although a historically strong literary culture had already existed in many places outside Havana, the *talleres*, often building on existing traditions but also creating new spaces, provided a crucial route for those local cultures to gain national recognition [NC]. The poet and scholar Roberto Manzano underlined the multiple levels at which the *talleres* contributed to the consolidation of a literary culture in Ciego de Ávila:

> Entonces, pues, el Estado tenía institucionalmente un asesor literario por cada municipio, por cada provincia y se dedicaba este individuo a buscar a los jóvenes a quienes les interesara escribir para organizarlos en talleres. Yo tuve esa suerte, rápidamente me incorporé a un taller. [RM][22]

However, he also underlined, again in the context of the provinces, the effect on the individual that a collectivist or mass movement such as the *talleres* could have: 'Tenía una enorme importancia, era el espacio que yo tenía para respirar vocacionalmente, porque imagínese, no tenía acceso a la capital' [RM] ('it was enormously important, it was the space I had in which to breathe vocationally, because, just imagine, I couldn't get to the capital'). Therefore, for those who lacked access to the intrinsic national (i.e. Havana-based) value, the existence of such a collective public space *taller* provided an important catalyst for self-identification as a writer and dialogue with peers [NC].

While the consensus about the early *talleres* movement is that it provided much-needed mechanisms and networks to promote aspiring writers and those whose social background did not imply an 'ambiente creativo' [AAB] ('creative atmosphere'), there was also some agreement that, as it became more established, it began to ossify, becoming less dynamic or responsive to local and individual needs and styles: the writer Alberto Garrandés, accepting the influence of Soviet science-fiction texts on his own literary development, highlighted the more negative aspects of the movement:

> No sé si decir 'por suerte' o decir 'por desgracia', el taller literario era un poco uniforme, ¿no?, había reglas, y cuando hay reglas – o sea hay reglas generales de retórica, de gramática, ortografía, etc – pero en un taller cuando alguien te dice que un relato breve debe ser así, ya eso no funciona bien, ¿no?' [AG][23]

Heras León (whose transformation of the *talleres* idea after 2000 is the subject of Chapter 6) also saw one of the movement's eventual flaws as being that the same climate of institutionalisation and massification which facilitated the growth of a mass movement also meant that writers could only develop to a certain point, after which the *taller*'s closed environment ceased to be of use: 'los talleres ya se cocinan en su propia salsa' [EHL] ('literary workshops end up following their own narrow rules').

However, alongside these potential writers, the national movement had a much wider importance for young readers, an aspect which is often neglected. A central figure of book publishing and the promotion of children's reading, Esteban Llorach Ramos, described how the *talleres* also incorporated prominent publishing houses, such as Gente Nueva, in order to promote literary culture among schoolchildren. Following Gente Nueva's research into young readerships in the early 1970s, and building on their existing contributions to *cultura comunitaria* (local community culture), the *talleres* added a level of prestige and status to the work already done by schoolteachers or school and public librarians, and, importantly, reinforced the potential for young readers to develop academically (and even imagine themselves as writers) and for schools to promote literary culture:

> Desde aquel entonces, se notó en todas las escuelas que había un grupo de Abelarditos, así los llaman a los que van muy delante, muy delanteros, que tenían las siguientes características. Ellos, aparte de leer, querían escribir. ... Te preguntaban aquellas cosas que a lo mejor no les preguntaban a los bibliotecarios o no le preguntaban al profesor. Porque tú venías rodeado de la aureola de que tú eras el editor, de una casa editorial. ... Por eso, cuando a la editorial se le acercaron desde el primer momento para hacer los talleres literarios, yo me sumé a ese empeño. [ELR][24]

Perhaps most importantly, Llorach described the movement as a complex network of contributions from different types of agent, working in a multitude of spaces. In this sense, the *talleres*' national success was entirely dependent on local individual and group commitment and participation:

> Ese empeño durante muchísimos años fue a nivel municipal. O sea, se hacían los concursos, y se quedaban a nivel municipal, y después a nivel provincial. A los que habíamos trabajado todo el tiempo nos parecía terrible que se perdiera, que no se viera a nivel nacional, ese esfuerzo del país, que además no es sólo ese esfuerzo estatal, gubernamental, sino el esfuerzo de ese maestro de la escuela, de ese trabajador de la Casa de la Cultura, de ese director de la Casa de Cultura, de esos padres, porque detrás de todo está el papá que tiene que coger el niño y llevarlo hasta la Casa de Cultura. [ELR][25]

The early 1970s' institutionalisation of the *talleres*, therefore, provided alternative mechanisms to mitigate a range of factors: geographical isolation, distance from the capital, lack of access to the traditional spaces of literary culture, and the inability to imagine oneself as a writer (or a reader?) of literature. Though the movement was clearly plagued by contradictions and problems, explaining why it has often been synonymous with the worst characteristics of the period, the evidence suggests that, without the drive for institutionalisation that they represented, the *talleres* were perhaps the only way to attempt to create a mass culture around literature. As Norberto Codina expressed it: 'Fue indiscutiblemente una experiencia importante y con un apoyo institucional, porque si no ¿cómo ibas a hacer eso?' [NC] ('It was undeniably an important experience that required institutional support, because without that support, how would you have achieved it?').

The same drive to accelerate the expansion of literary culture through institutionalisation, can be seen in publishing, likewise viewed from a variety of perspectives. Here it is clear that institutionalisation was a prerequisite for the further development of infrastucture, the lack of which made literary culture vulnerable to the power struggles of the *quinquenio*:

> La falta de un sistema institucional coherente y una política cultural consecuente con el desarrollo alcanzado por la cultura y el pensamiento revolucionarios de vanguardia afectaron a la dinámica social que habian alcanzado las revistas que expresaban ese desarrollo y los actores – autores, editores, lectores – de las mismas. (Zurbano, 1997: 5–6)[26]

Fornet's contribution to the 2007 *Encuentros* provided a more nuanced idea of the essential terms of debate – between a top-down and a bottom-up vision of culture – and its implications for publishing, drawing especially on the trajectory established in the 1960s. Now that the population was literate and increasingly educated, the question of what they should read became more pressing and complex: '¿Lo que le "gusta" al pueblo, dejándolo así estancado en su más bajo nivel, o lo que me gusta a mí, para que el pueblo vaya refinando sus gustos y un buen día llegue a ser tan culto como yo?' (*La política cultural*, 2008: 5) ('Is it a question of what the *pueblo* "likes", leaving things stuck at their most basic level, or what I like, so that the *pueblo* can start to refine its tastes and one fine day be as educated as I am?'). According to Fornet, the struggles between populism, paternalism and elitism – and the effect on publishing – coupled with the power struggles between different visions of literature, highlighting its aesthetic, ideological, educational or social value, led to a narrower understanding of the value of the literary text, focused on its educational function:

> De las distintas funciones que desempeñan o pueden desempeñar la literatura y el arte – la estética, la recreativa, la informativa, la didáctica – los comisarios trasladaron esa última al primer plano, en detrimento de las otras. Lo que el pueblo y en particular la clase obrera necesitaban no era simplemente leer – abrirse a nuevos horizontes de expectativas – sino educarse, asimilar através de la lectura las normas y valores de la nueva sociedad. (*La política cultural*, 2008: 6)[27]

The imperative for literature to educate (as the value system formalised at the 1971 Congreso) can be seen in the subsequent explosion of publishing. However, the evidence also points to a less monolithic, politicised and 'grey' vision of publishing: the Editorial Arte y Literatura was crucial, especially when viewed as the 'embrión inicial de la Editorial Letras Cubanas' (Pacheco, 2000: 47) ('the initial embryo of the Letras Cubanas publishing house') in promoting and distributing Cuban literature. Pablo Pacheco described the work of Arte y Literatura in the 1970s:

> Mirado desde hoy, es una gestión editorial que habla claramente de la seriedad con que se enfrentaba la delicada tarea de ofrecer a los cubanos los más prestigiosos frutos de la literatura mundial, aún en medio de las incomprensiones y controversias de la época. (Pacheco, 2000: 47)[28]

Publishers thus attempted to achieve a balance between the world and Cuba:

> Todo un esfuerzo conjunto hizo posible un arranque que devendría rumbo ascendente, sobre todo en el trabajo realizado en cuanto a la literatura cubana, de América Latina, de Europa oriental y de modo sobresaliente con la literatura africana, que era prácticamente inexistente en Cuba. (Pacheco, 2000: 47)[29]

This examination of the *quinquenio gris* has therefore offered a diverse range of perspectives. For established and emerging writers who were considered problematic, the period clearly brought marginalisation, silence, neglect and persecution, on the basis of judgments which were often arbitrary and contradictory, and often clearly determined by extra-literary assumptions, indicating how different regimes of value (social, political, ideological) were operationalised in order to prompt or justify decisions. While few literary figures in Cuba today would deny the often traumatic reality of the *quinquenio gris*, contradictions abound. The most significant for an understanding of literary culture during the period is seen in the contrast between the perspectives and experiences of i) those individuals suffering most and those of other groups and individuals, ii) those not living in Cuba at the time [LO], iii) those living in Havana but not part of the literary environment and thus unaware of the *quinquenio* [EDL] and iv) those soon to emerge as writers – in the more isolated provinces, in those spaces not traditionally associated with literary production, and, specifically, the case of young people who were just entering the field of literary culture as readers or writers. For these last groups, the process of institutionalisation and massification, within which both the *quinquenio* and the *talleres* must be located, provided opportunities to fill gaps and vacuums left by marginalised figures, or provided an unproblematic, 'natural' entrance into the world of letters. Arturo Arango, for example, has talked of having to 'inventar escritores para llenar los vacíos creados por las medidas administrativas (ideológicas, en el fondo) aplicadas por muchos compañeros' (Abreu Arcia, 2007: 178) ('invent writers to fill the void created by the (essentially ideological) administrative measures applied by many *compañeros*').

Furthermore, and despite the incommensurability of regimes of value which emerged then, one type of value in particular seems to have been a binding force, or common ground, at a time of intense and complex categorisation: the social value of literature. Even the writers who directly suffered most used their writing and social relationships as a way to avoid isolation, bitterness or solitude [RGZ]; for others, it was precisely the polyvalent nature of their role that allowed connections between writing, publishing and promotion to be developed most effectively during this period. It could thus be argued that it was an understanding of, and commitment to, the social value of literature, rather than the all-powerful influence of monolithic state control (as is often thought) that provided a measure of commensurability and created alternative spaces, ultimately allowing the Cuban literary culture to survive a potentially disastrous period.

Finally, while contemporary perspectives (such as those of the 2007 *Encuentros*) reveal the full importance of the errors and tragic decisions of the CNC, under the guise of creating a revolutionary culture, there is also evidence that the cases of at least some of those marginalised by the CNC were examined, and even compensated, during the 1970s themselves. One well-known case is of some victims appealing against

1961–89: Radicalisation and consolidation

the CNC decisions on legal grounds, arguing that there was no proof under labour law that they had not fulfilled the terms of their work contract; once these cases reached the Supreme Court, it ruled in their favour in 1975, forcing the CNC to pay five years' salary to each individual concerned, eating up the CNC's entire budget for 1975. In Rodríguez Rivera's words: 'Empezó como tragedia y acabó siendo comedia, ¿no?' [GRR] ('It started off as a tragedy and ended up as a comedy, right?').

The creation of MINCULT, announced in the National Assembly on 30 November 1976 and replacing the now-discredited CNC, clearly ushered in a new era of tolerance, which Fornet has described as 'un suspiro de alivio'(*La política cultural*, 2008: 21) ('a sigh of relief'). Whilst all scholars concur that MINCULT's creation was essential for the recovery of diverse cultural, social and political spaces, many are tempted to view 1976 as a rupture with the errors of the *quinquenio*; certainly, the founding of new educational and cultural sites affiliated to MINCULT (such as the Instituto Superior de Arte (1976) and the Centro de Estudios Martianos) marked new directions. What is less commonly discussed, however, is the extent to which certain strands of cultural policy – and the emerging opportunities provided for writers and readers – were not entirely discarded, but, rather, redeveloped and consolidated, after 1976. In this sense, the so-called 'golden age' (of opportunities) of the 1980s can be argued to have begun in the 1970s. The *talleres* movement certainly gained its own character and momentum in certain specific sites, under the direction of young writers: one interesting example, commented on by several interviewees, was the *taller Roque Dalton* at the university (in the so-called Parque de los Cabezones), with Margaret Randall as a mentoring figure ([AP]; [AA]; Codina, 2003: 187–9), providing a seedbed for emerging cultural figures. The importance of individual mentors now assumed a more central, but less urgent, role: those figures and institutional spaces connected to the university, including the publishing space of the *Revista de la Universidad de La Habana*, seem to have been especially significant in the late 1970s, encouraging young artists and writers to participate by thinking more critically. As Prieto expressed it: 'O sea, había un real interés por buscar perspectivas contradictorias y que el alumno tomara una posición razonada' [AP] ('in other words, there was a geuine interest in finding contradictory perspectives and allowing students to establish their position based on reason').

This new breathing space cannot be attributed solely to the CNC's elimination and MINCULT's creation, but also to the continued social mobility accompanying the educational initiatives of the 1960s and 1970s, highlighting the presence of young individuals and groupings then moving into positions of responsibility, especially after the earlier marginalisation of established figures. While these same generational issues had clearly been part of the tensions of the 1960s and the *quinquenio*, there were still many instances of conflict. As Prieto expressed it: 'También, no fue un proceso tampoco transparente, como nada en la sociedad es transparente, sino que en los años 80 hubo cierto recelo por parte de ciertos burócratas que era … echarte en cara el pecado de la juventud … "Estás muy joven para ser Director, estás muy joven para asumir una responsabilidad"' [AP] ('on top of that, nor was it a transparent process, just as nothing in society is transparent; in fact, in the 80s there was a level of suspicion on the part of certain bureaucrats that consisted in … throwing back in your face the sin of being young. … "You're very young to be Director, you're very young to be taking on such a lot of responsibility"'). Nevertheless, there are also strong indications that the process of *parametración* had not penetrated every sphere of literary culture: Roberto Méndez recalls the number of second-hand bookshops in Havana in 1976 that supplied his self-motivated reading programme, as well as access to the BNJM where he could read indiscriminately and eclectically (Codina, 2003: 187–9).

It is generally recognised that the late 1970s and the 1980s saw a second boom of literary activity, with massively increased publishing opportunities and a new publishing infrastructure, all rectifying the errors of the *quinquenio*. What is less clearly understood is that this boom built on the continued commitment to institutionalisation. For the new publishing environment saw the division of the single Instituto del Libro into separate publishing houses, each specialising in different genres and readerships. It is important to underline, then, that with the influence of emerging younger writers, editors and policymakers, and the experience gained from the *quinquenio*, the 1980s saw not a rejection of the institutional model (which had built the foundations for a revolutionary culture in the 1960s and had become paralysed by ideological concerns), but a refinement and consolidation of it. Zurbano described the most important changes to literary production as the rectification of the early 1970s' over-emphasis on ideology in literature; but, interestingly, he also argued that the 1980s favoured book production over magazines, and that, within those general tendencies, the decade did much to 'rectify' the marginalisation of particular texts and authors:

El replanteo institucional que arribó a las casas editoriales cubanas, aunque no satisfizo todas las expectativas de la efervescente produccion artística-literaria e investigativa en las más diversas ramas, si colocó al libro en camino de las problemáticas (...) del momento, y a través de una politica de reediciones y recuperaciones de obras y autores olvidados o marginados, fue participando en la apertura del cánon cultural cubano que comienza justamente en esos años ochenta y sólo podría definirse un poco después del año dos mil. (Zurbano, 1997: 6)[30]

In publishing terms, therefore, the 1980s did begin to correct the *quinquenio*'s errors regarding individual writers and works, and the Cuban literary canon was further transformed through the instigation, under MINCULT auspices, of the *Premio Nacional de Literatura* in 1982 (*La Revista*, 1998: 52).

However, revealingly, many initiatives to promote the new era of Rectification and effervescence were not only related to book production and the national promotion of writers but also promoted cultural exchange between nations. There were also significant initiatives aiming to forge further links with new political and cultural allies; these acquired new force with the Sandinista Revolution in Nicaragua, which provided an important impetus. February 1981, for example, saw the opening of the Encuentro de Escritores de América Latina y del Caribe, with the respective Ministers of Culture for Nicaragua and Cuba opening and closing the proceedings, and September 1981 saw the Encuentro de Intclectuales por la Soberanía de los Pueblos de Nuestra América (conference of intellectuals for the sovereignty of the peoples of 'Our America'), in the Palacio de las Convenciones, bringing together over 200 participants, and with both Castro and Hart in attendance. Against the backdrop of the 1980 Mariel exodus, and with the expansion of US-backed interventions in Central America, the idea of Cuban sovereignty being under siege was thus still prevalent, giving cultural institutions an important role in mobilising political opposition to the 'new imperialism', reflected in the UNEAC Congress of 1982.

However, in parallel with MINCULT's new international initiatives, there was also renewed impetus to develop literary culture in Cuba, significantly through reading as much as writing. The *talleres* movement, as mentioned, continued to expand through formal institutional and less formal networks, while a series of new commemorative days were decreed to further encourage reading on a mass scale: in 1981, 26 March was declared henceforth as *Día del libro cubano* (Cuban Book Day) and 12 March as *Día de la biblioteca* (Library Day). In early 1985, the Campaña Nacional por la Lectura was begun, again opened by Hart, who, speaking in a tobacco factory in La Habana Vieja, again underlined the importance of instilling reading habits across Cuba. The message was reinforced further by the twenty-fifth anniversary celebrations of the Literacy Campaign in mid-December 1986, when the national coordinators and over 170,000 participants were decorated. Although recent scholars warn against seeing 1971–89 as a period of continuity, this chapter argues against a tendency to look only for signs of rupture and new beginnings. The grassroots element which had disappeared from view with the 1970s' centralisation resurfaced with the emergence of newly consolidated groups, the most important being the new Asociación Hermanos Saíz (AHS), founded in October 1986 to bring together various pre-existing groups for those under thirty-five, representing all cultural forms under an umbrella organisation:

> La AHS surge como una fusión entre la Brigada Raúl Gómez García (compuesta por instructores, promotores y técnicos de la cultura), la Brigada Hermanos Saíz (formada por jóvenes escritores y artistas, en aquel entonces pertenecientes a la UNEAC, así como por intelectuales) y el Movimiento de la Nueva Trova, por decisión de la Unión de Jóvenes Comunistas (UJC), en noble empeño por concentrar y sistematizar esfuerzos a favor de estimular la creación literaria y artística e insuflar nuevos bríos a esa zona de participación cultural y social que es hoy la organización. (www.juventudrebelde.cu/secciones/ujc/htm/jovenes_ cubanos/ahs.htm)[31]

Other cultural figures described more local projects emerging or surviving in the 1980s. Soleída Ríos recalled the *Arenas Negras* project for young people in Nueva Gerona, which built on the first two decades' cultural projects but then lost momentum (Codina, 2003: 211–16), while Sigfredo Ariel described his affilation, as a twenty-year old, to a *brigada artística* in Manzanillo (Codina, 2003: 217–19), and Alpidio Alonso commented on an important *taller* in Santa Clara in the late 1980s as the impetus for his 'vida autoral' ('work as an author'), later also providing publishing opportunities in the form of the new Editorial Capiro [AAG]. However, some of those responsible for defining the 'parameters' of the worst years were still culturally or politically active in the late 1980s: Teresa Melo recalled a 1988 poetry reading at *El Pensamiento* bookshop in Matanzas, where she and Carilda Oliver Labra were subjected to physical violence by the 'authorities' (Codina 2003: 223–5; *La política cultural*, 2008: 24).

While the perspective offered by people such as Abreu Arcia, that the

1980s brought new postmodern currents, rupturing and reconfiguring literary culture, and creating spaces for more 'autonomous' cultural practices and beliefs, clearly contains some measure of truth, there is more significant evidence from across the breadth of Cuban cultural practitioners emerging or active during the 1980s that this reorientation and reinvigoration of literary culture was not solely due to the efforts of individuals', but, more accurately, was because these individuals functioned within a collective framework (Arango, 2009: 59). The experience of the 1970s and early 1980s thus highlights one essential truth: that in revolutionary Cuba, the 'regulation' of literature was never simply a matter of control, but, rather – equally importantly – also one of visible and accountable structures and mechanisms for the production and promotion of, and participation in, literature. Therefore, while institutionalisation meant a strengthening of the state, it also provided more coherent spaces within which writers and readers could move, and which could also offer a degree of autonomy and agency for individuals and groups. Even the two cultural groups which emerged at the end of the decade (Paideia and Castillo de la Fuerza), although advocating a pluralistic and often contestatory role for culture, were both underpinned by a continued commitment to using art to question and critique social reality (Abreu Arcia, 2007: 190–6).

Most significantly of all, in contrast to conventional views which assume the dominance of the political and ideological value of literature during the 1970s and beyond, the evidence seems to indicate that social value continued to be a primary motor for the development of a revolutionary Cuban literary culture. In fact the 1988 UNEAC Congress, which closed this whole post-1961 period, took for granted the pre-eminence of this value, and, instead, opened up for debate a new concern for writers: namely the conditions in which they worked and the material rewards which they received. The dual expression of self-confidence and self-criticism was also reflected in the frequency and diverse tones of many of the cultural debates of the early 1980s, organised to celebrate the landmark of twenty-five years of Revolution. Many of the more critical, less celebratory declarations were concerned with the material and practical inadequacies of the cultural environment for writers, implying that some of the deeper qualitative or ideological issues surrounding the role of the writer had at last been resolved (Marqués Ravelo, 1985: 20). The implication was clear: the corruption and stagnation that accompanied the institutionalisation of the political establishment in the 1970s had continued to affect cultural establishments such as

UNEAC, and thus the output of the individual writer. Other reports of the campaign emphasised its importance for culture in recognising past weaknesses and setting future objectives. The reorientation of UNEAC therefore depended on the reduced interference of political leaders and on a renewed debate between artists, and thus it appears that writers too responded publicly to Castro's 1986 call, once again, to overcome objective conditions with subjective commitment. In 1987, UNEAC organised the *Forum de la Crítica e Investigación Literaria* (Forum for Literary Criticism and Research), which called once again for greater critical thought and rigour, with the general mood of reassessment being ratified at the 1988 UNEAC Congress.

The recovery, reorientation, boom and stability of opportunity enjoyed throughout the 1980s were, however, brought to an abrupt end by the 1990s' crisis, which, by 1992, had virtually paralysed the mechanisms and institutions developed in every sphere over the preceding thirty years, shaking up all previous spaces. If social value had been the adhesive to ensure that political and cultural activity shared some common ground, this was to be severely weakened by the social fragmentation and economic austerity that were to ensue, and the delicate balance on the individual–collective continuum was about to be severely challenged.

Notes

1 'This book has a great value. That is why it is given to you free of charge. Its value lies in the accumulated labour implied in the knowledge contained within its pages, in the hours of effort spent producing it and because it constitutes a leap forward in the struggle for man to be himself. Its greatest value will, however, lie in the use that you make of it. We are certain of that use, and of its great value, and so it is given to you free of charge'.
2 'One wakes every morning thinking to oneself that one cannot bear those artists any longer, those conversations, those exclamations, one cannot bear oneself; that that's enough about Art, Beauty, Rigour, Seriousness; that there is no such predestination, no such state of ecstasy, no such destiny ... that we were are all freemasons of art – how awful!: I show you mine and you show me yours, and we all show each other; that the goal is close by, that we can attain it, of course! That's all that is needed!'
3 'The dynamic between national and Latin American, for the writer, America as a community imagined by its lettered subjects, concerns over the social value of the literary work, tensions between autonomous and heteronomous representations, between realism and anti-realism, are the

1961–89: Radicalisation and consolidation

dilemmas and choices that cultural producers on both sides face as they take up the challenge of writing either the novel of the Cuban Revolution, or the long-awaited Latin American novel.'

4 'Cultural decolonisation is an inevitable product of that new awareness. By discovering our reality and, along with it, the ineffectiveness of the theoretical instruments that we have hurriedly incorporated in the course of our readings and travels, we understand what we are not, what we do not share with intellectuals in the industrialised world'.

5 'Quite simply, to "get up-to-date". We believed that the Revolution represented – in publishing as well – the stimulus necessary for us to move out of backwardness and project ourselves into the future, and thus we arrived at the arrogant and ingenuous conclusion that it was enough to read the vanguard authors of the twentieth century in order to be considered cultured and, above all, "modern"'.

6 The Instituto del Libro (IL) became known as the Instituto Cubano del Libro (ICL) after 1976; although precise details of when it resumed its overarching supervision role for Cuban publishing are not clear, it seems that this happened after MINCULT's reorganisation in 1989.

7 'To maintain (without prejudice to that absolute freedom to attempt, to seek, to create, and indeed as an incentive for that freedom) a constant critical attitude, favouring the work of critics and subjecting that work to the crucible of the harshest self-criticism … in which can (and must) participate the true protagonist of the Revolution, in short the subject of the new aesthetic expression: the pueblo'.

8 'Huracán kept us calm. Why? Because we didn't have to be concerned about publishing Galdós, or publishing Dickens. You know? We already wanted to be doing something else… going a step further. So we could do that because, let's say, the consumption of literature on a mass scale was guaranteed by Huracán'.

9 'In spite of my literary inclinations, it never occurred to me to write, and, when the time came to choose a degree course […], I opted for biological sciences out of a sense of … let's say, duty at that moment. In other words, there was a nationwide call put out to the effect that the future lay in the sciences and that we had to develop our country, and that whole story, right? The story which I followed and would follow again – of contributing to and developing our country'.

10 'What I have done is read a lot. When I decided to start writing … First I began to read… and afterwards, when I began to write, I set out to read all the great writers whose work fell into my hands, in other words, Quiroga, Onelio Jorge Cardoso, Guy de Maupassant, and, after that, of course, the great North American writers, Faulkner, Salinger, Hemingway, who influenced me a lot'.

11 'And so, if officially we ceased to exist, and many people didn't even come to our houses, others – the great figures of Cuban culture – never kept their

distance, they always remained close to us, if sometimes just by phone. That's important if we are to understand what is happening in Cuba. That, although some cultural and political leaders – the political falls within the cultural – displayed miserable attitudes, there were also people who treated us with respect ... All those people encouraged us explicitly or implicitly to continue working for Cuban culture, for our country, for our homeland'.

12 'I always thought that these things happen to writers and that writers always have a kind of dispute with the state, although they might participate, like me, in the general principles of the state in which they live, but at the same time they have a series of differences in terms of the ways that those principles are implemented and put into practice'.

13 'I think that in Cuba it was never possible to implant socialist realism fully, because there were spaces where that vision never had any impact, right? It never took hold, for example, in ICAIC, in cinema. It never took hold there because there was one intellectual there who carried considerable weight, at the head of ICAIC, and who had his own views and opinions which were very distant from those of socialist realism, and that was Alfredo Guevara'.

14 'Well, Pensamiento Crítico was the child of that period of opening up, and was greatly disliked by the Soviets during that period ... We never ... and besides, they always sent us the ... Novosti news bulletin, so that we could publish something from it. We never published... never ... it has to be said that we put in a lot of effort because we wanted to publish something from it, but we never felt that there was anything worth publishing [laughs], that we could accept in theoretical terms and we ourselves exercised a kind of censorship right there'.

15 'As Victor Fowler put it so well, at that last meeting, talking about Pavón, no less, you know who that is. So ... Fowler stood up and said, "He might well have been all of these things but we have to remember that he is one of our compañeros". I recall that afterwards Sacha says to him outside, he says to Fowler, "that man is not my compañero", and Fowler, with his wonky eye and ironic expression, says to him, "No, the day one if us is down in the trenches, I'm going to see who's right by your side, and you can bet that it's going to be Pavón"'.

16 'By now institutionalisation was getting involved in all the things it shouldn't have been involved in, it was all too much, all very normative; even the regulations of UNEAC, you should look at them, it's all in there; they were very specific and there's a reality, or rather, there's a truth in Cuban reality that there's always a kind of transposition towards cultural institutions, they become a kind of imitation of sociopolitical organisations, which is logical enough because they're part of the Cuban social mechanism'.

17 'To explain it to you as best I can, the philosophy that I wanted to study was not exactly the philosophy that was taught officially at the university.

1961–89: Radicalisation and consolidation

Because I knew of certain debates that had taken place in Cuba in the 1960s, I was well informed about the existence of something that in the 60s was called the Department of Philosophy, the studies that were carried out at that time, a humanist Marxism which was very different from official Soviet bureaucratised Marxism'.

18 'I am a journalist because it was the space where they left me some freedom because of the contempt that they felt towards journalism, they undervalued it and that's why I was able to be a journalist, but they closed many doors to me, with Marinello, with Guillén, with Fabio Grobart, even with Mirta (Aguirre), they told me it was down to my own crazy whim'.

19 'There are many authors who now enjoy recognition who came out of the literary workshops. What happened? It would all get a bit stale. What I always think is that the person who made it as a writer might well have benefited from the literary workshops, but a writer who was always going to make it would have been a writer anyway, however many literary workshops they'd been through [laughs]. But it was an important phenomenon, above all, because, if the workshop didn't necessarily produce a writer, at least it produced a reader'.

20 'Because the programme began in 69, in other words, in a country that was only newly literate, we thought it was a programme that wouldn't be of interest to anybody – not to the masses because they didn't have the faintest idea (about literature), or were just beginning to take their first steps; and, as for those who were in the know, why would they watch a programme like that if whatever was asked, whatever was discussed there, was supposedly basic knowledge for an educated person? To our surprise, the programme lasted – we had initially planned for two years – we've now been around for thirty-nine years [laughs]. In other words, as I like to say, I have grown old on the TV'.

21 'And so we selected the books that were read least. The librarians selected them on the basis of the statistics that they had on what was read and what wasn't read. That's what we call "moving the collection" ... And as it was Casa de las Américas, well [laughs], the best writers in Cuba and writers who were passing through Cuba, everyone went there to talk about books.'

22 'And so the state had created institutionally a literary advisor for every municipality and for every province and these individuals devoted their time to finding young people interested in writing in order to organise them into workshops. I was lucky to be found, I quickly joined a workshop'.

23 'I don't know if I should say it was fortunate or unfortunate, the literary workshop was rather uniform, right? There were rules, and when there are rules – of course there are general rules of rhetoric, grammar, spelling, etc. – but in a workshop when someone tells you that a short story should be like this or that, that doesn't really work, does it?'

24 'From that time, we noticed that in every school there was a group of Abelarditos, that's what they call the kids who are way ahead, way way

ahead, of the rest. And these kids, along with reading, also wanted to write ... They'd ask you those things that perhaps they hadn't asked the librarian or teacher. Because you came surrounded with the aura of the editor, of the publishing house ... That's why, when they first approached the publishing house to set up the literary workshops, I joined in the initiative'.

25 'For very many years, this endeavour was at municipal level. In other words, the contests took place, and continued to take place, at municipal or provincial level. Those of us who worked on it all the time thought it was terrible that the effort of the entire country should be lost, and should not exist at a national level, especially as it was not just the effort made by the state or government, but also the effort made by the schoolteacher, the cultural worker in the Casa de Cultura, the effort made by the parents, because behind all of this is the dad who has to take his kid along to the Casa de Cultura'.

26 'The lack of a coherent institutional system and cultural policy that was consistent with the development already achieved in vanguard revolutionary culture and thought affected the social dynamic of the magazines that expressed this development, as well as the actors – authors, editors, readers – of those magazines'.

27 'Out of the various functions that literature and art can perform – aesthetic, recreational, informative, didactic – the commissars moved that last function to centre stage, to the detriment of the others. What the pueblo, and particularly the working class, needed was not simply to read – to open up to new horizons of expectation – but to be educated, to assimilate via reading the norms and values of the new society'.

28 'When you look at it today, it is a way of managing publishing which speaks clearly of the seriousness with which we undertook the delicate task of offering Cubans the most prestigious fruits of world literature, and all of that in the midst of the misunderstandings and controversies of the era'.

29 'The joint effort of many made it possible to kickstart a project which would gain increasing momentum, above all in the work carried out to publish Cuban, Latin American, Eastern European literature, but also – and most impressively – African literature, which was practically non-existent in Cuba'.

30 'The institutional redefining that reached Cuban publishing houses – although it didn't meet all expectations of an effervescent artistic, literary and research-based production across the most diverse areas – certainly located the book within a discussion of those concerns at the time [...] and, via a policy of reprinting and rescuing forgotten or marginalised works and authors, began to play a part in the opening up of the Cuban cultural canon, a process which began exactly in the 80s but was only able to be defined more clearly just after the year 2000'.

31 'The AHS arose from the merger – by the decision of the Union of Communist Youth (UJC) – between the Raúl Gómez García Brigade

(consisting of cultural teachers, cultural workers and technicians as well as young writers and artists and intellectuals, all belonging to UNEAC) and the Nueva Trova movement, as part of the noble endeavour to concentrate and systematise our efforts in order to stimulate literary and artistic creativity and breathe new life into that area of sociocultural participation which is now our organisation'.

5
1990s–2000s: The years of crisis and reassessment[1]

The artistic and intellectual concerns of the late 1980s, in the context of Rectification and the changes in the Socialist Bloc, were brought into sharp relief by the economic collapse from 1989 and the Special Period. Despite some semblance of 'normal business' (especially the quinquennial congresses of UNEAC, the UJC and the Party, but also – in 1994, in the worst year of the crisis – the sixth Feria Internacional del Libro, with over 250 titles published, albeit predominantly through new 'joint-venture' publishing initiatives), the collapse significantly weakened the state, creating fundamental challenges for the Revolution's survival and painful changes to daily existence, placing other concerns into perspective. Indeed, although many of those interviewed for this study hinted at the personal traumas of the experience, few chose to express it in terms of personal anguish, stressing that intellectual and cultural life was subordinated to more pressing needs.

However, the economic and social dimensions of the crisis could not help but affect culture, given its centrality to the revolutionary project, and, within that, literary culture specifically; the retrenchment in terms of expectations, provision and purchasing power, the reversal of policies forbidding access to the dollar and private trading, and massively increased emigration (which now became a recurrent theme in social life, fragmenting families and localities even further) all had a huge impact. In this context, however, literature provided a means of escape into a world by offering a sense of community and intellectual life. Reina María Rodríguez, active in the 1970s and 1980s in many cultural initiatives (notably Paideia), created a small, locally focused group, *La Azotea* ('the rooftop', named after its location at her Centro Habana house), providing consolation against the emigration of friends and the survival mode into which all Cubans had been plunged: 'Quise como sacarme todo aquello, vino una época de mucho hastío, se habían ido

1990s–2000s: Crisis and reassessment

casi todos los amigos míos ... aquí empezamos a construír ... durante cinco o siete años, venían todos mis amigos a dar sus lecturas' [RMR] ('I wanted to sort of shake off all of that, that era of weariness that came along, the fact that almost all of my friends had left ... we began to build ... for five or six years, all of my friends would come along to share their readings'); however, their objective was not nostalgia, but rather, through contact with exogenous readings in critical theory, self-protection against an apparently moribund and inward-looking system. Although many emigrated, this option was less accessible to writers than to artists working in other cultural forms:

> Primero se fueron los pintores porque tuvieron más suerte en el sentido del dinero, vendieron los cuadros, no tuvieron nada que perder en venir e irse, porque muchos van y vienen. Y después se fueron los escritores porque fue más difícil salir. [RMR][2]

While the influence of postmodernism, and many of the identity-based areas of literary focus, had already begun to emerge, Campuzano drawing attention to the work of women writers, for example (Campuzano, 1988), these specific interests were now overlaid by a preoccupation with the individual, rather than collective, experience of the crisis. A *narrativa de la interioridad* (inner narrative), the cultural representation of *desencanto* (disenchantment), a loss of faith in socialism, nation and Revolution, a rupture with existing value systems, a changing attitude to the diaspora all became the driving forces for a cultural production whose principal recourse and remit – rather than transforming or critiquing social and political life – was to represent and narrate traumatic experiences through art [NAG]. Simply, meeting basic needs (food and other domestic commodities) left little time for recreational, vocational or professional pursuits, and the paralysis of public transport, fuel shortages and resulting *apagones*, with an inability to plan ahead in private and public spheres alike, all prevented any sustained commitment to writing. Shortages and necessarily changed priorities substantially worsened conditions for literary culture, as the three-decade-old nationwide system of cultural participation (through Casas de Cultura, museums, bookshops and libraries) was paralysed through lack of basic infrastructure and materials.

The most important shortage was that of paper for printing, now coupled with a new set of priorities, born out of extreme austerity: presses now were to be predominantly used for education. Around 1993, journalistic production was also strictly rationalised, newspapers reducing their frequency (from daily to weekly) to maintain print runs as far as possible (although soon cut, until 1998), while other and specialist or local journals ceased to publish. For writers and journalists accustomed to the availability of textual space, these reductions led some to abandon their profession [MR], while those still staffing these fragile publications had to negotiate a constantly changing series of funding decisions, affecting frequency of publication, number of pages, editorial policy and content [AAT].

Literary texts soon dropped off the list of state-funded publications, bringing to a sudden halt the successful, three-decade old, network of national *editoriales*. Contracts, and even manuscripts already in production, remained unhonoured, forming a *colchón editorial* (stock of unpublished texts) [AAB]. Writers later observed that many such manuscripts were not only lost, in a now paralysed system, but, once the publishing infrastructure recovered, they were no longer suitable for publication since the post-1990 social changes made their themes less relevant and lacking in symbolic capital. Those who had begun to publish in the late 1980s, the *novísimos* (the new wave of writers), suffered particularly acutely, unable to disseminate their work through normal routes; indeed, one of that generation described how, although occasionally anthologised in Cuba and often better known outside Cuba than on the island, they suffered most from publishing delays, in some cases being 'leapfrogged' by writers of more recent texts: 'Yo tuve la desgracia de que me cogiese el Período Especial y el libro no pudo ser publicado hasta nueve años después' [AAB] ('I was unlucky to be hit by the Special Period and my book didn't come out for nine years'). In this context, the efforts of individual mentors (notably Redonet, Mateo Palmer, and Pogolotti) were evidently crucial in responding pragmatically to the crisis; Francisco López Sacha, then President of UNEAC's Unión de Escritores, even changed the statutes for UNEAC membership to reflect the collapse of the publishing infrastructure: 'Sacha como que violenta ligeramente los estatutos de la UNEAC en muchos casos y nos convierte en miembros de la UNEAC a la mayoría' ('Sacha gently shook up the UNEAC statutes in many cases and made the majority of us members of UNEAC') [AAB].

Furthermore, the publishing system could no longer afford to publish previously 'normal-length' texts, a factor decisive for the short-term future of certain genres: even by 2000, once the publishing recovery was under way, material costs continued to determine the choice of genres, the short story (especially within anthologies) and poetry being favoured over substantial prose narrative, such as the novel. All writers were also handicapped by the lack of basic equipment: one recalled the conditions under which she completed her doctoral thesis on Lezama:

> yo la hice en condiciones espantosas. No tenía bombillo, tenía que trabajar de día porque de noche [...] había que estar rotando el bombillo para el cuarto de mi hijo para hacer la tarea, para el baño. Era un bombillo itinerante, ¿no? (risa) No tenía bolígrafo, tenía que escribir con lápiz en unos papeles viejos, amarillos, que casi no se veía. Por supuesto, no tenía computadora. [MMP][3]

Put simply, with the end of the previously positive conditions, many felt obliged to embark on careers bringing them into contact with foreign currency. The implications for the survival of an always dynamic and coherent value system and mechanisms of communication were stark.

However, an unexpected, and less negative, by-product of the state's impoverishment was a weakening of the structures and processes of regulation. Indeed, although the *novísimos* might have felt disadvantaged in terms of publishing opportunities, they also recognised a new freedom from institutional structures and commitments and regulatory mechanisms:

> Es decir, se dice por allí, y no es una frase mía, que los *novísimos* no tenían otro compromiso que no fuera con su propia, su propia labor creadora. Y es cierto, es decir esta generación que irrumpió a finales de los años ochenta, principio de los noventa, era un poco más iconoclasta, era un poco más irreverente, y encontró que de pronto la política editorial del país estaba como abierto también para que ellos dijeran sus cosas. [RR][4]

Hence, despite the institutional collapse or paralysis, the lack of expectations (stressing dialogue between writer and reader) partially freed writers from their obligation, not only to state and nation, but also to the *público lector* (reading public).

The same idea (of enforced 'freedom', now enabled by crisis, and its impact on literary production and culture) was articulated by Mateo Palmer: 'Bueno, eso te iba a decir, es que yo realmente comienzo a escribir con un carácter mucho más creativo [...], justamente en medio de esa situación muy asfixiante económicamente, ¿no?' [MMP] ('Well, that's what I was going to say, that I really began to write in a more creative way [...], right in the midst of that situation that was completely suffocating us economically, right?'); for her, it was precisely the lack of infrastructure (and, therefore, the absence of the symbolic contract between writer and reader) which allowed writers to express themselves more individually [MMP]. There was, therefore, a clear shift for some writers regarding their place on the individual–collective continuum, from the traditional vision of the writer as mouthpiece, gatekeeper or mediator, to one where the writing voice itself became the subject:

> Pero yo siempre había visto mi trabajo como algo útil, en función de rescatar una historia olvidada, como era la de la trova tradicional ... Y en esos textos yo me anulaba como sujeto que escribía, lo importante eran los trovadores y yo era un simple vehículo para rescatar esa memoria y yo no tenía voz, prácticamente. Y de pronto esa voz se fue imponiendo, trató de aparecer, de hecho apareció y el resultado fue muy bueno. [MMP][5]

Moreover, once the cultural authorities gave artists the green light to follow other Cubans and seek economic solutions through hard currency, either abroad or through access to the emerging domestic dollar economy, material conditions changed for some, although, as already observed, this benefited non-literary cultural forms most. Speaking of an artist's subsidy of another writer's publication, one writer observed:

> Y tiene dinero para publicar quinientos ejemplares porque un pintor hizo una donación. Hoy en Cuba tenemos unas contradicciones muy graves: pintores y músicos, a veces un cantante de quinta fila o un pintor, incluso naïf, puede tener una vida con un confort superior al de los escritores y, sin duda alguna, puede ganar muchísimo más que un escritor, tanto por derecho de autor, como por otros planos de la vida ... Y entonces un pintor puede darse el lujo de subvencionar algunas ediciones de libros. Un escritor no se puede dar el lujo de subvencionar ni la suya propia. [VLL][6]

Indeed, for writers such opportunities were limited; language alone meant that overseas publication depended on translation or interest from Spanish-speaking countries. Even then, many foreign publishers followed their own market expectations and audience design, seeing Cuba in terms of the exotic, the erotic, the decadent and the dissident. Moreover, many overseas contracts were negotiated arbitrarily, were extremely exploitative, or were conditional on winning a major prize, mostly in Spain [LPF; PJG]. Some interviewees indicated that, whereas before 1990 the Cuban criteria for prizes were based on everything but market forces (ideology, social value, aesthetic qualities), the new world of international prizes brought a new set of regimes of value and expectations, conditioning the form and content of writing, especially given writers' material situation:

> Por lo tanto, el premio prostituye. Hace que tú te inclines para ganar ese premio. Te inclines hacia lo de moda, a lo que tenga mayor aceptación, etc.

Por eso tú has visto, por ejemplo, que la narrativa cubana contemporánea se ha inclinado hacia el realismo sucio. El realismo sucio tiene mucha suerte, tiene mucho éxito. La gente en España y en muchos otros lugares, no sé qué pasa con el actual estado de la humanidad que tendemos a lo sórdido. [VLL][7]

One mitigating factor was the intervention of left-wing foreign publishers (predominantly Latin American, North American and Spanish) to offer Cubans publishing contracts, just as foreign nongovernmental organisations (NGOs) and cultural institutions, and even foreign governments, were also mitigating material and production issues. While many interviewees were keen to stress that their precarious survival in those years depended on international allies, individual and collective, all framed this experience as one born of necessity rather than choice.

However, even in the depths of the crisis, there were some major publishing initiatives: the Pinos Nuevos collection, proposed at the 1993 Buenos Aires Book Fair, was immediately launched to promote some kind of publishing recovery, through opportunities for unpublished writers, perhaps to rescue the *novísimos* whose work was lost after 1989 or whose first manuscripts had coincided with the crisis. The response to the call for manuscripts was overwhelming; within a month of the *convocatoria* (call for manuscripts), 571 manuscripts had been received, of which 100 were published, 'veinticinco títulos de narrativa, veinticinco de poesía, veinticinco de literatura científica y veinticinco de teatro' ('twenty-five prose titles, twenty-five poetry titles, twenty-five scientific texts and twenty-five theatre titles') and duly launched at the 1994 Feria (Soler Cedre, 1997: 21–3; [AFJ]). The influx fell in the next two years, presumably since the initial rush had included pre-existing material and because the press's lack of self-generated funding meant that the production–purchase price correlation was complex and precarious. Unsurprisingly, given the limited textual space available, over the three years, poetry dominated (22.1 per cent), compared with other genres (Soler Cedre, 1997: 23).

Tourism, as the immediate response to the crisis, also raised questions for literary culture. While many aspects of Cuban culture, especially performance-based forms, were more easily marketable to tourists, already attracting a minority of visitors, literature did not enjoy the same market appeal. Inside Cuba, only Spanish-speaking visitors were allowed to purchase a writer's work, and, even then, such consumers (in a market distorted by Cuba's long-term isolation from the international publishing scene) were largely ignorant of anything but the pre-1959 'great' writers. Hence, freedom in principle actually meant limited benefit in practice. Moreover, although this became the subject of debates between cultural practitioners of various forms (Aróstegui and Zamora Fernández, 1991: 89–99), it also reflected an old, pre-1959 reality: that few Cuban writers had ever been able to make a living solely from their creative writing. In this sense, the figure of the polyvalent writer was already universalised, and the writer was, in the best of cases, obliged to recalibrate their various roles:

> [E]n Cuba, yo diría que el noventa por ciento de los escritores que ya tienen obras publicadas no viven de su profesión literaria. Tienen que ser asesores literarios, editores de libros, maestros, periodistas, teatristas, promotores culturales, algunos médicos, abogados, ingenieros; es decir, no puedes vivir de la literatura. [MSM][8]

Nevertheless, the emerging tourist industry did at least consider literature's ability to generate foreign currency: a 1991 Centro Juan Marinello research paper summarised the results of an earlier study into culture and tourism (published under the Programa Cultural para el Desarrollo del Turismo of 1991–92, and based on 1987–90 research), examining the way in which culture in general was made available to tourists, suggesting an awareness that the cultural world should also earn hard currency, although literature played a small part in the fieldwork and analysis (the researchers visiting a number of bookshops in La Habana Vieja). The report was damning of the whole cultural sector: only around 10 per cent of several thousand tourists interviewed had identified Cuban culture (in all forms) as a motivation for visiting Cuba, well below the percentage motivated by Cuba's more predictable tourist assets: beaches, climate, people, curiosity and cheapness. Moreover, if only 10 per cent had originally perceived that Cuban culture would interest them, this figure fell to 5 after their visit; in other words, culture had had a negative impact, blame falling squarely on the failure by institutions, hotels and tourist agencies to advertise their 'wares', on the poor level of knowledge of those needing to either advertise or sell culture, or on a poor attitude to display (Pérez Prats *et al*, 1991: 12–20).

Meanwhile, as print-runs ground to a halt, declining production levels had more far-reaching consequences for all Cubans, as the internal mass readership, whose capacity to purchase books or have leisure time for reading declined sharply. A 1997–98 series of Centro

Marinello studies of reception and reading habits revealed the extent of the decline: unsurprisingly, literature fared poorly in terms of mass popularity, compared with other cultural forms (Correa Cajigas *et al*, 1998: 9), indicating that, in Cuba as in other countries, educational level and professional employment status were prerequisites for the enjoyment of literature (1998: 13). The idea that social class, profession and the predominance of mass media were the determining factors for access to literature must have proved a bitter pill to swallow, given the post-1959 commitment to socialising literary culture. However, the study ended defiantly, stressing the centrality of culture to the revolutionary project:

> La democratización de los bienes simbólicos constituye una meta a la cual una sociedad como la nuestra no puede renunciar. Defender los derechos culturales es construir y perfeccionar la democracia socialista, porque la cultura no es algo complementario, sino que ocupa un puesto central en los hechos políticos. (Correa Cajigas *et al*, 1998: 60)[9]

Other studies examined how children's literature had fared (Pérez, 1998: 10–11; Resik Aguirre, 1998: 42–5), including an interview with Omar González, then ICL President, who reported that price rises for childrens' books (from an average of under ninety centavos in 1989 to an average of seven Cuban pesos in 1994), as a result of rising production costs, had had a particularly negative impact on the consumption of children's literature. One article, based on the observations of the manager of the *Cuba Científica* second-hand bookshop in Vedado, reported that, by 1991, bookshops were so little used by the general public (Resik Aguirre, 1997: 43) that there had been an attempt to carry out informal market research and subsequently adapt stock to the needs of the most frequent customers, in this case (given its location) Universidad de la Habana students and staff (1997: 44); the article also indicated that the Special Period had led to an increase in second-hand bookselling (1997: 44), and that Cubans had begun to develop a different attitude to books: 'se utilizaba el libro para las cosas más insospechadas' (1997: 45) ('books were being used for the most unexpected things'). Although it was not clear what other uses these were, this implied a significant reduction in the book's social value. Even then, however, the article made clear that the *librería de uso* (second-hand bookshop), however under-utilised, was a far more efficient and responsive mechanism for finding specific books than the normal system for new books (based on the Distribuidora Nacional del

Libro, or 'national book distributor'(DNL)) (1997: 45), a phenomenon which still seems true today in some parts of Havana.

Another article described the DNL's difficulties: although 1,200 titles had been published in 1989, only just over 400 had been distributed in 1994, the rest presumably being stored because of lack of transport. The DNL's Director, Javier Jomarrón Rodiles, anticipated that, in relation to the 420 titles published in 1995, they would prioritise distribution to seventy-seven public libraries, plus those libraries included in the Plan Turquino (established in 1987 to integrate mountain populations economically and socially, but whose integrative focus had been severely undermined from 1989: www.ecured.cu/index.php/Plan_Turquino). Jomarrón Rodiles also indicated that distribution was being managed according to the type of book and 'las características socio-económicas de cada provincia' ('every province's socioeconomic features'); for example, of the books published by the Fondo de Desarrollo de la Educación y la Cultura (founded in 1992), 9 per cent were destined for Santiago. Editions emerging from the new Centros Provinciales del Libro y la Literatura (CPLL) were likewise distributed nationally, although there was some discussion about the inability of small print-runs to meet demand; Jomarrón argued that every book published was guaranteed a *lanzamiento*, or *presentación* (book launch), but he acknowledged complaints about insufficient copies on sale at these events. Clearly, as distribution problems would make such copies more crucial than ever for readers, he stressed that the 150–200 copies available for the general public at these *presentaciones*, although insufficient, were the only way of ensuring equitable access for the public ('La distribución del libro', 1996: 74). To support this, he outlined the DNL's obligation to give ten copies of every book to the BNJM, fifty-two copies to municipal libraries and fourteen to provincial libraries (1996: 75).

A coetaneous survey of the BNJM likewise suggested a massive decline in library visits: while, since the 1960s, the number of annual visitors had not changed much (averaging around 300,000–350,000 a year), after 1989 (362,000) it dropped by one-third, and then by half of the original figure by 1992, remaining thus until 1997. By 1998, however, the figure was beginning to creep up (139,339), the evidence suggesting that initiatives to tackle the problem were having some impact (Fernández Robaina, 2001: 105).

Given the scarcity of basic resources, the only pragmatic response was therefore to rely on the one reliable resource, the human, in the form of the *promotor cultural*. A 1992 Centro Marinello report, clearly the first study of their profile and impact, attempted to clarify their role as crucial to encouraging a new impetus in community-based cultural life:

> El promotor cultural debe ser la persona que pertenece a una comunidad o se integra en ella, apoyando las labores de animación sociocultural, instrumentando diversas acciones sistemáticamente, de tal forma que se favorezcan las condiciones para la toma de conciencia de los individuos y grupos sobre la importancia de la participación activa en la vida cultural y a través de un proceso gradual lograr una disposición favorable respecto al ámbito cultural. (Martín Rodríguez and Jiménez, 1992: 2)[10]

However, the report's evidence contradicted this aspiration, demonstrating, through a survey of eighteen *promotores* in the Casa de Cultura of Centro Habana, that they were (a) mostly not local, (b) rarely motivated by love of their subject or cultural form, and (c) poorly organised and lacking commitment, with *talleres* and other events often being cancelled. The report's conclusion accused *promotores* of failing to live up to both their self-professed goals and their self-perception of satisfaction with their work (Martín Rodríguez and Jiménez, 1992: 15).

Lastly, there were indications that the book as an economic resource had created another activity within literary culture: theft from municipal libraries and the depletion of stocks in state bookshops, in order to supply hard-currency booksellers (e.g. in the Plaza de Armas, an initiative set up precisely to subsidise state publishing and thus ensure the availability of books for Cuban readers). Although one interviewee described the phenomenon as the 'parte grotesca y picaresca del Período Especial en el comercio del libro' ('grotesque and picaresque aspect of the Special Period's impact on the book industry') [RV], it was perhaps inevitable that the book would become a commodity like any other product or service.

Clearly, then, more than half a decade of severe economic and social crisis had created a whole new set of practices and priorities, and a disaggregation and diversification of any uniform sense of literary culture, all demanding urgent responses, even for those working within the cultural environment. However, the mid- to late 1990s also showed some signs of recovery and a less reactive, and more proactive, phase of cultural policy, aptly summarised in Castro's words at the Fifth Communist Party Congress in October 1997: 'La cultura es lo primero que hay que salvar' (UNEAC, 1993) ('the first thing that must be saved is culture'). Indeed, far from a coherent and monolithic policy directive emanating from the highest levels (although there was some element of this), that Congress's decisions effectively formalised empirical policy initiatives, combining experiences of (often fairly unsophisticated) local cultural responses to the crisis.

1997 and 1998 were crucial years for the public examination of the problem and the creation of national projects to recuperate a lost readership and discover the new one which had come of age since 1990. The 1992 creation of MINCULT's Fondo para el Desarrollo de la Educación y la Cultura had allowed hard currency (gained from tourism) to be reinvested to subsidise culture – for literature, primarily through redeveloping a modest publishing infrastructure, as a basis for future growth (www.oei.es/cultura2/cuba/06.htm). As Daniel García Santos, then director of Letras Cubanas, explained:

> Era una institución que recibía fondos, en divisas, de las empresas del Ministerio de Cultura, que trabajaban para el mercado en divisas, tanto para la exportación como para la frontera, para el mercado de frontera ... Ese fondo fue financiando determinado tipo de publicaciones y ahí fue paulatinamente recuperándose la producción y, por otro lado, el Estado empezó también a invertir y a renovar en la medida en que se fue recuperando la base tecnológica. ([DGS]; Casanovas Pérez, 1997: 13)[11]

The ICL's potential to earn hard currency enjoyed some limited success, as a result of these new outwardly oriented policies to enable publishing subsidies. According to a 2000 report, the ICL's hard-currency earnings initially fell between 1991 and 1992 (from US$200.6 to US$169.3), then rising steadily between 1993 (US$448) and 1998 (US$1736.6) (Mas Zabala, 2000: 50), and by 1998, 23.3 per cent of all books published were produced with subsidies (Mas Zabala, 2000: 51).

23–25 July 1998 also witnessed a new event, running alongside the still biennial Feria, to promote the circulation of literature: the Primer Festival del Libro de la Plaza de Armas, with thirty-six stands and 23,000 books sold (Sánchez, 1998: 8), indicating a tentative awareness of some recovery, or at least an attempt to stimulate further hard-currency revenue for literature.[12]

The decline of reading was also tackled by seeking to increase readership through tried and trusted means (reading clubs, reading campaigns, etc.), largely through the BNJM. Under the directorship of Elíades Acosta (Director from 1997 to 2007), several new initiatives were launched in 1998, one of the most significant being the *Club Minerva* (already tested in Acosta's previous post at Santiago's Ateneo), which created a network of borrowing libraries. Established by MINCULT

1990s–2000s: Crisis and reassessment 143

and MINED in 1997, and 'encaminada a la recuperación y enriquecimiento del hábito de lectura en la población cubana' [MMC] ('focused on recovering and enriching reading habits in the Cuban population'), with stocks purchased with funds from the Fondo de Desarrollo and through national and international donations [MTG], the project was aimed at Cubans aged over fifteen, who, joining for an annual fee, could borrow a book or magazine for a week, the ten best readers in any year getting some (unspecified) recognition. The first club was created in the BNJM in November 1997, but by 2006 there were twenty-seven across Cuba, and by 2007, thirty-three, all within public libraries and select bookshops [MMC]. The clubs also aimed to stimulate reading in local neighbourhoods through talks by cultural figures (Medina, 2001: 11; www.bnjm.cu/bnjm/espanol/acerca/info_general/minerva.htm). Further initiatives included the *Leer a Martí* (reading Martí) competition (to encourage reading and writing amongst children), the Proyecto Editorial 'Libertad' (to provide free reference books to 6,789 public and school libraries), and the Programa Biblioteca Familiar, distributing 100,000 copies of books (*colecciones integradas*) in tabloid newspaper format at the subsidised price of $25 *moneda nacional* (MN) (Medina, 2001: 12). The most comprehensive programme was undoubtedly the BNJM's Programa por la Lectura [MMM]. Finally, academic studies also aimed to understand the nature of reading and set objectives for integrated action across a range of institutions (Fernández Robaina, 2001: 110–11; Medina, 2001: 11); the most significant was conducted by the writer and critic Víctor Fowler Calzada, 'La lectura, ese poliedro' (Fowler Calzada, 2000), whose central thesis was to demonstrate the complexity of the reading process as a basis for effective policy development.

Despite these and other attempts, it was clear that the Special Period's first decade had thrown the pre-1989 individual–collective continuum into disarray, the collective having partly collapsed, or at best surviving under the threat of atomisation, and individualism given full rein, both de facto (with the growing pursuit of individual survival) and de jure (with official collective approval). With all old bilateral relationships (between reader and writer, individual and collective) being disarticulated, the cohesion of the four fundamental processes of literary culture – writing, reading, publishing and promotion – had been severely undermined.

However, there were also informal solutions to the problem, often underpinned by recognition of the social value of literary culture for both readers and writers. As early as 1994, there were signs of some recovery in publishing, primarily through the burgeoning and enterprising use of materials such as *plaquettes* (short books created from offcuts and recycled materials, including cardboard, paper and cloth). This now well-known format had been developed at Ediciones Vigía in Matanzas from 1985, although their aim then had been to create an artisanal form of book production (in contrast to the massified nature of the state-run publishing industry), to foreground the book as an object of pleasure and aesthetic value, rather than as an emergency response to material shortages [LRM]. From around 1994, however, primarily through the enthusiasm of a few writers and editors, they became more generalised to offer at least some publishing outlets for writers – although it is unclear whether these were available for readers outside the inner circles of literary culture [AGN; MY; OMP; AG]. Interestingly, some *novísimos* saw their first publication via this medium, including one who described how plaquettes of his writing had been created using the materials left over at a printing press on Reina in Centro Habana; while he recognised it as a spontaneous and inventive response to the publishing crisis, he also underlined that 'obedecía a una necesidad' [AG] ('it responded to a need'). Several editors likewise saw the *plaquette* as a collective response to the publishing paralysis, led by writers and editors unwilling to abandon the collective value of literature: 'Yo creo que hubo una cosa positiva que, más que resignarse, lo que se trató de buscar fueron alternativas dentro de aquellas circunstancias tan precarias ... que, de alguna manera, daban la posibilidad de hacer algún tipo de publicación [DGS] ('I think that the one positive thing was that, instead of resigning ourselves in the midst of such precarious circumstances, what we did was look for alternatives ... which, in some shape or form, allowed us to produce some kind of publication').

Olga Marta Pérez also described how her own experience after 1990 led her and others to create *minilibros* (mini-books) of her own and others' writing, from leftover paper margins from the national newspapers, prompted primarily by the urge to get books of some form into the public sphere. She also stressed that the impossibility and reductiveness of daily life also provided a stimulus for vocational activity as a form of therapy and spiritual and intellectual survival. The early producers of *plaquettes*, with print runs of 250–500 ('tiradas familiares' [OMP] (family-size runs)), had little regard for material or aesthetic concerns, and even less for any economic value or profit; one critic even

1990s–2000s: Crisis and reassessment

remarked, optimistically, that they were a useful filtering mechanism for a selectiveness hitherto absent in the old process of massification and socialisation of literary texts [RZ]. Interestingly, given the editors' seminal, but hitherto largely unrecognised, role in the survival and slow recovery of literary production, a new *Premio Nacional de Edición*, ranking alongside the *Premio Nacional de Literatura*, was founded in 1998, now being awarded with significant prestige at the annual Feria.

The ideological and political dimensions of self-regulation were further inflected by economic decisions, born out of necessity rather than a desire to prosper financially. The dichotomy of 'art vs. money' thus began to emerge for the first time since 1959, complicating – and potentially undermining – the other regimes of value, and making literary culture more complex and potentially conflictive, a harder terrain for writers to negotiate, a harder structure for agents to manage, and a harder environment for readers to participate in literature. With limited economic liberalisation, literature assumed the function of a predominantly economic solution for some (e.g. those selling books or second-hand book-dealers): tourism and 'dollarisation' made it a marginally more viable cultural activity than before 1989, introducing the notion of the literary text as a potential commodity.

For writers in particular, but also for editors hoping to resurrect the old publishing system, the negotiation of regimes of value was a delicate task, calling into question personal and social objectives, as well as political loyalty and sense of nationhood, and creating seemingly unavoidable contradictions. Some of these tensions and contradictions were still evident a decade later, particularly in the ways that writers sought to justify their decisions to publish abroad, especially when this appeared to fellow Cuban writers as 'selling out' or compromising one's aesthetic or ethical position. Although, until 1989, writers had had to negotiate the minefield of different interest groups with political and aesthetic agendas, with an inevitable element of self-censorship in play, depending on the 'space' where one hoped to be published [AAT], the need to publish abroad meant negotiating a much wider set of agreements, some seemingly impossible to reconcile with loyalty to one's individual and collective vision. Again, the necessity of operating in a more individual and less collective way also brought its share of personal and professional dilemmas, naturally pushing some individuals into survival mode, protecting their own interests and those of peers and friends, through the few mechanisms for publication that existed.

One of the most telling ways in which the value of mechanisms of literary culture shifted was in publishing via *concursos* (competitions) and prizes. Although, up until 1989, writers' publishing needs had been largely met by the internal network of *editoriales* – and prizes had served the important function of bestowing individual and collective prestige, occasionally 'fast-tracking' individual writers and allowing them to apply for UNEAC membership – the new survival mode created a new set of functions and value. With the decriminalisation of the dollar, swiftly followed by Law-Decree No 145 (November 1993), on labour conditions for creators of literary works (www.min.cult. cu/loader.php?sec=legislacion&cont=decretoley145), writers now had unprecedented freedom to seek contracts outside state mechanisms.

The theme of money and culture in the Special Period has been amply discussed outside Cuba (Fernandes, 2003; Whitfield, 2004, 2008, 2009; Stock, 2008). Whitfield, in particular, has explored the appearance of money as a textual component and the way that a new binarism of truth (national, non-lucrative writing) versus fiction (international, for economic gain) entered the debate, drawing interesting parallels between the 1960s and 1990s, and the emergence of a postcolonial exotic representation of Cuba (Whitfield, 2009). While they are correct not to underplay the crisis, and while the metaphor of the *jineterismo* (hustling, prostitution) or seduction of writers in the international literary marketplace has some validity (Whitfield, 2009: 30; de Aguila, 1998), some of these analyses propose a perhaps somewhat simplistic dichotomy of space and value which warrants further examination.

A late 1990s' article reflected the multiple and diverse forces operating on writers in the wake of the publishing crisis, from the social to the literary:

> en lo literario, la ruptura definitiva de una norma más o menos dominante hasta pocos años atrás y el reconocimiento explícito de la diversidad como valor; en lo promocional, más participación en premios y concursos convocados en el exterior, invitaciones sistemáticas a eventos – literarios o no – realizados en otros países, presencia cada día mayor de editores extranjeros a la caza de originales valiosos, frecuentes reseñas en la prensa internacional sobre la literatura cubana. Todo dibujado con un aura de prestigio dizque bien ganado y, muchas veces, apoyado en el necesario respiro económico que un buen fajo de billetes supone. (Morales, 1998: 7–8)[13]

Although all writers were keen to distance themselves from any hint of writing or publishing for gain, or through nepotism, their comments

1990s–2000s: Crisis and reassessment

on writing and publishing in the early 1990s express a much more complex reality and a diversity of perspectives. Most importantly, many framed their decisions to participate in the international market as born of economic necessity, as relatively insignificant monetary recognition became vitally important to survival but carried a huge moral cost.

Two of the writers best known outside Cuba – Padura Fuentes and Gutiérrez – have especially noteworthy and unexpected stories to tell of their experiences. Padura Fuentes described his first real relationship with the international market, when, in 1992, his third novel *Máscaras* won the Spanish Premio Gijón (the call for which he had spotted by chance in a magazine), which awarded him US$16,000 on 13 January 1996, when he had only $400 left in his bank account. After this, he became a Cuban-based writer whose books were, and still are, published in Spain before Cuba, through a special deal with the Cuban press and with translations also starting to be published. He also described the problematic relationship created by straddling the two systems: if his Cuban publishers print too many copies it can affect overseas sales, with Spanish tourists who buy his books cheaply in Cuba no longer buying more expensive editions in Spain [LPF].

For Gutiérrez, although travel abroad (Mexico, 1990) had represented an opportunity to broaden his personal and intellectual horizons, his first experience of publishing abroad, with Anagrama, was a necessary but negative experience. Speaking of the now iconic *Trilogía de la Habana Sucia*, he said:

> Por supuesto me dieron una miseria por esos libros, me da hasta pena decirlo. Me dieron US$2,000 de adelanto (pausa), US$2,000 de adelanto por *Trilogía* completa. Después, por *El Rey de La Habana* me hicieron lo mismo – yo no tenía la más mínima idea de nada, de en cuánto se puede vender un libro, de cómo funcionan las cosas en ese mundo. Y se aprovecharon miserablemente de mí, tanto esa gente como el editor de Anagrama, que como editor al fin y al cabo es un hombre de negocios que trata de comprar ... esa es su función, comprar lo más barato posible y después venderlo más caro. [PJG][14]

Other writers commented on the prestige or added value from publishing abroad, even if only through foreign anthologies, which were at one point the only recourse for writers [RLA; EPD; MY]. Ultimately, all showed a level of pragmatism in their interpretations of the phenomenon, although some simultaneously described the essential incommensurability between publishing in Cuba and abroad. One writer of children's literature gave an especially revealing response:

No, yo siempre he mantenido dos mundos. Desde el primer momento, yo percaté de lo que se buscaba en el extranjero, y de lo que se buscaba aquí. Es decir, no quiere decir que haya trabajado para el mercado, ni para la ideología, pero siempre estuve muy consciente ... que en el extranjero te dicen 'Este libro es magnífico pero no te lo podemos publicar', hasta, no sé, por el título, por el tema. ... Pero no, las dos carreras han sido, es como si fueran dos escritores, el del extranjero y el de aquí. [EPD][15]

Alongside the need for international publishing markets, however, the national publishing environment began a gradual recovery, often supported by donations from foreign NGOs; thus the value of the prize system was transformed according to the vagaries of the domestic economy and foreign donations [NAG]. While, for three decades, island-based prizes had provided a stimulus and a value structure within which writers could locate themselves, they were now predominantly a means to monetary recognition. Again, many commented on how the prize had become essential to survival, one painting an especially vivid picture:

Tan es así que llega un día una amiga mía que me dice –¡qué vergüenza!, pero es así – que hay un concurso que pagan mucho. Es de la Casa del Caribe o algo así, una cosa aquí en Cuba, y por un cuento, si te lo ganas, te dan 3,000 pesos cubanos – ¡ojo y cuidado! Hoy no representan una cifra apreciable – cualquier cantante maluco por pararse ahí te pide tres mil pesos, sí, 3,000 pesos es una cifra decorosa, pero no es para asombrarse; pero en aquella época en Cuba, con la crisis que había, no eran como para despreciar pensando que podría comprar un puré grande para los niños o pomos, yo no sé, y le digo: ay, chica, pero ¿tú crees? Y ella me dice: 'Laidy, escribe algo', y me estimula para que escriba. [AFJ][16]

For many, then, the prize system was a necessary evil, a complicated mechanism or 'lottery', where the rewards – in some cases four-figure amounts in Euros – were visible but the criteria never fully transparent [EHL; NRG; NAG]. Especially during the worst of the Special Period, the national and international systems of prizes had to be negotiated in order to be published or enter the formal spaces of literary culture, and perhaps also gain access to hard currency through associated events, such as book festivals or launches. However, the decentralisation, deregulation and extension of writers' opportunities also meant an increasingly confused network of internal spaces in which to function: the emerging writer was often disadvantaged by having to compete with established figures for the same prize, monetary recognition did not always closely match symbolic prestige (yet also carried the assumption that this was so), the list of prizes available was fragile and ever-changing, and the scenario, largely Havana-based, was complicated even further in the 2000s through the formal expansion of literary culture across the island by the accumulation of prizes attached to the CPLL [EPD; JAP; SH]. One writer (now director of Letras Cubanas) described the contemporary function of prizes as 'un mecanismo al menos práctico de publicación y de retribución. Algunos son más importantes que otros, algunos señalan caminos hacia la canonización, digamos, y estoy hablando en términos grandilocuentes, más claros que otros' [RR] ('at least a practical mechanism for publishing and financial retribution. Some prizes are more important than others, some prizes, let's say, show you which are the roads to having your work enter the canon, and I'm using rather grandiloquent language here'). What is also clear is that, despite a common recognition that the marketisation of literary culture from the early 1990s had been principally a practical solution – both individual and collective – to sustain a virtually paralysed publishing system and its writers, there was also a parallel recognition that the link with an internal readership had been severely compromised, if not lost altogether. For many of those coming of age during the euphoric early 1960s, when literature's economic value was not even considered worthy of discussion (unless it implied collective political resistance via *piratería*), the changes occasioned by the crisis, and especially the introduction of some market elements, were more difficult to comprehend. Some twenty years after the initial crisis, Fernández Retamar commented:

> En lo que toca al mercado, es inevitable recordar que tengo setenta y ocho años, y me formé viendo a Víctor Manuel dando sus cuadros para pagar la cerveza que habíamos bebido; a Portocarrero y Milián viviendo en un solar; a Carpentier, Guillén, Lezama, Virgilio, Feijóo, Eliseo, Cintio, Fina y tantos y tantas más (ni hablar de los jóvenes) pagando sus libros, que después enviaban a amigos. Los escritores no teníamos derechos sino deberes de autor. (Fernández Retamar, 2008: 18)[17]

While the 1990s introduced a new level of individual strategic positioning for some writers, it would be wrong to suggest that this necessarily implied the end of agents' participation in literary culture in any collectively oriented initiatives. Just as the *plaquettes* had been developed to satisfy writers' and editors' (and some readers') needs, there were many projects pre-dating 1989 which survived and underwent radical transformations of motive, function, scale, possibilities and personnel. There is evidence that, although publishing in Cuba had virtually ground to a halt, the system of *presentaciones* continued, albeit more modestly [JAP]; similarly, organisations such as the AHS, having survived the early crisis, were ready by 1995 to re-evaluate membership and functions, and to seek to reinvigorate themselves by finding younger leaders, representing new generations of artists. Interestingly, one AHS activist described it as a 'depuración de la membresía' [FLJ] ('cleansing of the membership') – not, as might be expected by some external commentators, a 'purging' in order to staff the organisation with loyal and unquestioning young 'bureaucrats' but, rather, an overhaul to correct two issues: that both emigration and the deregulation of cultural life had led to a rather uneven and arbitrarily chosen membership, which lacked creative and organisational talent (rather than loyalty); and that the membership was not necessarily in touch with the pressing sociocultural concerns of the moment.

Similarly, in the area of cultural promotion, and with the emerging emphasis on local *cultura comunitaria*, there was a fresh drive to rebuild social networks via cultural practice, using specialists in cultural activism and building on the skills and local knowledge gained through research, contacts and lived experience. One example in Centro Habana, badly affected by the crisis, indicated how the project of sociocultural 'reconstruction' was seen holistically:

> Cuando a mí me pidieron en el año 95, por la UNEAC, que yo fuera representante para el consejo popular por lo menos en el municipio donde estamos clavados ... me dijeron, '¿En qué línea tu vas a trabajar la cultura comunitaria?' Yo dije 'En la única que yo sé, con los niños, con los bibliotecarios. Y con los autores. Yo no sé hacerlo de otra forma, porque yo soy un editor...'. Por lo tanto, eso fue lo que hice ... O sea, en este sentido, Centro Habana vio con una luz muy amplia por parte de todas instituciones del territorio, de cómo vincularnos a la comunidad. [ELR][18]

However, perhaps the most interesting and long-lasting publishing response to the crisis, given its consequences for literary culture, contributing to a new expansion in the provinces, came in 1991 in the form of provincial publishing outlets, grouped in 1994 under the network of Fondos Territoriales (provincial collections), to structure and manage what was an essentially deregulated cultural economy, especially outside the capital, and, in 2000, mostly incorporated into the ICL under the Sistema de Ediciones Territoriales (SET). Again, the response combined local initiatives and adaptation with state-level policy, the latter through the acquisition of Xerox Photocopiers (called

1990s–2000s: Crisis and reassessment 151

RISO, from the Japanese brand name) which allowed for a nationwide network of literary spaces (UNEAC's provincial branches, local publishers and Casas de Cultura) to reproduce small print-runs of, initially, up to 500 copies (now more often 1,000 copies) of short texts. The RISO phenomenon, still an essential part of the Cuban publishing system, provided an inventive solution at that time to material shortage, with a profound effect on literary culture, although, given the semi-autonomous nature of many of these outlets (making them difficult to detect and evaluate), it was a long time before data which revealed the extent of their impact was available. Although numbers (titles and copies) were low and the books' physical quality decidedly modest, they nevertheless filled an important gap in the provinces; many Havana-based writers argued that the RISO and SET provided a vital means of survival for publishing, even creating an anomalous situation where provincial conditions were sometimes more favourable than those in Havana. Some, comparing it to the more centralised structures of Havana-based publishing, attributed this to the greater immediacy of small-scale publishing, 'porque son menos y disponen de sus instrumentos de publicación, los tienen ahí a mano y hay muchos sellos editoriales, yo creo que realmente se ha creado una gran posibilidad' [RLA] ('because there are fewer of them and they have their own means of production, near at hand, and there are many publishing brands, I think they really have created many possibilities'); it is certainly true that, in Havana, the RISO/SET lessened the pressure to meet writers' demands and deal with the ever-increasing *colchón editorial* of manuscripts [AG]. Hence, their impact was felt in complex ways across Cuba, not just affecting provincial literary culture; many Havana-based writers also used them to publish texts quickly, albeit with very small print-runs, but their greatest effect was to open up possibilities for unknown or emerging provincial writers, echoing the earlier *talleres* movement in having created a new national network of spaces for literary culture. However, just as the *talleres* had aroused fears about standardisation, centralisation, proliferation and even qualitative impoverishment of literature, most interviewees recognised that, although it would be foolish to assume that the RISO/SET could have guaranteed the dissemination of only 'good' writers, they at least provided the opportunity for those writers to be discovered and disseminated. One poet now based in Havana (originally from Ciego de Avila) described both experiences – *talleres* and RISO – as having been vital to his literary career:

[E]l Taller era mi espacio particular, personal, como creador de provincia, porque allí o generábamos una pequeña publicación, hecha en mimeógrafo, muy humilde, o mandábamos a concursos nacionales, que daban la vía para publicar de inmediato y sin retroceso, sin rechazo, o luchábamos por ver cómo podíamos meter nuestros pequeños cuadernos primerizos de poesía en esas editoriales nacionales, donde el filtro era poderoso. [RM][19]

Others questioned the qualitative hierarchy which privileges Havana, stressing that many provincial writers benefiting from the RISO/SET were already well-respected figures in their own areas [NRG], and, for many who had published via the SET, their selection mechanisms were as rigorous as any in Havana. There were, nevertheless, suspicions that the proliferation of publishing opportunities had created an 'apertura indiscriminada' ('indiscriminate opening up') in some cases (although of course the same argument could hold for any new technologies which, from Cuba's entry into the internet environment in 1996 (Uxó 2009), had expanded the possibilities of dissemination), or that the provincial publishers had developed cartels or *mafias provinciales* in order to help one another [VLL].

There was also a range of responses regarding critical reception. One prominent scholar recognised that the critic might review a published work, rather than a manuscript, with greater respect [MMP], others pointed to shortcomings deriving from small print-runs and distribution failings, and Havana-based critics stressed that, given the impossibility of systematic access to RISO/SET publications, there was an urgent need for the decentralisation of *crítica literaria* alongside literary production [JF]. One critic also noted another unforeseen consequence of the decentralisation, fragmentation and atomisation of a national system: that recently published literature was hard to uncover and thus analyse in its own context, for the purpose of constructing accurate literary histories and bibliographies; the only exceptions were those books published via the CPLL:

> Antes de enmendar la crítica literaria en Cuba se requiere socializar sus discursos y reconocer sus funciones (descriptiva, interpretativa, valorativa, jerarquizadora y proyectiva) e integrarla a las estrategias editorial, creativa y de mercado de las letras cubanas del fin de siglo. (Zurbano, 1998: 22)[20]

While most studies of the post-1990 Cuban cultural scene tend to conflate the following two decades, assuming that the crisis continued unchanged, the year 2000 actually saw a significant change for literary culture, as with many other aspects of the Cuban system, although partly building on the lessons learnt since 1990: the immediate responses, the irreversible social and cultural changes and the need to maintain the more deregulated local and provincial-level organisations and activity that had replaced state-level or Havana-based operations.

A new emphasis on culture was already evident from 1997, with Abel Prieto (already notable for having revitalised UNEAC under his presidency over the preceding decade) being appointed Minister of Culture after the 1996 Party Congress, and already beginning to show his familiar mix of dynamism, energy and flexibility to the task of negotiating a new direction for culture in the rapidly changing 'new' Cuba. In November 1998, at its Fourth Congress (the Third having taken place, as normal in 1993, despite the crisis), UNEAC reinstated culture at the centre of the national project: 'Por eso, más que el congreso de un sector de la sociedad, se le considera un congreso de la cultura nacional' (Cantón Navarro and Duarte Hurtado, 2006b: 308) ('Therefore, more than a congress for a particular sector of society, we should consider it a congress for national culture'). Then, in June 1999, at the Primer Congreso Internacional sobre Cultura y Desarrollo, Fidel Castro demanded 'la urgente necesidad de propiciar, mediante la educación y la instrumentación de correctas políticas culturales, una verdadera revolución ética del hombre' (Cantón Navarro and Duarte Hurtado, 2006b: 333) ('The urgent need to bring about, through education and the implementation of cultural policies, a real ethical revolution for mankind').

Finally, in late 1999, the Elián González saga provided the focus for just such an ethical revolution, rallying Cubans in protest and reinvigorating mass mobilisation to an extent not seen since the 1960s. The return to a strongly moral underpinning for the social project, under the *Batalla de Ideas*, after a decade of enforced prioritisation of material concerns, created a very different environment for literary culture, where the work of the agents of literary culture was once again validated as vital to the social project of revolution and national sovereignty. The 1998 UNEAC Congress had clearly acted as an inspiration for the *Batalla*, and the 'political reverberation' (Stock, 2008: 8) of Elián in the cultural sphere further underlined the centrality of culture: 'Es darle un peso dentro de la Batalla a la cultura artístico-literaria, es apostar a la cultura como única vía para sostener un proyecto social, es decir, Fidel está diciendo: sin cultura no hay libertad posible' [AAG] ('it means giving weight within the *Batalla* to artistic and literary culture, it means pledging a commitment to culture as the only way of sustaining a social project, in other words, Fidel is saying: without culture there is no possibility of freedom').

However, it was not just a question of using cultural practice as an instrument to address social problems; there was also a renewed emphasis on understanding how social sectors, transformed by the Special Period (especially through limited economic liberalisation, tourism and mass emigration) now functioned, and how changing social patterns and attitudes might threaten the unity of the revolutionary project and its underlying development model. With the creation of fifteen schools for *instructores de arte* across Cuba, and the founding of the many projects under the remit of *trabajadores sociales*, these 'new' agents and researchers sought to raise levels of sociocultural awarenes and realise detailed studies of the social environment:

> Y había que crear condiciones para que esos jóvenes que también son cubanos y que son hijos de gente revolucionaria y que están también participando de este proyecto tuviera igualdad de posibilidades de hacerse médico, aún cuando las becas estaban ahí y venían para todos, y no te decían, "la puede coger un blanco, no un negro", no; las propias condiciones sociales te iban condicionando y entonces, las mejores notas las tenían los hijos de los profesionales y por tanto, podían coger las mejores carreras. Es complicado. Y así se visitó casa por casa, porque eso no se resuelve con disposiciones generales. [AAG][21]

Against all the odds, and within the context of a partially renewed siege mentality, the *Batalla de Ideas* sought to promote a new revolutionary spirit, 'un segundo aire de la revolución … una vuelta al humanismo de la revolución' [AAG] ('a second wind for the Revolution, a return to a humanist Revolution'), which itself provided the impetus for a reconsolidation of the mechanisms and spaces of literary culture begun in the mid-1990s with the notion of *cultura comunitaria*. However, as the expansion of initiatives such as the Feria indicate (see Chapter 8), 2000 was also a watershed in prioritising active participation in literary culture, i.e. readership and reading, principally through the initiation, development and consolidation of a multitude of reading-based projects, clearly echoing the mobilisation and cultural democratisation campaigns of the 1960s in scale and ambition. Post-2000 studies emphasised the socialisation of culture, 'la distribución y popularización del arte, el conocimiento científico y las demás formas de alta cultura' (Linares Fleites *et al*, 2004: 84) ('the distribution and popularisation of art, scientific knowledge and the other forms of high culture')

1990s–2000s: Crisis and reassessment 155

as the most effective element of cultural policy in the 1990s, seeing it as vital that any blueprint for cultural massification should focus on active and creative participation rather than passive consumption (Linares Fleites *et al*, 2004: 86–7). Such studies clearly aimed to assess the damage since 1990 and then revive cultural life within the spirit of the *Batalla*'s emerging discourses and values, addressing the post-1990 processes of withdrawal, individualisation and atomisation. The aim was to regain public cultural space – especially locally, and including cinemas, video clubs and the ailing network of Casas de Cultura – as the stage for a national project of reconstruction. Given the inherently solitary nature of reading, literature did not figure significantly in the studies' recommendations, but nor did their authors exclude literary culture from their proposals.

Instead, alongside more popular or performative cultural forms, literary culture assumed its place in a drive to collectivise and incentivise through social value and prestige gained via participation. The list of initiatives related to literary culture from 2000 is vast, each year seeing a proliferation of projects implemented by a wide range of cultural and educational institutions and networks, often under the energetic leadership of UJC *dirigentes*. Their key motive was to consolidate and reinforce the national coordination and regulation of initiatives that had emerged as local or provincial responses to the crisis, and thus to create a system whereby both local autonomy and national coherence could be delivered. Since the 1990s' experience had confirmed that a nationally institutionalised framework was the only way to implement policies with a national impact, the use of the existing framework of nationwide Casas de Cultura, libraries and educational institutions allowed for some level of structural coherence [ELR].

Furthermore, given its national scope, the ICL, which had been slowly incorporating provincial publishing from the 1990s, along with the CPLL, offered a comprehensive perspective of the spaces and networks for literary culture. Alongside a quantitative change (with steadily increasing resources), there was thus also a qualitative change, 'un vuelco sorprendente' ('a surprising upturn'), transforming the ICL's remit and functions through changes to publishing structures, to recognise the Ediciones Territoriales, since 'el razonamiento de Fidel era que deberíamos encontrar el modo de que un autor pudiera publicar su obra, independientemente del lugar donde vivía' [FLJ] ('Fidel's reasoning was that we should find the way for authors to publish their work, irrespective of where they lived'). The growing importance of youth, as the *Batalla*'s front-line, became clear, as did the increasing role of the UJC and AHS in promoting and regulating cultural life; with the AHS holding its First Congress in 2000 and the UJC's Grupo de Atención a los Proyectos Culturales del Consejo de Estado (group to execute the Council of State's cultural plans) becoming the vanguard for the new campaign, literary culture was evidently to be conceptualised differently and prioritised within the revolutionary project, in ways not seen since the 1960s [FLJ]. Given that active participation in the AHS often preceded UNEAC membership and participation, the AHS's growing profile also reflected the future-oriented objective of a seedbed for cultural life [ELR].

Thus, the ICL, having largely managed the publishing system for four decades, now had new roles and functions within a nationwide remit: to socialise literature effectively and cost-effectively where possible; again, the notion of mobilisation and utilisation of human resources as a pragmatic response to material shortages carried strong echoes of the 1960s, literary 'socialisation' replacing the ability to produce and distribute sufficient books for the population's needs [AP]. However, the drive also provided the potential for the ICL to act as one of many agents, or brokers, in shaping the reconstruction of sociocultural life after the crisis, and thus 'convertirse en ese espacio de concertación de voluntades' for Cuban society [MRA] ('become that space where desires could be harmonised'). Until 2009 at least, the expansion of the ICL's activities was staggering in its commitment to making literature accessible; often linked to the Feria, the range of weekly and annual activities grew exponentially each year in Havana. From the fifty annual *sábados del libro* (weekly Saturday-morning *presentaciones* at the ICL headquarters, the Palacio del Segundo Cabo in La Habana Vieja) to the rehabilitation of former spaces for literary culture and the creation of new ones (the Centro Dulce María Loynaz, the Ateneo bookshop, UNEAC, the BNJM, the Biblioteca Rubén Martínez Villena, Casa de las Américas), where new books could be launched and sold in limited numbers at additionally subsidised *moneda nacional* prices, but also where authors could read from their published and unfinished work, the weekly and annual calendar of events became an increasingly significant part of literary culture, providing an opportunity for authors and editors to promote their work, gain readers' feedback and also create semi-autonomous spaces for individuals and groups to pursue their own literary interests within the ICL's national framework.

For readers, likewise, there were quantitative and qualitative changes: although initially access to literary texts was centred in spaces with a tradition of literary culture, such as libraries, cultural centres, or cultural institutions, the mid-to-late 2000s saw a significant change in direction, with the decision to locate these readings, *miniferias* (mini-fairs) and *lanzamientos* in truly public spaces. This includes on the Malecón, *Lecturas frente al mar* (readings by the sea), on Calle 23, *La noche de los libros* (book night) – one of the most iconic spaces in the Havana cartography – in new *cafés literarios* (space for books in cafés already popular with youth), in the Hotel Inglaterra in the Parque Central (to resurrect the *tertulias* of earlier times, and challenge the sociocultural impact of tourism on Havana's iconic spaces), and, from 2008 onwards, on the main university campus in Havana (the Festival Universitaria del Libro y la Lectura), to improve students' reading habits.

These projects also went nationwide, using provincial capitals and often one other major city in each province. Hence, the sites for literary culture as a social phenomenon steadily proliferated and began to occupy symbolic public spaces previously dedicated to social life, especially for youth. Once again, these initiatives were both a clever attempt to find cost-effective 'new' spaces for literature's dissemination and discussion, and a prioritisation of the needs of both the existing readership and potential new ones, by locating events at the heart of everyday local social life.

A unique example of this came in 2008 with a new related project, again under the ICL/UJC, to bring books and texts into the most unlikely of spaces: a Havana-based programme which distributed a limited number of texts to spaces where Cubans spent time waiting their turn (barber shops, bus terminals, etc.), enabling them to occupy their always lengthy waiting-time in reading. Under the slogan *Leyendo Espero* (literally, 'reading while I wait') – printed on stickers identifying those locations participating in the project – people were encouraged and reminded to use their time reading [ISE; FLJ]. Despite the commitment of those involved, however, material limitations were clear, the texts distributed not always being the most attractive, engaging or even comprehensible [AP].

However, other initiatives were extremely successful in bringing literary texts to the public and making literature popular (some 50,000 books previously collecting dust in bookshops were sold in nine hours on Calle 23 during the 2008 *noche de los libros* [FLJ]); in immersing literature in everyday sociocultural life, literary events often being accompanied by other cultural performances; and in finding ways for publishers to circulate accumulated stagnant stock in state and second-hand bookshops and warehouses. Central to this drive to socialise the literary text was the understanding of the needs of both writers and readers, in ways which recognised local conditions and individual demands, but also coordinated these within a national project. Two phenomena were developed to answer this need: the *promotor cultural*, a category of 'agent' which, as we have seen, already existed but which was now given a much higher profile; and the Observatorio Cubano del Libro y la Literatura (OCLL).

The role of the *promotor cultural* was developed both at the level of specific *editoriales* and cultural centres (for example UNEAC, Casa de las Américas, Centro Dulce María Loynaz, the Instituto Superior de Arte (ISA)), but also more generally for the effective promotion of books per se, the two levels being coordinated through the joint meetings of Departamentos de Promoción of publishers, cultural centres and the ICL.The *promotor*'s basic function was to coordinate all aspects of the book's dissemination, through catalogues, the review or *crítica* system, media coverage and, finally, in the *presentación*, the 'momento culminante' (climax) of the process [EPD]. Their training, within MINCULT's Centros de Superación (centres for enhancing skills), now consisted of a two-year course, including communication studies and specialist courses in cultural forms and genres [YLG]. For the *promotor* attached to a (national) publisher, this might mean promoting up to forty books a year, taking each one from printing to *lanzamiento*, the latter including negotiations with writers, editors and critics to participate in the *presentación* panel, with institutions providing the event's location, and with interested journalists (mostly for high-profile authors and books, usually at the *sábado del libro*). In Ediciones Unión, in line with its semi-autonomous status and UNEAC link, every new book was first presented at UNEAC, and only then, if relevant, promoted elsewhere, depending on the author's particular networks. However, it is clear that the *presentación* was not always generated automatically with every new book, some authors being more willing than others to have their books presented in that way. Since the author decided the *presentación* panel's composition and suggested a suitable location, the *promotor* effectively became an 'events manager' for literary culture, a broker between book, author, insitutional agents involved (including the head of the publishing house and relevant ICL staff) and public – often a delicate task, incorporating the wishes and conditions of a range of actors, and the policies of several institutions, each with its own agenda.

Observation of *presentaciones* (2005–10) confirms that the audience (ranging from twenty to over 100, depending on the author's profile) is usually composed of the author's friends and family, students of literature, specialist readers (critics, academics), other *promotores culturales* (observing for their own professional training), and a more general public, predominantly female, perhaps with a specific interest in the book. Since the book is sold afterwards at a slightly subsidised Cuban peso price, some individuals evidently attend to purchase multiple copies; what is less clear, however, is whether these are to be distributed among friends or are intended for re-sale at a slightly higher price or even in hard currency. From 2008, it certainly became difficult to buy more than one or two copies per person, perhaps indicating a crackdown on re-sale. The *presentación* also has another economic dimension: following MINCULT's 2005 Resolución 35, to recognise 'la oralidad de la escritura' ('the oral dimension of writing'), panel members have received a modest financial remuneration (between 120 and 200 Cuban pesos), including payment for subsequent online publication of their contribution [EPD]. However, although the *promotor* leads and designs a marketing exercise not dissimilar to that in a capitalist system, economic considerations play a secondary role to the sociocultural and symbolic value of books and reading.

The OCLL was founded within ICL, under Iroel Sánchez Espinosa, in September 2008, as a response to the Centro Marinello's and BNJM's considerable research into cultural participation throughout the 1990s and 2000s [JLM]. Building on several studies of the cultural industries, it was created to consolidate understanding of publishing in particular, for a wider understanding of publishing and reception of literary texts. Thus, although many of the ICL's post-2000 initiatives were characterised by a drive for imaginative solutions and subjective commitment, by 2008, their need to coordinate a more methodical and systematic approach to the problems of sustaining literary culture, and to 'ejecutar la política' ('to enact policies') to reduce waste of resources, was recognised. As the unit's then Director, Jacqueline Laguardia Martínez, observed:

El Observatorio básicamente evalúa la política de muchas maneras y una de ellas es coordinando las investigaciones, viendo quiénes investigan, haciendo que el diálogo entre academia y políticos fluya, que es muy difícil en cualquier contexto del planeta por lo que yo he visto e investigado. [JLM][22]

Thus, using the ICL's authority, as the 'institución rectora de la política del libro en el país' ('the institution determining book-related policies in Cuba'), the OCLL was able to request publishing data from all literary institutions with a publishing component (CPLL, SET, *editoriales*), for the *balance anual* (annual analysis and evaluation), published every spring. However, since OCLL had less authority over mass organisations, educational establishments, and the Council of State, it was less successful in gaining a comprehensive picture of how literary publishing coexisted alongside other subject categories.

OCLL's report for 2009 (ICL, 2009), however, indicated some interesting features. With figures of both numbers of titles and copies published for most years since 1991, the data showed that, while, in the 1990s, the ICL's national publishing houses were still maintaining pre-1989 production levels, by 1993 their situation was critical (ICL, 2009: 6–7). While across the whole spectrum of national publishing, literary texts represented the largest single category (according to UNESCO criteria) of titles published for any year, in terms of print-runs or overall number of copies printed, educational textbooks exceeded literary texts sevenfold. RISO publishing was almost entirely oriented to publishing literary texts, with the exception of Havana and Santiago provinces, where the existence of literary publishers (Letras Cubanas and others in Havana, Oriente in Santiago), allowed the RISO effect to benefit a wider range of texts.

Furthermore, the 2009 data indicated that literary texts made up over 70 per cent of the SET books published across the provinces (with small and standardised print-runs, there is rarely a discrepancy between numbers of titles and copies), and that in Havana the one existing SET operation, Ediciones Extramuros, published only literary texts.

As an example of provincial publishing, Extramuros sheds important light on the challenges of small-scale publishing: although originally founded in 1976, from 1997 it began to use RISO, although increasingly using Cuban parts. Publishing on average fourteen to fifteen titles per year (compared with fifty titles across the whole SET network and eighty from Letras Cubanas), it has print-runs of about 1,000 copies. All production costs (paper, ink, machinery) are calculated in Cuban convertible pesos (CUC),[23] but all books are sold domestically in *moneda nacional*, at an average price between three and six pesos (compared with an average price of twenty for books published outside the SET). It has four staff, paid in *moneda nacional* (editor, secretary, designer and one other), plus four contracted *editores*. The number of pages for a book is agreed in advance (taking costs into account), and, since such outlets were incorporated into the ICL, they are expected to send three copies of each title published to all Cuban libraries (with over 400, that goal is not always met) and obliged to lodge copies of each title in the BNJM and local libraries. Although they distribute their published texts through the Distribuidora Nacional de Libros (DNL) to the main Havana bookshops and occasionally, to the provinces via the CPLL, their publishing plans are increasingly geared to the Feria so that they can manage sales and production costs more directly.

Thus, the OCLL aimed to reveal areas of duplication in publishing, to assess the extent of national and provincial coordination and to identify training needs for the various agents in the system; in other words, to study the economy of the book as 'una cadena de producción, un ciclo productivo', to eliminate inefficiencies. However, as publishing continued to recover, OCLL's remit also extended to reception and consumption, including pricing and effective marketing: 'Hay que saber quién es el consumidor para el que se produce, porque el objetivo final del libro es que se lea. Y cuando pienso en consumidor, pienso en consumo activo, no sólo en quién compra' [JLM] ('we need to know more accurately who exactly is the consumer for whom we are producing, because the final aim of the book is that it is read. And when I think of a consumer, I think of an active consumer, not just someone who buys the book'). Again, an important dimension of that understanding was to consider not only the national evolution of publishing, but also local conditions and variations in tastes and habits, with important work still to be done in gaining feedback from booksellers with first-hand knowledge of customers and reading/sales trends, of weaknesses in distribution, and so on, and in training booksellers to understand their public and shape their reading habits, needs and tastes.

The potential existed, then, for a new important broker in the systems of literary culture: echoing the views of many interviewees that the old network of skilled booksellers had been impoverished during the crisis, Laguardia explained that the ICL was running new courses for booksellers (except those in the Plaza de Armas and those affiliated directly to MINCULT), to train them in the mechanisms of pricing, marketing and *promoción*, as well as to collate sales information for analysis within the ICL.

Given the massively expanded emphasisis on both the reader and the collective experience of literature, as part of the *Batalla*'s social and ideological reinvigoration, what were the implications for writers, many having withdrawn into an individualistic survival mode, negotiating the difficult terrain of domestic and foreign prizes and publishing contracts? How far did they recover their prominent role in literary culture, and how did the provincialisation and the new socialisation affect their role and self-perception?

Firstly, just as in the 1960s and 1970s, the massification of literary production through *talleres* (professional – as in the Centro Onelio (see Chapter 6) – and community-based through *cultura comunitaria*) and the provincialisation of publishing had clearly transformed their environment in ways which writers embraced but also saw as problematic. While many recognised the significance of an improved publishing system, providing spaces for established and emerging writers, the renewed drive to reconnect writers with a public and the *Batalla*'s increased focus on readership also meant a more public and collective role. For many, this was a welcome corrective to the 1990s' isolation [RV], allowing them to be part of a larger project of public *trabajo cultural* (cultural work), based on their expertise and authority, rather than simply being assigned to administrative or bureaucratic functions. The annual Ferias and weekly *presentaciones* thus became an important element of local and national community-building, both within the cultural and intellectual communities and between writers and the general public [MSM; MY; NAG; RGZ; ECP].

In particular, the newly formalised provincial sites of literary culture provided an opportunity for new connections between geographical areas and previously isolated literary groups. Indeed, for many provincial writers, these emerging networks meant opportunities for professional development and some element of social mobility, some becoming established in Havana, and thus nationally, thanks to increased exposure [RM; JDC; JAP; FLJ]; these writers also spoke of the hierarchical nature of the new networks for literary culture, with Havana as the ultimate standard and mechanism of canonisation, but clearly they attributed these inequalities to poor distribution mechanisms, reinforcing the peripheral nature of provincial literary work:

> Pero tienen un talón de Aquiles – el sistema distributivo. La distribución es pobre, limitada y a veces se quedan en los márgenes provinciales, con lo cual entonces, ese producto cultural pasa trabajo para moverse. Es decir un santiaguero puede pasar trabajo para saber qué publican los poetas camagüeyanos, pero no pasa trabajo para saber qué publica un poeta habanero, ¿entienden?. [RM][24]

Many also emphasised the renewed local interest, with writers' or literary specialists' residence in a given neighbourhood often becoming an informal but effective way for books to circulate, reading to be promoted and *talleres* to be developed [RGZ; RV; ECP; AAL; ELR; MDO; MR; AGN]. Indeed, most interviewees (even the most apparently reclusive) mentioned their informal neighbourhood cultural work to socialise the literary text.

As for printed mass media, although some space is dedicated to the promotion of literature in the national dailies, it is more often through *revistas* (magazines) – initially Havana-based/national and now also the burgeoning range of provincial organs enabled by the SET, some distributed successfully across Cuba – that textual space is afforded to literary culture [RR; RM; MSM; AAB]. *Gaceta de Cuba*, having survived the 1990s, is now the most successful national cultural magazine, seeking actively to promote literary texts from writers across Cuba [NC; RR]. As Codina, *Gaceta* Director in 2007, explained, its nationwide impact can be attributed to several factors: with an overall print-run then of 5,000, 2,000 were distributed by mail to *estanquillos* (newstands), 1,000 to state bookshops, 1,000 via subscriptions (of which, inexplicably, 550 emanated from one province, Las Tunas), and 200–300 copies were complimentary copies for contributors – although Codina also explained that, before the 1990s, all UNEAC members were entitled to a free copy. This circulation was achieved through a delicate combination of funding from the state (MINCULT, Fondo de Desarrollo de la Cultura) and foreign NGOs, occasionally supplemented by UNEAC's agreement – not uncontroversially – to advertising by non-Cuban companies, a scenario described wryly by Codina: 'Yo todavía no me encuentro un buen anunciante que me financie la revista, siempre que no me ponga una lata de chorizos ahí' [NC] ('I still haven't been able to find a good advertiser who'll pay for my magazine without insisting on putting an advert for tinned sausages in it').

Writers also commented on cultural programming on the national television and radio channels, the consensus being that, despite the commitment and expertise of a handful of influential individuals, such coverage was insufficient to boost significantly the reception of literature, especially compared with the coverage for more popular cultural forms. The cultural journalist and director of Radio Habana, Magda Resik Aguirre, whose radio spot, *Entre libros*, was mentioned by many, is one such individual with a regular public presence, attending and leading *presentaciones* at events such as the *Noche de los libros*.

Perhaps even more prominent in promoting reading and literature is María Dolores Ortiz, whose television programme *Escriba y Lea* has run since 1969, offering the general public some kind of literary education ([MDO]; also www.cubanradio.cu/index.php/cuban-radio-history/24–radio-memories/933–dr-maria-dolores-ortiz-cepero-brito-offered-me-the-job-as-a-panelist-for-escriba-y-lea-television-show-).

The genesis of the programme was the Ortiz-led nationwide network of Clubes de Amigos del Libro (clubs of friends of the book), existing since the 1970s as an offshoot of the Literacy Campaign but resurrected at ICL's request in the early 1990s, to reinforce the value of reading and literature, to 'formar lectores' (create readers). Supported by MINCULT, Clubes were founded across the country, in schools, local radio stations, the workplace, municipal libraries, and often organised according to age groups or responding to local figures, events and texts [MDO]. Importantly, they existed in parallel with other initiatives, but also acted to coordinate them. By harnessing the public's interaction with literature in the often private space of their television viewing, the overall project clearly maintains literary culture at the centre of social and cultural life – 'en este momento, después del noticiero, el programa que más audiencia tiene es *Escriba y Lea*' ('right now, after the TV news, the programme with the highest viewer ratings is *Escriba y Lea*'), and a recent attempt to move the programme to the Canal Educativo provoked viewer protests and was abandoned [MDO].

Although the success of such inititatives, in terms of readership, is unquestionable, some writers and literary figures see their raised public image as having 'un valor puramente ceremonial' [AF] ('a purely ceremonial value'), little more than a performance of a successful literary culture, highlighting the sometimes unwelcome demands made on their writing time by such community work:

> Tanto es así que a [...] se le atribuye una frase que ha pasado a ser clásica entre nosotros que dice 'Las actividades culturales van a terminar acabando con la cultura' porque tú no tienes tiempo ni de leer ni de estudiar, todo el tiempo estás en una actividad cultural presentando un libro, yendo a la presentación de un libro de un amigo, la presentación de una revista ... chico, déjame tranquilo, déjame leer, hace varios años que yo no me leo un libro de trescientas páginas. [AF][25]

On balance, therefore, although there is considerable consensus that the prestige generated by these collective spaces has enormous social and symbolic value, the unavoidable problem is still a lack of economic

1990s–2000s: Crisis and reassessment

recognition for writers, whether through publication in sufficiently large print-runs – and the concomitant royalties and extended recognition through associated events and awards – or through a coherent policy of promoting Cuban writers abroad.

Hence, these interviews indicated that, some twenty years after the start of the Special Period, and regardless of writers' commitment to a revolutionary project to recognise the value of literary culture, it was the financial aspects of their participation in that culture that proved most problematic. Since around 2000, the formalisation (via Resolución 42) of a dual approach to royalties, depending on whether a book was sold in CUC or MN, created a mixed environment, combining several types of value, ultimately difficult to negotiate for all involved. Given that any cultural producer was entitled to a percentage of hard-currency earnings from their work, authors were entitled to 10 per cent of the income from hard-currency sales, following 'un concepto de mercado' [DGS] ('market concepts'). However, in the case of MN earnings, and even with advances from *editoriales* to established authors, the value of the work resided not in its sales potential but in a calculation of another kind, determined by an assessment of its aesthetic, social or symbolic value, and agreed by all parties: as Daniel García explained, with reference to Letras Cubanas in 2007:

> Es un problema de consideración que el editor tenga del libro, de la calidad del libro ... y del nivel del autor. Entonces me dice, 'Bueno, yo por este libro puedo pagar tres mil pesos.' Se lo decimos al autor, 'Mira, yo por esto te pago tres mil. ¿Estás de acuerdo?'. 'Sí. No, yo creo que cuatro mil'. Ahí empieza un diálogo y se llega a un acuerdo. Y eso es lo que se paga. Y se paga cuando el libro ya está aquí en la editorial. No tiene que ver con la venta. Y tiene la intención, el objetivo, de beneficiar, precisamente, al autor. No adscribiéndolo a la venta y haciéndolo de mutuo acuerdo. Es una resolución perfectible. [DGS][26]

Despite the fact that authors may also have been subsequently remunerated for *la oralidad de la literatura*, there was clearly a notable imbalance between sales figures in CUC and MN (which rose to a maximum of $10,000 MN on rare occasions, but was more often around $3,000 MN). Although the system attempted to offer a fair recompense to writers after 1989, with *editoriales* working closely with UNEAC to negotiate new policies, a fair resolution was elusive. Hence, Resolución 42 was overtaken by Resolución 34 'que quita todo ese análisis cuantitativo y prioriza el análisis cualitativo de la obra, y el pago en función de ese análisis cualitativo' [DGS] ('which removes all that quantitative analysis and prioritises the qualititative analysis of the book, as well as payment which is tied to that qualitative analysis'). On the other hand, perhaps partly to compensate for a lack of economic recognition, authors were also keen to see their work read and enjoyed by as large a readership as possible. As a result, when decisions were taken to send copies to hard-currency bookshops, as part of a policy to generate hard currency for national publishing (or, according to the more cynical, merely to report that this income was being generated), many authors protested that the books were unlikely to be bought by tourists, thus entering a vacuum of reception [AF].

The situation became even more complicated by the actions of individuals who attempted to transfer the book as an object from the non-commercial, heavily subsidised, domestic system (in MN) to the market-driven hard-currency market. Along with observations at *lanzamientos* that second-hand booksellers were profiting from the subsidised *moneda nacional* prices by selling the same books in hard currency in the Plaza de Armas, many writers and editors indicated that the 'clash of cultures' between market-driven global publishing systems and the subsidised Cuban system also created significant difficulties, establishing copyright agreements that made impossible the publication of several Cuban authors on the island:

> Porque ahora incluso cubanos, por ejemplo no podemos publicar Reinaldo Arenas, los herederos no dan autorización. No podemos publicar, bueno se publicó en realidad. Se hizo una publicación clandestina de Reinaldo, de *El Mundo Alucinante* pero no se puede, oficialmente no se puede. Y otros autores, otros que te dicen ... Guillermo Cabrera, no se puede. [AF][27]

Two mitigating factors must be mentioned. Firstly, the system of prizes, at least with the major national ones (*Alejo Carpentier* for prose and *Nicolás Guillén* for poetry), brought publication and national recognition at the Feria, and international exposure: 'Se hace una gira por todo el país, se le publican los libros, se llevan a la Feria de Guadalajara. En fin, tienen un nivel de promoción, porque son premios que tienen un pago importante en divisas, también su pago en derecho de autor, en fin' [DGS] ('they do a tour around the island, their books are published, they go to the Feria in Guadalajara. Anyway, they have a certain level of marketing, because these are prizes which carry a significant payment in hard currency, as well as royalty payments, anyway'). Secondly, the restricted textual space of publication opportunities was slightly

1990s–2000s: Crisis and reassessment

mitigated by a growing use of new technologies at individual and collective levels [AGN; AG; RR], perhaps favouring younger writers more able to adapt to new media.

The early 2000s also saw the further consolidation of the remit of state institutions to encourage and support emerging writers through the *talleres* movement [ELR; FR; EHL], while reading as a route to thinking and, ultimately, textual production was boosted by nationwide, holistic and multi-disciplinary phenomena such as *Leer a Martí* [ELR], which by 2005 had received half a million contributions. The Havana's Facultad de Artes y Letras also continued to provide an important space for the development of specialised readers and many agents in literary culture, from writers and literary critics to editors, *promotores culturales* and cultural journalists [SH]. Spaces which, in the depths of the Special Period, had had a survivalist or resistant function for young writers were consolidated in the early 2000s and brought under ICL auspices, to share resources [RMR; FLJ]. While this clearly meant some element of regulation of previously independent spaces, it also guaranteed support, including a locale for events, national publicity, and necessary resources; Reina María Rodríguez's *Azotea*, for instance, became the *Torre de Letras*, in the tower of the ICL's Palacio del Segundo Cabo: clearly remaining a cultural community with autonomy, it chose its own texts for publication through artisanal publishing, and, although its modest catalogue was included in the 2009 ICL annual report, it was able to negotiate and pursue its own cultural agenda.

UNEAC similarly developed after 2000 (celebrating congresses, as planned, in 2003 and 2008), Although many interviewees were keen to point out individual UNEAC leaders as especially effective (or ineffective) in supporting and promoting writers' work, the general consensus was that UNEAC continued to act as facilitator, rather than being the instrument of control that outside commentators often assume to be its function. The most telling but unexpected opinion (in view of the fact that his sordid narratives of Havana life have been published exclusively abroad and often embraced by opponents of the system) came from Gutiérrez; describing his experience of starting to gain recognition abroad, he stressed the support of key figures who recognised his long-standing contribution to Cuban cultural life and his inherent loyalty and stated:

> Bueno, nos gusta o no nos gusta lo que tú escribes, eso es lo importante: es importante que eres miembro de esta organización desde hace dieciocho años, y no eres un oportunista o un arribista, escribiste lo que querías

escribir en ese momento. Además tú vives en Centro Habana y eso es lo que tú estas viendo, eso es tu vida cotidiana. [PJG][28]

He attributed UNEAC's advice and support as a professional organisation to the fact that its members were writers and artists in their own right, rather than simply cultural bureaucrats [PJG].

The AHS was also often considered to be important in wider decision-making processes, especially for debating issues from new perspectives, being described as 'el sector de más inquietudes, o sea, suele ser el sector más propositivo, que más opiniones genera sobre las instituciones mismas, por lo tanto es un sector de gran utilidad para el desarrollo de la institución' [FLJ] ('the group which addresses the greatest number of concerns, that's to say, with the greatest number of propositions and opinions about the different organisations, and hence a group that is invaluable for the development of institutions'). The generational factor emerged with particular intensity in early 2007, with the television broadcasting of apparent homages to some of the figures (notably Pavón, Serguera and Armando Quesada) most associated with the worst of the *quinquenio gris*; the result was a fierce explosion of publicly protesting emails and a hastily arranged series of closed-door meetings with different groups of intellectuals. The debate curiously also provided a forum for young artists and intellectuals to voice their own grievances collectively, arguing that, while fully respecting the need to address the errors of the 1970s and recognise the loyal contributions of those who had suffered, there were also contemporary issues, affecting them, which were equally urgent (Kumaraswami, 2009b). As one prominent AHS figure stated, the debates indicated the continued commitment and intellectual and political maturity of younger generations of writers and artists:

> Ese taller verificó que los jóvenes estaban mucho más allá del *pavonato* y les interesaba un comino el *pavonato*, les interesaba discutir los problemas que había hoy con la cultura, sus inconformidades, sus insatisfacciones, que fue una discusión donde el nombre de Pavón salió bastante poco, los que salieron fueron los problemas de ahora, las discusiones contra las trabas burocráticas de hoy, el sentimiento de inconformidad que tiene la gente. [AAG][29]

Although reactions to the broadcasts varied (UNEAC being severely criticised for an initial declaration which appeared conciliatory and uncommitted), one outcome seemed to be some changes of personnel, especially the appointment of Elíades Acosta to the Dirección de Cultura

1990s–2000s: Crisis and reassessment

in the Party's Central Committee, and the promotion of Fernando Rojas to Vice-Ministro within MINCULT. However, the whole episode had other dimensions, especially reflecting Raúl Castro's new and more pragmatic 'open debate' policy, with Abel Prieto as Minister paying close attention to the discussions and complaints. Furthermore, within the context of the international attention being paid to groups such as Generación Y (perceived outside Cuba as representing the voices of all young Cubans), these debates indicated the emergence, at the end of the *Batalla de Ideas*, of a new, more responsive and realistic, openness to cultural and social problems.

Finally, there are several aspects of literary culture yet to be fully addressed here, which now constitute the core of those and other debates, most notably distribution systems (the DNL's weaknesses being evident and discussed frequently in the major professional organisations [VFC]), literary criticism and book publishing. Criticism (ranging from reviews in the mass media to literary scholarship) is an especially complicated issue. Firstly, the activity in Cuba is rarely comparable with the notion of critique that is so central to its function in 'marketised' literary cultures: critics may underline weaknesses in given literary texts, but their role is more frequently instructive, orienting the reader (whether specialist or general) towards which texts to buy and how to maximise the potential of their reading experience of the canon that is constantly created. One prominent critic explained that adverse reviews did not exist within the system, as 'bad' books were simply not reviewed by critics [JF]. For writers, then, although free from fear of being 'slated' by journalistic or academic criticism, the risk lay in being 'ignored'.

However, some critics also indicated that the explosion in publishing of provincial *revistas culturales* was going some way to paying critical attention to writers outside Havana [RR; JF], and that the recent increase in mass-media spaces for literary criticism (e.g. *Granma*, *Bohemia*) met some demand from writers and readers, at least in terms of a *crítica divulgativa* (criticism aiming to disseminate) for the general public. The need to provide this service and seek additional sources of income and the multi-tasking profile that is part of every writer's remit was also leading increasing numbers of writers to participate in literary culture as critics, with regular columns in *La Jiribilla*, *cubaliteraria*, etc. Two more institutional responses to the problem (the first, until recently, directed by Yáñez) came in the creation of the Círculo de la Crítica (critics' circle) – making up to twenty books a year available free of charge to the main critics and thus promoting the activities of writers and literary critics [MY] – and in the founding of the *Premio de la Crítica* to award the critics' prize (from a selection of ten books) to an already-published work, thus decoupling the *premio* system from publishing opportunities and awarding a prize that, although ICL-funded, emanates solely from the *gremio de escritores* (literally, 'writers' guild'), rather than institutions [JF; MY; AF].

For some writers, there was an urgent need for a 'crítica sistemática' ('systematic critique'), as in other countries, a professional system by which a wider range of books – Cuban and non-Cuban – could be regularly reviewed for all kinds of readerships [JTS]. The notion of favouritism or self-interest was also a controversial point, some interviewees acknowledging that a tendency for critics and heads of publishing houses to promote their own tastes had emerged during the Special Period [MSM]. For many, then, the power relations of the act of literary criticism presented more of a risk (of accusations of complicity or corruption) than an advantage:

> Los escritores no pueden estar al tanto de lo que los críticos evalúan sobre su obra. Pero no, tú tienes que seguir obstinadamente pensando por ti mismo. Y los críticos pueden pensar muy bien o muy mal, o lo que sea. Pero tú guardas esas críticas y tú sigues obstinadamente con un proyecto, con tu propio proyecto. No puedes estar pensando en si el crítico te adora o te odia. [PJG][30]

However, the most subtle evaluation of the relationship between writer and critic was its description as an ambiguous but mutual need, a love/hate relationship [JF].

In terms of publishers' editorial work, the most urgent contemporary issue for debate, given the constant economic pressures of a heavily subsidised publishing industry negotiating with markets for its basic resources, was the necessary development and improvement of the 'alta gerencia editorial ... sobre todo en comercialización, marketing, lo que es costo, elementos con los cuales durante nosotros durante una época estuvimos a espaldas, que son importantes a la larga' [OMP] ('senior management in publishing ... most of all in commercialisation, marketing, cost, aspects which for a time we were able to ignore, but which in the long term are important'); in other words, training in order to eliminate inefficiencies, measure demand, and 'compete' cooperatively with other Cuban publishers, in the interests of offering readers the best, most cost-effective and most comprehensive national catalogues. However, as a result of the proliferation of book production through the SET, the issue of *edición de libros* (the process by which a manuscript approved for publication becomes a published book) was the area most hotly debated between publishers at the *editores*' panels of the 2011 Feria del Libro. These debates mostly centred on the shortage of equipment as basic as electric staplers and paper suitable for the RISO machines (which need more expensive *papel cromado* rather than the usual *papel cartucho*, or cartridge paper), emphasising that these material deficiencies were leading to 'libros fallidos' ('poor-quality books') – books that may be of a high literary quality but were materially inadequate. Since many writers deprived of publishing opportunities in the 1990s had turned their hand to editing (the consensus being that editors should also be specialist readers), there had been a steady decrease in expertise in *gestión editorial* (publishing management), in seeking out the best manuscripts, and also in design, marketing and publicity. The future of RISO production was also debated, with varying recommendations: to create a 'niche' market which made a virtue of the simple aesthetic of RISO books, following the model of Ediciones Vigía; to centralise RISO production and brand it with a single format; to reduce SET production to ensure intellectual and material rigour, or, alternatively, to expand it further to create more publishing spaces; for similar reasons, to limit SET production to a few provinces (rather than the current fourteen) in order to concentrate resources. Subsequent *encuentros de editores* (meetings of publishers) at the Feria debated the role of a new Consejo Técnico Editorial (technical editorial committee) within the ICL which would focus on confronting challenges at a technical level, while heads of individual *editoriales* (Vigía, Unión) described their recent experience, focusing on economic challenges such as the unavailability or prohibitive costs of paper, the apparent unwillingness of printing presses to honour contracts with *editoriales*, and the controversial issue of the inadequate print-runs – in Cuban editions of works first published abroad or of re-editions of the most popular works – of one of Cuba's best-selling writers today, Padura Fuentes. On this last issue, the evident dissatisfaction of booksellers, *promotores* and general and specialist readers was addressed by Olga Marta Pérez in detail: firstly, that in the case of Padura Fuentes's most recent novels, Ediciones Unión (via the ICL) had had to *pactar* (come to an agreement) with the Spanish publishing house Tusquets for reprinting rights, and, despite the limitations imposed by having to buy these rights, had requested that the usual print-run of 2,000 be doubled. However, she also emphasised in no uncertain terms that all decisions to reprint or increase print-runs were based on detailed sales analysis rather than more subjective opinions – or even general feedback from the public on the perceived quality or success of any one book – and that Unión's distribution mechanisms (via UNEAC bookshops) ensured accurate sales data.

In conclusion, let us return to the question of value. Despite external – and even some Cuban writers' – expectations, the social value of literature had continued to be sustained, and had even been given a boost, after 2000. In other words, *pace* some writers' increased pursuit of commercial value and external prestige, literature in Cuba continued to be about social integration, literary culture resuming its essential role as an important mechanism in this project, its political value being thus reinscribed. Most importantly, however, its heightened symbolic value was now, as in 1961, related more to the reader than to the writer.

By the late 2000s, however, and under Raúl Castro's leadership, the *Batalla de Ideas* had largely been halted, shifting the emphasis throughout Cuban policymaking to prioritise economic efficiency and rationalisation. Despite the abrupt change of direction entailed for those responsible for designing and implementing cultural policy (ICL changing personnel, under the new leadership of Suleika Romay), despite reported reductions in publishing scale (one report suggesting that national book publication had fallen by 82 per cent in 2005–10 (http://entretenimiento.terra.com.pe/cultura/publicacion-de-libros-en-cuba-cayo-un-82-en-cinco-anos,bb1bda88f41e0310VgnVCM4000009bf154d0RCRD.html) and despite a reduction of the associated activities of *promoción cultural* (now designed to circulate existing stock as much as new stock), there is strong evidence that those responsible for directing literary culture are once again adapting to a changing context, and especially the complex network of value that underpins all policy and practice in Cuba. In other words, heightened emphasis on the economic value of all activity within literary culture does not imply that its social, political and symbolic value have been abandoned, although the negotiations are always fragile and changing. With the 2011 Feria inviting not a single country, but rather the whole of ALBA, as the *país invitado de honor* (honorary guest nation), and with the Casa del ALBA being inaugurated in Havana in late 2009, there are signs that relatively new political alliances and symbolic spaces are seen by policymakers as essential to the survival and development of literary culture on the island.

Notes

1 This chapter, more than others, is largely based on interviews conducted by the authors, supported by their own *in situ* observations of literary culture from 2005.
2 'First the artists left because they were more fortunate in financial terms, they sold their paintings, they didn't have anything to lose by going back and forth, because a lot of them just come and go. And then the writers left because it was harder for them to go'.
3 'I wrote it in awful conditions. I didn't have a lightbulb, so I had to work during the day because at night [...] I had to move the one bulb we had around the house to my son's bedroom so he could do his homework, and then to the bathroom. It was a nomadic lightbulb, right? (laughs) I didn't have a pen, but had to write with a pencil on some old yellowing paper, so you could hardly see what was written. Obviously, I didn't have a computer'.
4 'In other words, it's often said, and these are not my words, that the novísimos were only really committed to their own, to their own creative work. And that's true – in other words that generation which burst onto the scene between the end of the 1980s and the beginning of the 1990s, was a bit more iconoclastic, a bit more irreverent, and they found that suddenly Cuba's publishing policy was also more open to their saying things their way'.
5 'But I had always seen my work as something useful, as part of a project to rescue forgotten stories, such as the stories of the traditional trova movement ... And in those texts I deleted myself as the writing subject. What was important was the trovadores themselves and I was no more than a vehicle for rescuing those memories and so I practically had no voice. And suddenly that voice began to make itself heard, it began to appear, in fact it did appear and the result was great'.
6 'You have enough money to publish 500 copies because an artist donated some money to you. In Cuba today we have some very profound contradictions: artists and musicians, sometimes a third-rate singer or an artist – even a primitivist artist – can have a much more comfortable life than writers can and undoubtedly earns much more than a writer, as much as through royalties as through other means ... And so an artist can treat themself to subsidising the publication of some books. A writer can't even treat themself to subsidising the publication of their own book'.
7 'And so, the prize system makes us prostitute ourselves. It makes you bow down in order to win a prize. You bow towards what is in fashion, what is most accepted, etc. That's why you see that contemporary Cuban prose has bowed towards dirty realism. Writing dirty realism is very very lucky, it's very successful. People in Spain and lots of other places, who knows what

is happening to humanity right now that makes us all be drawn towards the sordid'.

8 '[I]n Cuba, I would say that 90 per cent of writers who are already published don't live solely from the proceeds of their literary profession. They have to be literary advisors, editors, teachers, journalists, theatre specialists, cultural promoters, sometimes doctors, lawyers, engineers; in other words, you can't make a living from literature'.

9 'The democratisation of symbolic goods constitutes a goal which a society like ours cannot abandon. The defence of the right to culture means building and perfecting socialist democracy, because culture, far from being something additional, occupies a central place in our political life'.

10 'The cultural promoter must be a person who belongs to a community or becomes part of one, supporting the various sociocultural activities within it, carrying out various projects systematically, in such a way that favourable conditions are created for individuals and groups to increase their awareness of the importance of active participation in cultural life, so that a favourable disposition towards the cultural environment can gradually be achieved'.

11 'It was an insitution which received funding, in hard currency, from the businesses under the Ministry of Culture, which worked in the hard currency market, in export as well as border markets ... The Fund began to finance a certain kind of publication and that's how production slowly began to recover, and on the other hand, the state also began to invest and renew investment as the technological conditions began to recover'.

12 Under the auspices of the Oficina del Historiador, it was agreed that, in the new millennium, a percentage of the revenue from the second-hand libreros in the Plaza de Armas would be used to fund the ICL's publishing plans.

13 'In the literary sphere, the breaking off from a norm which had been more or less dominant until a few years before and the explicit recognition of diversity as a value; in marketing and promotion, greater participation in foreign prizes and competitions, systematic invitiations to conferences – literary or otherwise – taking place in other countries, the day-by-day increase in foreign publishers in search of valuable original manuscripts, frequent reviews of Cuban literature in the international press. All of this portrayed with an aura of prestige which was apparently well-earned, and often backed up by the much-needed economic relief provided by a fat wad of cash'.

14 'They of course paid me a pittance for those books, I'm embarrassed to admit. They gave me an advance of US$2,000 [pause], an advance of US$2,000 for the whole Trilogía. After that, they did the same thing for El Rey de La Habana – I didn't have the first idea of any of all that, of how much a book could fetch, of how things work in that world. And they

1990s–2000s: Crisis and reassessment

took complete advantage of me, those people as well as the publisher at Anagrama, as after all, every publisher is a businessman who tries to buy … that's their job, but for as little as you can and then sell for as much as you can'.

15 'No, I've always been able to maintain two worlds. From the first moment, I figured out what they were looking for abroad, and what they were looking for here. In other words, that doesn't mean that I have written for the market, nor for ideology, but I was always very aware … that abroad they say to you "This book is magnificent but we can't publish it", because of anything – even the title, the subject matter … But no, the two careers I've had are as if I were two writers, one abroad and the other here'.

16 'And so much so that one day a friend of mine comes over and says – how embarrassing, but it's true! – that there's a competition where they pay a lot. It's the Casa del Caribe or something like that, something we have here, and for a short story, if you win, they give you 3,000 Cuban pesos – but hang on! Today that doesn't get you very far – any rubbish singer can charge you that amount for a couple of numbers, OK, 3,000 pesos is a decent amount but it's nothing to write home about; but at that time in Cuba, with the crisis and everything, it wasn't an amount you'd turn your nose up at, you could buy the kids a big pack of mashed potato or some tinned stuff, anything, and so I said: "Do you think I can, sweetie?" And she said: "Laidy, write something", and she encouraged me to write something for it'.

17 'As far as the market is concerned, it is impossible not to recall that seventy or eighty years ago, I learnt my craft as a writer while watching Víctor Manuel handing over his paintings to pay for the beers we'd just drunk; while Portocarrero and Millián lived in an old tenement building; while Carpentier, Guillén, Lezama, Virgilio, Feijóo, Eliseo, Cintio, Fina and so many others (never mind the younger writers) paid for their own books to be published, and then sent them to their friends. We writers didn't have authors' rights but rather authors' duties'.

18 'When UNEAC asked me, back in 1995, to be a representative on the People's Council, at least in the municipio where we were based … they said to me, "What kind of community cultural work are you going to focus on?" And I said "The only kind I know, working with children, with libraries. And with authors. Being an editor, that's the only way I know how to do it". And so, that's what I did. In other words, in that sense, Centro Habana experienced in a very broad way the process of creating community cultural links to all the national organisations'.

19 '[T]he publishing workshop was my own unique, personal space, as a provincial writer, because it was there that we either produced a small publication, in humble duplicated copies, or we sent texts to national competitions, which allowed us to be published immediately and without delay, without being rejected, or we struggled to work out how we could

position our first little collections of poetry with the national publishing houses, where there were powerful filtering mechanisms'.
20 'Before we modify literary criticism in Cuba we have to socialise its discourses and recognise its functions (to describe, interpret, evaluate, hierarchise, project) and integrate it into the publishing, creative and market-oriented strategies for Cuban literature at the end of the twentieth century'.
21 'And we had to create the conditions so that those young people, who are also Cuban and the children of revolutionary people and who are also participating in this project, would have an equal opportunity to become doctors; even when there were scholarships and they were open to everyone, no one said, "that's for white students, not for black students", no one said that. It was social conditions themselves that conditioned us all and so the children of professionals got the best grades and could choose the best degree course. It's complicated. And so people were visited house by house, because general resolutions don't resolve that kind of problem'.
22 'The Observatorio basically evaluates policy in many ways, and one of them is by coordinating research, seeing who is doing the research, making sure that the dialogue between academic and political elements is a fluent one, something which, from what I've seen and researched, is very difficult to achieve anywhere on the planet'.
23 In 2004, US dollars were replaced in general circulation by dollar-equivalent convertible pesos, denominated $CUC.
24 'But they have one Achilles heel – the distribution system. Distribution (of books) is poor and limited, and sometimes means that books remain in the peripheral provinces, which means that it takes quite a lot of effort to 'move' those cultural products. In other words, someone from Santiago de Cuba can have a hard time finding out what poets in Camagüey are publishing, but has no problem finding out what a poet in Havana is publishing, see?'
25 'It's so bad that they say that […] came up with a phrase which has become a classic of our times, which says "All these cultural activities will one day end up putting an end to culture" because you don't have time to read, or study, all the time you are at one cultural activity or another, attending a book launch, going to the launch of a friend's book, a magazine launch … Mate, give me a bit of peace, let me get on with some reading, I haven't read a 300-page book for years now'.
26 'It's to do with the editor's assessment of the book, the quality of the book, and the level of the author. And so the editor says to me, "OK, I can pay 3,000 pesos for this book". And we tell the author, "Look, I can pay you 3,000 for this. Do you agree?". "Yes. No, I think 4,000". The dialogue starts there and leads to an agreement. And that's what we pay. And we pay once the book is with the publishing house. It has nothing to do with sales. And actually the point is, the goal is, to benefit the author – by not tying the

1990s–2000s: Crisis and reassessment

payment to sales and by establishing it instead via mutual agreement. It's a resolution which could always be improved'.

27 'Because now even we Cubans, for example, can't publish Reinaldo Arenas, the heirs to his estate won't authorise it. We can't publish him, but actually we did. A clandestine edition of El Mundo Alucinante was produced, but we can't, officially we can't. And other writers, others who tell you … Guillermo Cabrera, we can't publish him'.

28 'Well, we either like or don't like what you write, that's the important thing: what's important is that you've belonged to the organisation for eighteen years and you're not an opportunist or arriviste, that you wrote what you wanted to write at a particular moment. Besides, you live in Centro Habana and that's what you see, that's your daily life'.

29 'That workshop made clear that young people had gone way beyond the pavonato and didn't give two hoots about the pavonato, they were interested in debating the cultural problems that exist today, their disagreements, their dissatisfaction, so it was a meeting where Pavón's name wasn't mentioned very much, it was the problems of today that were discussed, debates about the bureaucratic obstacles they face today, the feeling of disagreement that people have'.

30 'Writers cannot be following closely the assessments that critics make of their work. No, you have to carry on stubbornly thinking in your own way. And the critics can think very well or very badly of you, or think whatever they want. But you put those opinions aside and you continue stubbornly with your project, with your own project. You can't spend time wondering whether the critic loves you or hates you'.

6

The path to becoming a writer in contemporary Cuba: The role of the Centro de Formación Literaria Onelio Jorge Cardoso and the movement of *talleres literarios*[1]

Meesha Nehru

Since its establishment in 1998, more than 500 young aspiring Cuban writers of narrative have passed through the Centro de Formación Literaria Onelio Jorge Cardoso (henceforth 'the Centro' or 'Centro Onelio'). Run by its Directors, Eduardo Heras León and Ivonne Galeano, with Francisco López Sacha, the Centro Onelio is the only institution of its kind in Cuba. It offers an annual course in *técnicas narrativas* (narrative techniques) to sixty, nationally selected aspiring writers, aged between sixteen and thirty-five. The course began as a specialised literary workshop, in Heras León's house; however, in 2002, with grants from the Dutch NGO Hivos, and MINCULT, it gained its own premises, a beautiful, renovated building in the Miramar district, and began its transformation from *taller literario* to a permanent national institution, with full-time staff, a publishing wing, website and library, as well as excellent teaching facilities and a computer room. From early on, the Centro established itself as a focal point in the search for the country's new literary trends and emerging writers, gaining significant media visibility, with public endorsement by leading international intellectuals and with many graduates winning prestigious literary prizes.[2]

Yet this institution was only the latest development in a long history of state-backed assistance for aspiring and amateur writers in Cuba, beginning with the movement of the *talleres literarios*. While this chapter

Becoming a writer in contemporary Cuba 179

focuses on the Centro's evolution and role in contemporary literary culture, it should be placed in the context of the *talleres* movement as a whole. Spanning over forty years of the revolutionary process, these official literary workshops have been important mechanisms for developing literary culture all over the island. Aimed at encouraging creative writing at the grassroots, and run by either trained *asesores literarios* or established writers, a network of *talleres literarios* has been established in every *municipio* since the 1970s. Of the many writers becoming established in Cuba over this period, the vast majority spent some time participating in the movement.

The first *talleres* emerged organically during the transformations of the 1960s, as young writers, inspired by the new importance given to culture, established their own groups as a way of participating in the revolutionary process, improving on their writing and promoting literature locally. They were soon recognised and supported by the CNC, as they fitted in well with the Revolution's objectives of developing an accessible, participatory culture. They were also integrated into a general programme of literary development that included a range of initiatives aimed at encouraging reading and literary appreciation among the general population. It then became a central aim of literary policy to incentivise writing and to create the objective conditions for establishing more *talleres* [TFR].

As these initiatives began to produce results, the cultural authorities began to establish *talleres* in as many places as possible, even where there was little or no literary tradition. In 1974, they were formalised into a national movement, modelled on the *aficionado* movement already created for other artistic forms. New a*sesores literarios* were trained to lead workshops promoting creative writing in nine accepted genres (short story, *testimonio*, poetry, *décima* (oral poetry), theatre, essay, short story, poetry and children's theatre). They were primarily organised within *municipio*s, but provincial and national competitions (*Encuentro-Debates*) were also held, bringing together participants from different regions. As with the main *movimiento de aficionados*, the *talleres* prohibited established writers or members of UNEAC from participating (CNC 1975: 57). However, in contrast to the qualifications required to be a professional artist, musician or dancer, there was no educational barrier preventing workshop participants (*talleristas*) from later becoming professional writers. Thus, the movement became a breeding ground for future professional writers, as well as for thousands of amateurs encouraged to join.

Organised in this way, the number of *talleres* continued to increase more or less uninterrupted until the 1990s, when their development was paralysed by the economic crisis. As economic recovery began, the *talleres* were revitalised and expanded again, until they had around 45,000 participants, more than ever before. However, they were reborn with a new focus, reflecting the changes of the 1990s, with much less emphasis on the *talleres* being a dynamic national movement and the source of future literary styles and writers; instead, municipal *talleres* now concentrated on promoting community participation for amateur writers. Simultaneously, a trend that started in the 1980s, of setting up individual specialised *talleres*, affiliated to the main system yet also relatively independent, began to gather steam. This phenomenon received a boost with the success of the Centro Onelio, which, as a national-level *taller*, encouraged the creation of other *talleres de vanguardia* (vanguard workshops) across Cuba; run by established writers, these had a freer remit than the main *talleres*, offering courses on both theory and practice in a range of different genres.

By 2000, a two-tier system of *talleres literarios* had developed, with the large, non-selective municipal system encouraging grassroots cultural engagement and the selective Centro and *talleres de vanguardia* offering more vocational educational courses. Beyond the post-1990s' change in policy priorities, this diverse landscape of *talleres* was the culmination of over forty years of concerted literary development; it also reflected an internal hierarchy that had always existed within the *talleres* movement, between the drive to provide literary opportunity accessible to all and a growing demand for the provision of more intellectually advanced support. In fact, the *talleres*' close relationship with education, some argue, is why they never became a mass movement on the scale of the *movimiento de aficionados*. However, the existence of this two-tier system, and particularly the dominance of the Centro in the field of narrative, has also transformed the type of guidance sought and received by aspiring writers. Historically, the municipal *talleres literarios* had a near monopoly over the accepted path taken by new and emerging writers, as well as being an outlet for amateur writing.

Writers who have participated in the movement have claimed that their experience in *talleres* represented only a partial or initial stage in a much longer process of individual formation and did not guarantee publication. Nevertheless, the *talleres*' collective dimension to their training left a lasting legacy, helping to socialise them into, and give them their first experience of a voice in, literary culture. Although the conditions of this process were shaped by the Revolution's values and policy directions at the time, the *talleres* provided access to the resources, tools and spaces necessary for participants to become active contributors to the national literary tradition, if only at the local level. As such, they offered the means to develop cultural citizenship, whereby participants became cultural citizens through a dialectical process of 'self-making and being made within webs of power' (Pawley, 2008: 600). Furthermore, as communicative spaces, the *talleres* acted as mini-public spheres where that cultural citizenship could be enacted (Nehru, 2010).

The impact of this communication was limited for those who wished eventually to become writers, restricted as it was within the movement and local areas, yet it constituted a grassroots space for constructing, reinforcing, debating and challenging a shared culture, and fostered the emergence of new literary developments. In the contemporary period, the Centro and the *talleres de vanguardia* have largely taken over the provision of guidance and access to cultural citizenship for those who aspire to write as a vocation; yet, by being selective and fewer in number, they have much less of the ethos of egalitarianism and democratisation that characterised the earlier movement. The Centro's prestige and high visibility, in particular, aligns it much more closely with other central cultural institutions rather than with the grassroots. The following analysis of the Centro provides an insight into how this fascinating and important feature of Cuban literary culture has operated since 1998. For, although, as a *taller*, it shares many characteristics of the wider *talleres literarios* movement, as a unique institution it also raises new questions: about the incorporation of literary practice into official culture, about what it means to be a writer and about cultural citizenship, participation and the space to create in contemporary Cuba.[3]

The shaping of an institution

Despite its relative autonomy as an *institución adscripta* (a self-managed entity within the overall MINCULT framework), the Centro's mission, as with the wider *talleres* before it, has been shaped by certain fundamental values and beliefs about culture within the revolutionary process. However, although the Centro is in tune with the most consistent strands of cultural policy, a number of contextual factors contributed to its establishment in the late 1990s and helped to define its role.

According to Heras León, it had been his dream to create the Centro ever since the 1960s, when he learned about the success of the similar

Centro de Escritores Mexicanos in the 1950s [EHL MN]. However, at that time, he was unable to gain official backing for his idea, because official attention was directed more towards democratising literary practice, rather than creating a prestigious and selective training institution. In 1998, he was finally given approval to develop his project, having established a strong reputation for himself as a supporter of new writing talent. More importantly, by then, his Centro project chimed with the direction taken by the leadership during a critical political and ideological juncture for the Revolution. The response to the Special Period had precipitated a new 'turn to culture' in official policy: strengthening national culture was seen by the leadership as the only way of guaranteeing the Revolution's survival, preserving its values and redefining its position in the newly globalised world. As a consequence, official policy became less concerned with defining Cuban culture in explicitly political or ideological terms. As part of this process of redefinition, cultural producers, especially writers, gained new visibility, while the government embarked on a new campaign to democratise access to cultural consumption and production. It was believed that encouraging the population to participate in cultural and educational activities would re-engage people with some of the Revolution's core values and institutions.

The Centro Onelio project was particularly commended by the Cuban leadership for its focus on youth, since that social group was of particular concern for the government at the time and the need to encourage youth participation was becoming a priority; indeed, the Centro opened only a year before the Elián González mobilisations made engaging with youth an official priority. While, as a single institution, the Centro could not address all youth, it could provide a space for young educated writers who, unlike their counterparts in other artistic forms (with the institutional backing of formal qualifications), had traditionally found recognition elusive. In fact, by being designated a space specifically for young writers, the Centro began the process of institutionalising an idea of a youth literary tradition in Cuba; Heras León wrote: 'El Centro Onelio respondió al auge de la literatura nacional que, desde los fines de los 80 ha develado una nueva geografía de la literatura cubana' (Heras León, 2001: 5) ('the Centro Onelio responded to the boom in national literature which, since the end of the 1980s, has revealed a new geography of Cuban literature'). The Centro thus took up the task of giving young (especially female) writers formal recognition.

This institutionalisation was powerfully reinforced by practical factors, especially the fact that several of the permanent staff (including Sergio Cevedo, Raúl Aguiar, Ernesto Pérez Castillo and even Heras León) were recognised for the youthful energy of their former writing; the first two had been central figures in a rebellious strand of writing emerging in the 1980s, but by the time the Centro was founded, they had been included in the official panorama of Cuban literature. Hence, their inclusion symbolically linked the Centro to writers and writing that had relatively recently posed a challenge to conventional orthodoxies.[4] Both the Centro's thrice-yearly publication, *El Cuentero* (e.g. 'Punto 4' 2007), and its library also referenced youth, the library being named after Salvador Redonet, the literary critic, who, until his death in 1999, had been credited with encouraging young writers to experiment and renew Cuban literature [AGN MN;MM].

Two further elements define the Centro. The first is its international dimension: unlike the municipal *talleres*, rooted in a local literary tradition first and a national tradition second, the Centro encourages young writers to build connections with their counterparts outside Cuba. The second is its relationship with the wider cultural democratisation process: despite its prestige and orientation towards aspiring career writers, it has communicated its work though the mass media (Heras León's lectures on *técnicas narrativas* are broadcast through the *Universidad Para Todos* (open university) initiative) and uses *talleres* as a potential recruiting ground.

Old debates, new focus

Heras León defines the Centro's course not as exhaustive but rather as a process of acceleration, in which young *talleristas* learn what solitary writers usually take years to discover [EHL MN]; according to him, it is not about training writers per se, but about giving young writers a knowledge of theory and techniques, to help them better understand literature and approach their own and others' work more critically [EHL MN]. The course consists of a weekly *taller literario*, interspersed with a series of classes on *técnicas narrativas*, based on a textbook edited by Heras León, *Los desafíos de la ficción*, whose topics range from guidance on punctuation and grammar through to theoretical reflections on various literary genres and creative writing techniques, by major authors from Cuba, Latin America and beyond (Heras León, 2001).

Although Heras León estimates that only one or two writers will emerge from each course, the rest becoming simply better readers, the course (like the *talleres* before it) has sparked considerable controversy. In 2006, writer and ex-student Ernesto Pérez Chang wrote a scathing attack on the Centro in the online literary magazine *cubaliteraria*, accusing Heras León and the Centro of setting out to mould the latest generations of Cuban writers and claiming to see the influence of the textbook and formulas in the stories produced by *egresados* (graduates), some of whom had won prestigious national prizes (Pérez Chang, n.d). Interestingly, he simultaneously praised the main *talleres* movement, crediting it with having helped thousands of ordinary Cubans to engage with literature; his venom was clearly reserved for the Centro alone, because of its extra attention and prestige, above the rest of the system, and because, he felt, literary critics had hailed the institution and its Director as the saviours of young Cuban literature:

> Otros espacios similares, pero no tan famosos, a pesar de carencias económicas, esplendores o crisis, se han mantenido, a la sombra de una modesta casa de cultura de un municipio modesto, orientando lecturas, despertando el interés por la literatura (sí, por la LITERATURA, y no por el mero oficio de redactor de relatos). (Literatura es pensar el mundo, no hacer pasarelas como Naomi Campbell) (Pérez Chang, n.d)[5]

Soon after this article appeared, the website published several counter arguments by writers who were either Centro employees or *egresados* (Pérez Castillo, n.d.; Ramón Delgado, n.d.; Santiesteban, n.d.).

While the Centro seems to have more supporters than detractors, the arguments which it arouses reveal how the terms of the debate about the relationship of *talleres* to writing and writers have shifted over the decades. Until their contemporary incarnation (as a purely amateur movement), the municipal *talleres* also attracted criticism for producing formulaic writing (Sánchez Mejías, 2006). However, this criticism came largely because they were perceived to be mechanisms of ideological control, rather than sites offering privileged access to *técnicas narrativas* and literary prizes. For, in the past, the existence of the bureaucratic and centrally administered system aroused some suspicion that the government was trying to train 'obedient' writers, especially as many associated them with the *quinquenio gris*, when *talleres* were described as 'laboratorios de escritura' [EHL MN; MM] ('writing laboratories'). Through the *talleres*, it was suggested, the leadership could promote the idea that writing was not about individual talent and could encourage collective literature as a means of overcoming any individualism in writing.

Although this discourse did not automatically translate into practice on the ground, the *talleres* had posed a further threat to established writers, many already uncertain about their role. At that time, the boundaries were occasionally blurred between the *tallerista* and the fully-fledged writer: *talleristas* were given publication space in prestigious national magazines, and, when UNEAC's provincial branches were created, membership was automatically granted to many *talleristas*, some still without published books.

After the *quinquenio*, the official discourse about *talleres* softened, in keeping with the new cultural policy. From the early 1980s, the dominant perspective was that successful writing arose from a combination of talent and the acquisition of technical skills (Heras León, 1988: 9; [FR MN]). Later, of course, they focussed less on the ideological training of writers and, instead, emphasised the process of participation and the training of critical readers: the tradition that fed into the justification for both the contemporary *talleres* and the Centro. Indeed, the experience within the *talleres* both reflected and contributed to these changes: as the number of amateur writers swelled, and the criteria for judging literary merit changed, *talleristas* were no longer automatically considered fully-formed writers, and a hierarchy of writers became more clearly defined. Furthermore, the movement was by then able to engender diverse trends and even contestatory approaches.

Within these current debates about the *talleres* and the Centro, at one level they are united on the question of whether it is possible to teach literary writing at all. Although this concern has been voiced beyond Cuba, it has particular resonance in the context of evolving revolutionary cultural policy, for it questions what it means to be a writer and challenges traditional self-definition of the intellectual, issues at the heart of the cultural debates of the 1960s and 1970s. For its part, the Centro reignites these old debates in a radically different ideological and cultural context, one that is more concerned with unfair advantage and individual motivations. Summarising the Pérez Chang debate, one critic noted: '[hay] una cuestión que subyace la idea de "formación literaria": ¿Qué significa ser escritor? Preguntaría además, ¿por qué se desea serlo?' (Díaz Mantilla, 2006: 2) ([there is] one question which underlies the idea of "literary training": What does it mean to be a writer? I'd also ask, why does one want to be one'?)

The Centro Onelio and cultural citizenship[6]

True to Heras León's statement, not all of the Centro's *egresados* become writers after graduation; while some finish with book projects, aspiring to a career in writing, others choose to work in different fields or even give up writing altogether. However the *egresados*' accounts of their experiences of the course demonstrate how the Centro provides the context for the gaining and enactment of cultural citizenship.

Unlike the participants in the more community-focused *talleres*, the Centro graduates are fairly socially homogenous; as might be expected of an institution priding itself on intellectual rigour and drawing comparisons with postgraduate creative writing courses elsewhere, the young *egresados* all have, or are working towards, a university education, and all admit that their decision to try to gain a place on the course was motivated by a perception that the Centro offered the best possible writing training.

Without exception, the *egresados* interviewed for this project embarked on a learning process at the Centro which was initiated as much by the motivation to write, to engage in self-study and to exchange with other writers as by the specific focus on *técnicas narrativas*. In fact, reactions to this component of the course were decidedly mixed: some found that the emphasis on techniques had helped develop their critical faculties and approach to their own writing, while others disagreed with some of its premises and felt that they lacked the maturity to absorb the teaching, or even found that it resulted in a creative block. Nevertheless, they all refuted Pérez Chang's argument that the course produced formulaic writing, arguing that, during their time there, individuals wrote in a variety of styles about a range of subject matter. Much more important to them was the feedback which they received from established writers, which not only helped them to learn more about being a writer, but also gave them valuable future contacts.

Such contact enabled many *egresados* to be socialised into the literary world. However, unlike the wider movement, the Centro's complement of full-time teachers and their Havana location enabled them to enter this world at its centre. For participants in the wider *talleres*, especially now, introduction to the literary world has been largely restricted to *asesores literarios* and events within the movement and local area; while *asesores* might be writers themselves, and act as promoters for their participants' writing, they have often lacked sufficient literary training to provide the level of professional guidance offered by the Centro

Onelio. Moreover, the *asesor*'s primary role in a *taller* is as facilitator, differentiating them from the Centro, which makes a much clearer distinction between teacher and student. Although all agree that, in Centro discussions, all contributions are validated in an atmosphere of solidarity and respect, with room for disagreement even with the teacher, ultimately it is the teacher who passes judgment on the work in question, indicating that the Centro's main objective is to enable the students to write to an accepted literary standard.

As well as providing feedback on their work, the Centro has helped *egresados* gain confidence and improve their communication skills, as well as learning more about themselves. From learning to 'escuchar al otro' ('listen to others') in the *taller*, *egresados* have been able to develop their own sense of identity as writers, and as people with shared interests and dislikes. Thus, the Centro's communicative dimension, as in the wider *talleres*, includes space for a variety of approaches and disagreements but, simultaneously, fosters shared frames of reference and sets the terms of debates, allowing the Centro to provide a context for participants to reinforce a common culture. However, it should be said that this is not restricted to the local area, as in the *talleres*, but rather is framed as being at the forefront of emerging national literary trends.

This process is particularly important at the point of the year when the thirty participants from the provinces join those from Havana in their own condensed version of the course. One *egresado* described a heated debate during one such encounter, when he read out a story which he had written about emigration; his provincial counterparts accused him of ignoring the wider Cuban experience by promoting *habanidad* (Havana-ness). Although he took their opinions into account when later preparing the story for publication, he did not substantially change it. Equally, several *egresados* recounted how, on another occasion, the space offered by the Centro fostered the emergence of two separate literary cliques: one that concentrated on the national space in its subject matter, and another that looked beyond the borders into other imaginaries. Despite this gulf between approaches, the shared space of the Centro forced them to engage in a dialogue, and this discovery of shared interests within the *taller* also often led to productive collaborations outside.

Although the Centro Onelio does not offer a formal qualification, many *egresados* recognise that completing the course successfully is highly regarded by potential employers, especially in the cultural world. Many have found work in cultural institutions, and several provincial graduates returned to their home areas as *asesores*, to establish their own *talleres*. More than one *egresado* said that completion of the course 'me ha abierto puertas' ('has opened doors for me') when it came to looking for work or applying for other prestigious courses. Completion of the course afforded several *egresados* minor celebrity status, with some graduates often featured in the cultural press. Moreover, for those pursuing a writing career, the Centro offered multiple opportunities to gain recognition: as a 'mini-public sphere', it convenes its own literary prizes and its publishing wing promotes the work of young authors. The Centro's name also carries weight in the wider public sphere; two *egresados* admitted that having the Centro Onelio on their CV may have improved their chances of winning a literary prize or getting published, although, responding again to Pérez Chang's criticism, they were quick to assert that literary merit was always the ultimate deciding factor.

A young cultural community

In many ways, the full impact on Cuban literature and culture of this validation and empowerment of Centro *egresados* may not be known for years, as it will take time to measure how these individuals have exerted their enhanced capacity to influence literary culture. However, it is possible to gauge a more immediate consequence of this national-level space for youth participation, in terms of the forging of a young cultural community. The testimonies of the *egresados* confirm that connection with the Centro facilitated their participation in a national cultural community, albeit one that, in contrast to that fostered by the older *talleres*, was largely concentrated in Havana. Membership of that community clearly meant different things for different people: possibilities included participating in an active, 'cultural' social life and maintaining close contact with contemporaries and other cultural producers through events and activities, the latter included producing internet-based digital magazines, participating in literary competitions and activities, or being involved more indirectly through the reading of particular literary magazines.

For the *egresados*, one dimension of this community is centred physically in the Centro itself. Despite completing the course, many *egresados* still regularly visit the institution; they go in order to take advantage of its resources, such as the computer cluster and other teaching rooms, the internet and printers [LCL; IH; AO]. The computer room in particular is an invaluable resource for these aspiring writers, who otherwise lack easy access to such equipment or information. As *egresados* are encouraged to enter international literary competitions, as well as national ones, having their own email account and use of the internet is extremely important. One *egresada* used the Centro premises to run a *cine-club* which she organised and publicised [YLG MN]; the institutional backing for the club helped to attract important directors as visiting speakers.

Many *egresados* also remain connected to the Centro because of the personal relationships forged there. Furthermore, the Directors are keen to reinforce the idea of a community based around the institution, with Ivonne Galeano introducing everyone working there as the *gran familia* (one big family), explaining that the majority of the *especialistas* employed are also *egresados* [IG MN]. One *egresado* echoed her notion, saying: 'Creas amigos de escritores o familia de escritores – se acerca a la literatura mucho la gente, para mí eso es lo fundamental del Taller' [AO] ('you create friendship networks of writers or families of writers – it gets people close to literature – that's the main thing about the Taller'). *Egresados* are also often asked to help with the organisation of the Centro's events, such as presentations at the Feria or the Primer Festival Internacional de Jóvenes Narradores (First International Festival of Young Prose Writers), held at the Centro in 2008 [YLG MN; AO].

Some of the *egresados* interviewed had formed literary groups through their participation in the Centro; these consisted of circles of friends with shared interests in literary styles, as well as other philosophical and cultural ideas. However, those so involved maintained that these were not *grupitos literarios* (literary cliques), thereby distancing themselves from the more pejorative notion of writers grouped around political issues. They also distinguished such groups from the artistic groups of the 1980s, directed against a clearly defined establishment [LCL]; one *egresada* insisted that, in her time, it was more a case of individual writers forming groups based on certain shared ideas and artistic viewpoints, some of which produced their own digital magazines [LCL; AE]. Many more *egresados* also wrote their own blogs from the Centro's computers. In this way, the official institutional space of the Centro also provided the community with access to non-official, non-institutional spaces in which to express itself.

The shared experience of the Centro also reinforced *egresados*' sense of belonging to a cultural world not confined to literature: 'en el grupo hay gente que estudia teatro, filología, pero a pesar de la variedad en cuanto a estética e intereses, lo que nos une paradójicamente es esa diferencia. Compartimos literatura, seriales, música, pintura' [AE] ('in the group there are people who study theatre, philology, but in spite of the variety of interests and aesthetics, we are all paradoxically united by that difference. We share literature, TV series, music, art').

This deeper sense of belonging was more accessible to Havana-based *egresados*, because of the ease of convening in cultural spaces in Havana, but also had connections in the rest of the country. In particular, many *egresados* had links to other cultural forms; not only were *egresados* graduates or students of film or the arts, or working in the wider cultural apparatus, but they also participated in other cultural activities, which provided further spaces in which they could interact [MB MN; LCL; YLG MN]. Some of these allowed them to forge relations, and to work creatively, with an international cultural community [LCL; YLG MN].

Although people participated in this cultural life at different levels, depending on their personal commitments, there was a clear sense that they shared certain spaces in the city and that it was important to be in contact with this life in order to learn from creative activity across all the arts: 'El lobo marca un terreno, pero al mismo tiempo necesita vivir en comunidad, alimentarse, defenderse ... El creador tiene que ser como un lobo, ser capaz de comer carroña y al mismo tiempo ir a la manada' [AE] ('the wolf marks its territory but at the same time it needs to live in a community, feed itself, defend itself ... The creator has to be like a wolf, be able to feed off carrion but at the same time travel with the pack'). The notion that this community was at the forefront of new cultural practice was also reinforced by the fact that most *egresados* were also members of the AHS, membership of which, while not considered as helpful as the Centro in terms of access to publication or space for those wishing to pursue a literary career, was nevertheless valuable for organising and supporting cultural events and meeting young cultural producers from the provinces [VB; LCL; YM].

Reflecting on their involvement with the youth cultural community, *egresados* broadly supported the idea that being engaged with culture was, as well as being a creative and productive pursuit, a way of living a better, more enriched, existence. This was why many *egresados* had changed profession to work in the cultural field, were studying culture, or remained connected to culture in some other way [MB MN; LCL; AE; IH; YLG MN; YM; AO]. For these *egresados*, working in culture and being part of the youth cultural community had real benefits, even if the material rewards were sparse.

Conclusion

As a creative writing course and literary public sphere, the Centro Onelio both shapes and encourages the development of a shared culture among its students and *egresados*: young educated Cubans who write. Like the *talleres*, the Centro shapes this culture by ensuring that participants are exposed to, and engaged with, the values and institutions of official culture and provides them with the tools and space necessary to make a contribution to that culture. However, as a unique and prestigious institution, it also reflects the changing nature of wider Cuban literary culture since the 1990s. By giving official recognition to young writers, the Centro shows a more inclusive approach towards the concept of a national literary tradition. The main *talleres* movement had vastly increased inclusiveness in literary culture at a local level, yet, in the past, young people had had to wait years to gain the national-level acceptance and exposure offered to them by the Centro. For the first time, then, the Centro gives young writers of narrative an institutional context within which to work.

This incorporation of young writers into hegemonic culture can be viewed in different ways. On the one hand, it can be interpreted as a means to neutralise a group often associated with rebellion and challenges to authority. On the other hand, it can be seen as providing young people with the tools to help define and redefine the boundaries of that hegemony. The Centro Onelio teaches and gives recognition to young writers who use their cultural citizenship to debate and discuss issues of importance to them. It provides space for these debates in the form of the building, classes, its magazine and publishing wing. However, it is not all-encompassing; participants can also use their voices in other non-institutional and transnational contexts that are linked to the Centro, such as blogs and electronic magazines and the Primer Festival Internacional de Jóvenes Narradores that took place in 2008. According to Heras León, the Centro's international dimension is particularly important; he describes it as a Casa de las Américas for young people that can foster a fruitful exchange of ideas across the whole of the continent.

Beyond its institutionalisation of a literary tradition of youth, the Centro also manifests a changing attitude towards writers and writing in Cuba. Its focus on the technical aspects of the vocation and its close links to the professional world projects a rather different ethos from that of the original *talleres*, whose underlying idea was that anybody could, and even should, become a writer. In part, the Centro is a response to the requirements of a more complex cultural field and the growing demand for specialised training from an increasingly educated and culturally aware population. However, it also demonstrates an emphasis on professionalisation and individual talent, over and above any idea about the social function of writers. This attitude, confirmed by the Centro's *egresados*, seems a far cry from earlier cultural policy prescriptions that writers should be actively engaged in, and in dialogue with, the whole of society. Although the Centro is ostensibly open to all and fosters a tangible community, how far that community is able to communicate with broader sections of society is open to question. There is evidence that *egresados* do spread their technical knowledge through teaching; nevertheless, it is unclear whether they use these opportunities to gain further feedback on their writing.

In a sense, then, although the Centro Onelio is a mechanism for making literary culture more inclusive through the incorporation of young people, the education which it offers and extra attention which it receives, as well as its location in a smart Havana district, can also appear exclusive. Although it provides an important space for young writers, its prestigious reputation potentially reduces opportunities for young writers who are unable or unwilling to attend. Moreover, it is because of the privileged status which it bestows on its *egresados* that the Centro has been accused of unfairness; critics such as Pérez Chang have used its level of recognition to question the motivations of both students and teachers, questioning whether the new visibility given to cultural producers and writers generally since the 1990s, and reinforced by the Centro, has made writing into a more attractive career option for young people who are motivated more by individual 'success' rather than a vocational calling. While he denies that this is the purpose of the Centro, Heras León confirms that cultural initiatives, more than political ones, capture the imagination of young people and attract them into the revolutionary project.

In general the debates provoked by the Centro reveal wider tensions within the literary world over who assigns authority and sets the criteria for judging literary merit. These become particularly contentious when criteria are established specifically for young writers, as the path to becoming a writer is usually associated with a long process of maturation. The criteria employed by the Centro have evolved considerably from the more overtly political objectives of the early *talleres* and, as a consequence, the institution invites a renewed discussion of what it means to be a writer in contemporary Cuba. Beyond this wider question, however, what remains clear is that the Centro has succeeded in its objectives, both politically and culturally motivated, of inserting young talented people into a national culture. Although the success of the institution adds legitimacy to the revolutionary project, a deeper analysis of its overall impact will have to wait, while it advances the careers of the people who shape Cuban literary culture in the years to come.

Notes

1 I would like to thank my thesis supervisors, Antoni Kapcia and Par Kumaraswami, for all their support and encouragement with this project and to acknowledge how much I have learned about Cuban culture while working at the Centre for Research on Cuba at the University of Nottingham. I should also like to acknowledge the help of Nottingham's Graduate School Travel Prize in funding my fieldwork research. In Cuba, I would like to express my gratitude to Eduardo Heras León and Ivonne Galeano, the Directors of the Centro Onelio, for supporting my investigation into their fascinating institution. Finally, I am indebted to all my Cuban interviewees, who kindly offered their time, friendship and insights into their experiences of the Centro Onelio and the wider literary workshop movement, in particular – Ahmel Echevarría, Abraham Ortiz, Lien Carranza Lau and especially Yannis Lobaina González.
2 These intellectuals include Eduardo Galeano (uncle of Ivonne), Abelardo Castillo, Mempo Giardinelli, Augusto Monterroso, Luisa Valenzuela and Mario Benedetti ('Mensajes de los intelectuales', 2002).
3 The evidence for this case study is taken from my doctoral thesis, *A Literary Culture in Common: The Movement of Talleres Literarios in Cuba 1960s-2000s* (Nehru, 2010).
4 That period had produced groups such as *Seis del Ochenta* and *El Establo*, and the *novísmos*, often self-identified as marginal characters, such as *roqueros* (rockers), *friquis* (freaks/punks/hippies), drug users or other *delincuentes*, or wrote about them in their work (Rosales, 2002; Fornet, 2006: 5). Often long unpublished, these groups initially existed on the periphery of the literary establishment.
5 'In spite of economic shortages, moments of splendour or moments of crisis, other similar, but less famous, spaces have been maintained, in the shade thrown by a humble Casa de Cultura in a humble *municipio*, orienting readings, awakening an interest in literature (yes, in LITERATURE, not in the mere trade of editing stories). (Literature means thinking the world, not performing on the catwalk like Naomi Campbell)'.
6 Much of this section is based on interviews with Centro students and graduates in 2006.

/ 7

The history of a novel: Alberto Ajón León's ¿Qué bolá? (What's Up?)

This chapter deals with the illustrative trajectory of a typical new work of literature – a novel by the relatively unknown author, Alberto Ajón León, called ¿Qué bolá? (What's Up?) – the title referring to the common greeting in Cuban street slang equating to either the 'What's up?' of the subtitle, or, more commonly, 'How's it going?' or 'What's new?'. The purpose here is to illustrate the earlier analysis of the institutional context and the decision-making processes for Cuban writers and readers, highlighting especially the complex set of pressures – circumstantial and political – which shape the normal operations of contemporary Cuban publishing and create Cuba's unusual literary culture.

The process of selecting the novel for this study began in 2007, with discussions with the then Director of Letras Cubanas, Daniel García Santos. In 2009, further discussions were held with the interim ICL President, Fernando León Jacomino, the new Director of Letras Cubanas (and former head of the Sección de Narrativa), Rogelio Riverón, and Jacqueline Laguardia Martínez, Director of the ICL's new OCLL. Out of those discussions came the identification of the latest manuscript by Ajón, who, as a relative newcomer (although already known for his regular slot for the national radio station Radio Reloj), met one of this study's key aims of examining the existence and experience of the majority of less established Cuban writers. Thereupon began a series of meetings and email correspondence with Ajón.

The context

The institutional context here is vast: from the different actors in the publishing house itself (commissioning editor, critical reader, copyeditor, designer and *promotor*), to UNEAC, booksellers, critics, readers and the many actors of the Feria del Libro and other similar spaces. Indeed, what this small history demonstrates is that no single actor operates in isolation or exercises more power in decision making than any other, making the whole process one of constant negotiation.

The publishing house is logically the starting point of the context. Although Cuba now boasts around 130 separate publishers [ELR], most produce educational and academic texts, and relatively few specialise in literature. Nonetheless, Cuban literature currently boasts about fifty different prizes at some level or other (national, provincial or local), with about twenty of these in turn leading to publication; hence, even outside the larger presses, there are still many smaller outlets that make up the range of opportunities available to authors and would-be authors. Of these outlets, however, the largest is Letras Cubanas, part of the overarching ICL and created (as already seen in Chapter 4) in response to the concerns – not least expressed at the 1975 Party Congress – about the lack of publishing facilities to match the growth in writers' output (Smorkaloff, 1997: 164–5). It was immediately successful, publishing around 60 per cent as many titles (958) in 1977–86 as had been published in the whole of 1959–76 (1,544) (Smorkaloff, 1997: 165); within this, the lion's share, responding to public demand, went to prose fiction, which, although constituting only 53 per cent of the titles, accounted for 81.1 per cent of the copies printed (compared with poetry's 20.4 per cent of titles and only 8.3 per cent of the copies (Smorkaloff, 1997: 165). Hence, Letras Cubanas has always been the clear national leader in prose fiction, although Ediciones Unión probably enjoys greater prestige because, by publishing only UNEAC members, it produces work of more firmly established quality.

Within Letras Cubanas, the internal structures and processes tend to set the norm for other, smaller presses, to follow: it has four sub-departments – a commercial department (addressing questions of accounting), a marketing department (dealing with promotional activities), an economics department (addressing budget issues) and an editorial department (which drafts and executes publishing plans). The latter consists of four editorial sections: poetry, theatre, narrative and visual arts [DGS], plus production and design departments (see Figure 1).

For comparison, it is worth commenting that Ediciones Unión, although smaller, follows the same pattern, but operates on different principles given its institutional character; this necessarily limits the scope of its publishing decisions (to UNEAC members) and may make

Instituto Cubano del Libro

Director Letras Cubanas → Advisory Board (24)

Economics department	Commercial department	Marketing department	Editorial department

Editorial Committee – Director, Senior Editors, Heads of Accounts and Commercial

Editorial department →

Editor Theatre/Poetry	Editor Prose	Editor Critical/Literary Theory	Editor Visual Art	Production department	Design department

Figure 1. Organisational structure of Letras Cubanas

it more immediately responsive to those it publishes. Its size, publishing only around sixty titles a year [OMP], inevitably affects its scope and operation – giving it perhaps less international presence than Letras Cubanas (and thus less hard-currency income) and a lesser capacity for realistic long-term plans – but, conversely, it seems to bring some benefits, such as a more intimate atmosphere and the multi-skilling which a smaller staff base implies. Moreover, Unión enjoys considerable autonomy of criteria and publication, and enjoys precedence in UNEAC's national network of bookshops [OMP].

Within all publishing houses, the annual plan is the basis of all strategy and decisions. Including details of all proposed books – prices, costs, print-runs – this is the formal responsibility of an advisory board (*consejo asesor*), which, consisting of high-profile writers and intellectuals, meets annually to monitor the old plan and agree the next one. For Ediciones Unión, in 2006, its chair was Ambrosio Fornet, while for Letras Cubanas the chair was the leading University of Havana critic, Rogelio Rodríguez Coronel, with twenty-three other members, including Arrufat, Nancy Morejón and Fernández Retamar. However, the plan itself is constructed by the lower, more hands-on editorial committee (*consejo de redacción*), which in Letras Cubanas consists of the heads of all four genre sections, plus leading representatives from the commercial arm, all of whom discuss and agree the proposed list of books from each section, seeking some balance between genres, and between Havana and the provinces. It is essentially this committee which, taking decisions on cultural criteria, continues to ensure the plan's execution, meeting weekly to monitor progress and find solutions to any unforeseen obstacles [DGS]. Hence, for all presses, there is a need for flexibility in the plan's execution, not least to adapt to outside developments over which the publisher has little control [DGS; OMP].

Once the plan is active, the next stage is the submission, evaluation and processing of manuscripts. After a manuscript is submitted by an author, the press in question is obliged to respond within ninety days, confirming (after the initial reading by one or more of the commissioning editors) either that it is rejected (with a clear set of reasons given) or that it is considered good enough to be sent out for review; in the latter case, the text will then be sent out to a minimum of three anonymous specialist (and paid) readers, the number of readers varying according to the publisher's size. The text itself is rarely anonymous, unless written by someone well-known (which, of course, does also send a message to the assessor).

When two positive assessments have been received, those responsible for future plans must decide whether and, if so, when, to include the book in the plans (the current year's plan being relatively sacrosanct, with new manuscripts being included very exceptionally); inevitably, there are some cases where positive reader assessment does not mean the publisher's acceptance, if there is no room in immediate plans [RR], although a book not deemed to fit into the normal publishing criteria would normally be weeded out by the commissioning editor's initial judgment.

Thereafter, the process starts in earnest, the manuscript's assigned editor liaising directly and regularly with the author, guiding book and author through the publication stages. Mostly, the choice of editor depends on availability, experience and specific expertise, although some more experienced writers occasionally ask for specific editors [OMP].

The final stages of the process are printing (starting with the agreed *ficha*, or mock-up, which then gets burned onto a CD), pricing, distribution and publicity. Printing of course means decisions about print-runs, an aspect of publishing which still shows the impact of the post-1990 crisis. The usual print-run for larger publishers is still 2,000–3,000 [DGS; OMP], well down on the prodigious figures for the 1980s' 'boom' years, but a figure which, for all its problems of accessibility for a voracious reading public, does have the advantage of allowing the publishers to publish more authors [DGS]. Of course, for most books, a figure of 2,000 is so low that many books are sold out quickly, thereby running into another publishing problem: the improbability of reprinting. Given continuing shortages and the cost of imported paper, only the high-profile Cuban classics (such as the works of Lezama or Carpentier) or the very popular modern authors (such as Padura Fuentes) generally benefit from decisions to reprint, together with key works by leading politicians, especially Fidel Castro (for which the demand is, anyway, likely to be massive, as exemplified in 2005 by the published interview with Ignacio Ramonet, *Cien horas con Fidel*). A special Fondo de Población – provided from Ediciones Cubanas' hard-currency sales – funds the small number of titles (in Letras Cubanas, about thirty) which are earmarked, according to a Plan Especial, for larger runs, i.e. between 5,000 and 40,000 [DGS; OMP]. What this means for new authors is that, since a successful first book means a rapid exhaustion of stocks and the near impossibility of reprinting, they need to build on fame with a second book, or find other means of recognition (e.g. through publicity), rather than through increased sales of the original book [AAL].

Print-runs, of course, are also part of the picture for an author to consider when choosing a publisher. The easiest place to be published may well be a provincial Edición Territorial or other local press, and some authors publish prolifically through these means. However, their drawback is the relative lack of recognition that results; not only do provincial presses print fewer copies (usually 500) for a localised circulation (although the ICL's Havana bookshop, *Fayad Jamís* on Obispo, is committed to stocking Territoriales publications) – leaving locally successful writers unknown at a national level [AAL] – but they also lack the prestige of the big Havana publishers, who compound this advantage with much bigger print-runs [ELR].

Distribution is at present handled by two separate institutions, the DNL, taking care of the Cuban distribution, and the export entity, Ediciones Cubanas, managing sales abroad. The latter's role is complemented by a new post-1999 phenomenon of co-publication in collaboration with foreign presses, enabling much larger print-runs; these even reach 700,000 in some cases, albeit only 15,000–20,000 of those reaching Cubans, the remainder being sold abroad [OMP].

Equally, the vexed decisions about pricing will have been taken already, driven by economic considerations (by the commercial department) but also by the overriding need to keep books within the price range of the average reader. Whereas in a more commercially oriented system, pricing is intimately linked to authors' royalties or projected sales, that is inevitably less true in Cuba, where the relative lack of commercial criteria underpinning publishing, coupled with the patterns of payment which operated between 1976 and the 1990s (i.e. until opportunities broadened for some), means that very few Cuban authors can survive on royalties from Cuban sales (sales abroad are, of course, a very different matter, but for even fewer authors). However, eventual sales do play a part in decisions on royalties, because of the economic constraints on publication; hence, a commissioning editor must negotiate any advance payments based largely on a judgment of the quality of the book and the author, rather than on projected sales [DGS].

Equally, print-runs and royalties imply the need to address another key stage of the process: promotion. This not only brings in the commercial department, but also another key player: the *promotor cultural*, clearly crucial in the decisions of which author and which book to promote, and how and where to publicise, based on their very specific training, their experience, and their knowledge of the most appropriate space, public and type of reader for the book. The central moment here is the *lanzamiento* or *presentación*, an event in the Cuban book cycle of far greater importance than in the UK, for example. For Letras Cubanas, and any ICL press, the major *presentación* usually takes place in the ICL headquarters, in the weekly *sábado del libro* series (with space for up to 100 people); until 2010, this was held in the courtyard of the eighteenth-century Palacio del Segundo Cabo, on the Plaza de Armas, but is now located in the ICL's new premises on Obispo. For higher profile authors, there are usually several other launches in other cultural centres (most notably the Centro Dulce María Loynaz, the University of Havana, Casa de las Américas, the Instituto Superior de Arte or even a secondary school or prison). Ediciones Unión's launches, logically, tend to be held in the Sala Martínez Villena of the UNEAC headquarters (accommodating 150 people). Wherever the main launch is, of course, it is the February Feria del Libro which takes the publishers' pride of place, all their annual plans being increasingly geared to that event – although Feria launches tend to mean several books being presented simultaneously, and is therefore perhaps less significant for the individual writer. For a single-book launch, the event is presided over by the director of the press, accompanied by the writer, the editor, the person speaking about the book, and, occasionally, the *promotor cultural* responsible for publicity [YLG].

Wherever the launch, since all decisions must be agreed with the author, the press's management and the main distributors, its planning can be a complicated process, finding a free date at the chosen institution (which usually means planning it at least a month in advance), but also agreeing with that institution (which usually expects to have some sort of interest in the book or author). However, before that process begins, the *promotor* must read the book (to be sure of making the right decisions), and then prepare a small review or press release [YLG]. Once all is agreed, the public has to be invited, making sure that the space is either large or small enough (depending on likely numbers) and that there are sufficient copies of the book for the likely audience (or at least the capacity of the space, in the event that many uninvited people turn up). Even then, however, there may well be insufficient copies, especially with a small print-run, once the publisher has set aside the required number for libraries and specific bookshops, and also those to be given to the author [YLG].

The question of the launch also returns to the issues of pricing and print-runs, since one attraction of a launch (for would-be readers) is that a number of books are available (to be signed by the author) in Cuban pesos; although almost all Cuban books are sold in local bookshops in this currency, the low print-runs and, for some, the need to meet the hard-currency demand, can mean that numbers run out rapidly, making attendance at the launch attractive. The needs of the launch, however, also mean a key decision has to be made about the number of copies to be held back for this purpose, and guessing at sales according to the author's fame.

After that, of course, bookshops become the key players. Here the question of qualification and expertise gives a mixed picture, most shops' staff being selected for their experience rather than training, although writers and publishers clearly value the role of the more literature-aware booksellers: 'Pero el librero tiene que tener un gusto; tú no puedes poner a trabajar a cualquiera. Hay que tener el placer, el arte, la distensión de ese libro ... Y los hay muy buenos'[JLM] ('but the bookseller must have taste; you can't put just anyone in a job like that. You have to feel the pleasure, the art, the mood of that book ... And there are some excellent booksellers').

A study of one of Havana's better bookshops – the Ateneo (on Línea and 12), known for specialising in literature and as a focal point for literary activities, although no longer hosting *presentaciones* – serves to highlight the characteristics and challenges of the whole book system. The manager is clearly one of the better educated and more respected booksellers, a literature graduate who, having no formal specific training, was appointed on the basis of experience in other bookshops (specifically the *Centenario* bookshop on 25 and O) [SO]. The Ateneo is one of Havana's largest, with seventeen staff (partly because it covers the Café Literario on 23 and 12, which, catching much passing trade, is a valuable sales outlet) and stocking about 1,300 titles at any one time (the average for most bookshops being around 600); indeed, at the 2009 *Noche de los libros*, its stall sold 10,000 books, the highest number of all such outlets [SO].

However, although a leader in its field, even the Ateneo struggles within a system that, at this level, is surprisingly disarticulated and inevitably resource-constrained. The disarticulation refers to a complaint common among those in the book circuit: the lack of a direct link between publishers and booksellers. Hence, although publishers and selected sellers do occasionally collaborate in one-off studies of book sales and demand, there is no systematic link between those deciding on prices and print-runs and those selling to the public; instead, the former receive periodic reports from the DNL on total sales [DGS]. Moreover, the disarticulation is heightened by the fact that the distribution of specific books is left in the hands of local government (OPP), since the DNL does not disseminate directly to sellers but via the network of CPLL, which belong not to the ICL (as might be thought logical) but the provincial Poder Popular [DGS]. This leaves the publishers without direct feedback from sellers and leaves the sellers with no say in which or how many books they receive; moreover, unlike sellers in the second-hand sector, the latter have no control over prices, except when selling off unsold books at a lower price (some of which are off-loaded to smaller bookshops). While this has its advantages (in that the lack of a sense of competition with other bookshops can lead to helpful cooperation if a specific book is requested at one shop), it also limits the scope for imagination and adaptation to a local demand. Moreover, record keeping is elementary and somewhat basic, each purchase being recorded by hand by the seller (noting title, author and price), with the manager totalling up each day's sales, listing according to category (but not title). At the end of each month, the totals (again by category) are sent to the Centro Provincial and thence upwards to the ICL. There is thus a central record of sorts of the total number of books sold (and their value), but there is no central recording system for the individual titles; in fact, the only record of the latter is found on the daily tickets made out by each seller for each purchase, which are kept (although it is not clear for how long) by the bookshop itself. What this means, of course, is that the ICL cannot systematically know which titles sell well, leaving such knowledge to impressions by sellers (who, of course, know very well which books are 'best-sellers' and which are 'non-sellers', even if no one asks that question centrally). Therefore, there is no market mechanism built into the system at all, and feedback to the publishers can only be by informal contact with booksellers.

Second-hand bookshops, however, do operate with much greater flexibility, even those (the majority) which are state-run, since their market is by definition one geared to specific demand and since they depend on finding books wherever they can, rather than receiving a fixed number from a central distributor. Hence, these shops can be a vital link in the chain of supply and demand, but in very limited ways, i.e. for specific texts, and usually for books which, by definition, tend to be in less demand, given that, although the 1990s saw an increase in the number of Cubans selling their own books to help make ends meet, few Cuban readers actually sell the books which they really value [MTG]. In one key respect, however, second-hand book sellers have a critical freedom: they can set their own prices, which, unlike in the new-book shops, vary according to the seller's knowledge of the demand and the price which he or she knows buyers will pay for a given book. Hence, even the Ateneo's small second-hand section (stocking only thirty books or so) is sold at prices set by the second-hand specialist. Moreover, second-hand shops (apart from those close to large hotels or in the more tourist-oriented areas) almost always sell in Cuban pesos, allowing them to gauge the Cuban domestic market better than those shops or stalls (usually privately owned) which sell primarily to tourists in CUC (most notably in the Plaza de Armas).

Pricing of course leads us logically to the final element in the whole process and chain: the reader. In one sense, there is little that, perhaps, can be added at this point to what has already been observed in Chapter 5, about reading practices; later in this chapter, reference will be made to the readers' reception of the specific novel studied here. However, some comments are apposite. Firstly, if the comparative rigidity of the Cuban book-production and book-selling systems (so clearly designed to ensure maximum spread within strict financial constraints) frustrate publishers and writers, it is equally frustrating for those readers whose appetite for ever more books – an appetite fed systematically since 1961, and well met in the 1980s – is simply not satisfied by the numbers of books available, making the search for specific books an ongoing occupation of many average readers. In part, the lack of available books is offset by initiatives such as the *Club Minerva*. Usually located in libraries or bookshops and consisting of books made available by the Feria (from among the most popular ones), these clubs lend books to readers at one Cuban peso per book per week (the Ateneo stocks about 300 such titles for this purpose); however, this is always a small-scale operation and merely scratches the surface of the problem.

Moreover, it is not just the numbers which frustrate, for many Cubans will complain vociferously about the high prices which they pay, even in Cuban pesos (CUC-priced books are simply out of the reach of most Cubans) – an issue about which the Cuban authorities are understandably sensitive, given the central importance in the Revolution's collective psyche of the idea of cheap books available to all. Hence, while everyone recognises objectively that the cost of book production must be very high, given the cost of the paper, ink, chemicals and the printing presses themselves (all having to be bought abroad with hard currency), many readers, nurtured until 1989 on heavily subsidised cheap books (often sold at fifty centavos), resent paying five, or even ten or fifteen, Cuban pesos [MTG], although such expectations clearly do not take into account the unaffordability of the old subsidies.

However, readers' perceptions have changed in one respect: while in the 1960s the improvisation mentality was appropriate for a more 'heroic' epoch of nation-rebuilding, expectations of physical quality are now much higher, perhaps driven by the increased access to a globalised market-place, with many readers also resenting the often poor-quality paper being used, the better paper being reserved for luxury editions [HC]. Hence, Cuban publishers now have to consider visual appeal more than before, because the traditional reader's appreciation of the book as object – 'El contacto con algo tangible, tocable, palpable, olible, la cosa de poderlo atesorar' [GFL] ('the contact with something you can feel, touch, sense, smell, the whole idea of being able to accumulate books') – now seems to be translated into an expectation that it should also look better, acknowledged necessarily by publishers: 'Tampoco vamos a perder, que el libro no sea un objeto bello'[OMP] ('we're not going to forget the fact that a book should be a beautiful object'). Equally, expectations have been raised by greater access to the internet, increasing Cubans' awareness of, and demand for, books which they know to be available. Hence the discerning reader is increasingly the subject of publishers' concerns and planning.

From this picture of the publishing processes, we can draw two highly relevant conclusions. Firstly, there is an increasing tension between the traditional commitment to promoting the reading of as much literature as possible and the straitened economic context for Cuban literary culture since 1989, with the latter being greater as a result of the post-2008 imperative to save and to cover costs. Hence, growing pressures affect publishers who remain loyal to the political value of the book and of reading: 'Por lo tanto, las necesidades primeras que uno tiene en cuenta son las culturales, [...] no es el criterio básicamente comercial el que predomina [DGS] ('and so the most important criterion that one takes into account is cultural needs, [...] it's not the commercial criterion that has greatest weight').

Secondly, the long-standing tension between the traditional focus on the reader and the post-*quinquenio gris* need to treat and reward writers better has become sharper, reinforced by the contrast between the post-1993 opportunities for many cultural actors and writers' relative lack of access to those opportunities. This extends to publishing opportunities, which, although expanded beyond recognition (with accompanying fears of a potential devaluation effect), cannot keep pace with the number of writers which old and new initiatives continue to produce: 'hay autores cubanos que tienen en un año tres libros publicados, pero cinco guardados' [ELR] ('there are Cuban authors with three books published, but five books waiting to be published').

One logical outcome is a greater tendency towards small print-runs and greater delays for most books, while another – reflecting the traditional need to value quality rather than quantity – is the need to prioritise some authors and some books: 'pero después al final yo tengo que tratar de hacer una pirámide, con escalones, y decidir incluso a la hora de la tirada a quién le doy mayor cantidad de papel. Eso no siempre se entiende' [ELR] ('but after that, in the end, I have to build a kind of pyramid, with steps, and even decide when it comes to print-runs which author I am giving more paper to. That's not something that's always understood'). These tensions in turn make negotiations between the author and everyone in the publishing process potentially more complex and vexed.

The author [AAL][1]

Alberto Ajón León was born in 1950 in Jobabo, a small, isolated ('prácticamente perdido') sugar town in Oriente. Like many other writers, he acknowledges the influence of his mother, whose frustrated ambitions to be a teacher meant that she passed on her love of reading to her children, especially Alberto who, at four, could recite poems by Rubén Darío and Martí, especially at the weekly school *acto cívico* (civic ceremony). This early ability to memorise and recite sprang from his mother's inculcation of an appreciation of the rhythms of Spanish and the pleasure of language. His father ran a small *fonda* (canteen), providing cheap meals for migrant sugar workers whose mixture of speech provided another boost to Alberto's appreciation of language. This early love of both *lo popular* (popular literature), for example, Guillén) and the 'classical' (for example, Martí) developed further when, often forced to remain indoors for safety during the insurrection, he began to create his own stories about characters from comics.

In January 1959, shortly after the rebel victory, he wrote his first poem, dedicated to a family friend whose brutal death and immolation in the recent repression had affected him greatly, the friend having visited and eaten in Alberto's house until the day of his murder;

while visiting his grave he wrote and recited his first poems. Later he suggested that those days marked him indelibly, giving him a context which later generations lacked, a time of 'actividad necesaria que ha de tener el individuo para inculcarse emociones' ('the activity which an individual needs in order to instil emotions') and an opportunity to participate which made him a child of the Revolution. Indeed, when twelve, like thousands of others and against his mother's wishes, he left home for the first time to take part in the 1961 Literacy Campaign, a life-shaping eight-month experience, when he taught ten peasants in all. In 1962 (again like many others), he harvested coffee in the Sierra Maestra, a much harder three-month experience in far-flung places, where – exposed to parasites, travelling primitively, surviving the cold and illness, and even going hungry as they catered for themselves inadequately – his eyes were opened.

At home his older brothers were also influential, not least in their clandestine reading of (quasi erotic) love poetry (including Neruda) and in one brother's love of romantic *boleros* (ballads), awakening his pre-adolescent interest in sex. School also played a part, especially after moving to Havana to attend a *preuniversitario* school (their village having no secondary school), where one teacher – whose confidence in him, she later admitted, made her give him high grades without reading his work, and who would later attend the launch of his first book – regularly asked him to read to the class. His membership of the school's UJC led him briefly to contemplate a career in much-needed medicine or agronomy, but, after two years of what he called 'tortura' in Medicine (where his love of literature stayed with him, almost clandestinely – he even hid a poetry book inside a larger book of anatomy or physiology), he finally persuaded his parents to let him change direction, a decision which immediately triggered a period of obligatory military service, in the Escuela de Ingeniería Militar (military engineering academy). There, while learning chemistry, he was given charge of classes on politics, where he employed his skills and knowledge in literature and where he learned to teach. Once demobilised (in the late 1960s), he entered a teacher-training course, where, before emerging with top grades, he employed his love of theatre and performance to teach him to project himself, which, together with his old ability to memorise, later enabled him to recite to his pupils, evidently memorably so for many.

In 1987 he left teaching, having moved into an Escuela de Perfeccionamiento Educacional (teacher-training school), and, in the last five years of that period, he studied part-time for a degree in literature in Spanish. He then took up radio journalism, beginning as a style editor on Radio Reloj, another experience which shaped his literary approach by sharpening his attention to language and making him determined to resist overblown style, linguistic fashion, mediocrity and other linguistic distortions: 'los maniqueísmos, del acomodamiento, del comodín, del circunloquio, el dar vueltas y vueltas, y no decir nada' ('Manicheanisms, complacency, pet-words, wordiness, going round in verbal circles and not saying anything').

Meanwhile, he had created a small theatre group for his students, taking them to the theatre on Saturdays and instilling a love of drama which spilled over into the vacations and saw them win *aficionado* competitions over three years. He had also begun to write, fitfully, but, as work and study allowed him little time, his first book was never published – a metaphorical work, unlikely (he feels) to have anything other than historical value. Before that, however, three months after starting in radio, he had written stories, eventually winning a prize in a national *talleres* competition, representing Havana. His experience in the school-based *taller* was clearly more an opportunity than a formative experience (given his years of training and experience in literature), enabling him to participate in provincial *encuentros*, gaining acclaim for one story (published in 1987 in the anthology of that year's winning entries), with a different take on the counter-revolutionary *bandidos* (literally, 'bandits') of the 1960s.

In 1990, he progressed from the *aficionado* circuit to the Fuerzas Armadas Revolucionarias's (FAR) *Premio 26 de Julio*, gaining an honourable mention (i.e. second place) for a book of stories; although the winning work was never published (coinciding with the 1990s' crisis), his own was published by FAR, albeit in the most rudimentary form. This was followed by a Pinos Nuevos prize (i.e. a prize for new authors), for the story collection *Pesquisas en Castalia*, where he consciously sought to expound his ideas on literature. That ended his search for recognition through prizes (not least having seen such competitions from the other side, after serving on a prize jury), after which he began to submit his manuscripts directly to publishers, starting with *Ancora*, his first novel. However, although it was well received, its small print-run and the impossibility of reprinting left him still relatively unknown.

Throughout this whole trajectory, Ajón developed a particular, almost magisterial, approach to literature and to the art of writing. While a teacher and after starting in radio, he developed an ability to write quickly, between other commitments, ideal for someone still writing part-time. He also became rigorous in his approach to writing correctly, but he was less interested in the judgments of critics than in the opinions of his immediate neighbours, the poorest of whom might have something useful to say. That (essentially moral) attitude to correctness has also extended to different aspects of his work, as teacher (vigilant and demanding) and as radio journalist, especially in his Sunday programme, where he habitually talks about language, orthography, the meanings of words, and other aspects, in a personal drive to resist the use of poor language.

That rigour also means welcoming criticism, recognising its role in improvement: 'Para mí, la crítica es fundamental ... Por eso me gusta que me critiquen, que me digan "Esto está mal, pudiste hacerlo mejor", que eso me ayuda, y no me creo jamás, jamás – yo siempre me consideraré un aficionado. Por eso reviso y reviso tanto' ('for me, criticism is fundamental ... That's why I like it when people criticise me, when they say "This is wrong, you could have got this better", that helps me, and I never ever think of myself as – I always consider myself an amateur. That's why I go over what I've written so much'). This is driven by a desire to seek greater perfection, which he knows is unattainable: 'si no podemos serlo nosotros, como personas, lo que produzcamos, debemos tratar de que sea mejor' ('if we can't be better as people, we should try to make sure that what we produce is better'). Indeed, his passion for literature and perfection drives his respect for art as 'el deseo de la perfección' ('the desire for perfection'), although, as befits someone with an evident ludic sense, he recognises that art must also entertain: 'La literatura es juego' ('literature is a game').

The book

The action of the novel is set in the suburb of Alamar, built in the 1970s, east of Havana Bay and famous for its once prestigious but now dilapidated and somewhat under-provided complex of dozens of *microbrigada*-constructed apartment blocks; in fact, it is essentially set in one single block. The novel is most notable for the overall lack of a definable single 'plot', consisting essentially of a mixture of almost 'snapshot' pictures of life as lived in one block, the larger-than-life stories of the equally larger-than-life characters who live there (all given bizarre names or nicknames to enhance their characters), and the events and processes that develop around them, all in a short time-span. However, the novel's most obvious trait is its pervasive and always clever sense of humour – in the descriptions, the narrative, the characters, the events – which partly disguises its additional purpose: to reflect something of the social fabric of post-1990 Havana. For, although the characters hardly constitute a representative collection of types (prostitutes, transvestites, American tourists, hustlers, bureaucrats and so on), the circumstances in which they live and the challenges which they have to confront daily are all too recognisable to most Cubans – the bus queue (lovingly and lengthily described), the wait at the dentist's, the confrontations with bureaucracy. Moreover, all of it is written with a gift for language which shows erudition, a love of the power of words, and also a familiarity with the most recondite street slang; one minute it recalls Carpentier's erudite and baroque language, then it recalls Cabrera Infante's word-games and then it reflects the most incomprehensible but very familiar working-class argot – and all of it used to narrate lives in an almost Rabelaisian picture of the 'dark' side of daily life.

The novel's genesis lay in an older short story, which one friend had originally suggested might be the basis for a novel. Eventually, after increased success, Ajón returned to the story, working it up into the novel and eventually being shortlisted for the 2009 *Premio Alejo Carpentier*. This began the book's publication stage, when the jury, led by the journalist Marta Rojas, unusually decided not to award any prize (declaring the outcome *desierto*, literally 'abandoned'), a decision which caused shock and resentment among those affected, reinforced in some by an elitist disbelief that a journalist had presided over a literary jury. One of Ajón's friends, knowing the wife of Rogelio Riverón, the head of Narrativa in Letras Cubanas, was so outraged by the decision and by Rojas's judgment (that the manuscript was nothing special) that she contacted Riverón indirectly. The next that Ajón heard was from Riverón himself, expressing Letras Cubanas' interest – and also informing him of the decision to make his book the subject of this case study.

Ajón then met the assigned editor, Anet Rodríguez-Ojea, and Riverón, three times, firstly to agree issues such as the contract and probable date of publication, and then, after Rodríguez-Ojea's perusal, to discuss the manuscript itself, focusing largely on questions of syntax, spelling and punctuation. However, Rodríguez-Ojea did question the realism of having the improbable scenario of *marginales* and a transvestite talking on a beach and using quotes from Lorca's

Romancero Gitano (something which Ajón was content to concede, making the appropriate changes), although his choice of title remained, despite her doubts. In fact, throughout, Ajón found their discussions positive, with no attempt by Letras Cubanas to impose any preferences on him; moreover, he found Rodríguez-Ojea's attention to detail remarkable, even drafting a plan of the residential block in question in order to locate the characters.

Equally, discussions about design were straightforward, especially as the book was part of a regular Letras Cubanas novel series, with a set pattern of typeface, size and price. The only debate here affected the cover: Ajón wanted a design based on overlapping transparencies of an Alamar building, to reflect the view of the omniscient narrator and the novel's different perspectives, but the designer, using the style of Carlos Enríquez, came up with the final version, which Ajón happily accepted.

All that remained to be decided was the publication date. This was originally scheduled for April or May 2010, although Ajón (already used to delays) told friends that it would probably be June or July. However, at this point, extraneous factors entered into calculations: the death of Carpentier's widow in February 2008 and the release of his unpublished manuscripts and letters meant the sudden prioritisation, in 2009–10, of texts by, and on, Carpentier; the death of Cintio Vitier in October 2009 similarly intervened in production plans; finally, in 2009, the ICL prioritised the first of Fidel Castro's accounts of the 1956–8 insurrection – *La victoria estratégica* – published in August 2010, with 896 pages, complete with graphs, photographs and illustrations, and with a total initial print-run of 60,000, demanding a considerable and rapid revision of all national publishing plans. The eventual price of that volume (twenty Cuban pesos) indicates the general principles guiding the subsidisation of books with a special political, ideological or symbolic worth. What this of course meant for *¿Qué bola? (What's up?)* was an indeterminate delay, everyone concerned hoping that it might be out in time for the February 2011 Feria del Libro.

At this point, it is worth reflecting on the reaction of those within the publishing structures to these developments; for, while most Cubans seemed content to buy Fidel's book, receiving news of its publication with emotions ranging from national pride to affection, those whose own work was directly affected by the news that this volume had effectively soaked up reserves originally destined for their own books showed an equally interesting awareness of the necessarily more important priority accorded to Fidel's work, a recognition (maybe with differing levels of resignation and tolerance) that such a book must inevitably take precedence over any others. Hence, while it might be tempting to see an irony in Castro's surprise (in his *Reflexiones* a few days before the book's release) that it was published remarkably quickly, the overriding reaction of all of the agents in this publishing process was constructive and pragmatic.

The final obstacle to publication came in late 2010, with the prioritisation of hundreds of thousands of copies of the document which all Cubans, through their many collective entities, were asked to consider and debate (the so-called *lineamientos*, or 'guidelines'), in the build-up to the April 2011 Communist Party Congress, containing all of the new Raúl Castro-led leadership's proposed economic reforms; this massive demand on paper exceeded even Fidel Castro's memoirs.

Ultimately, Letras Cubanas did find space for Ajón's novel in its schedules, with the first printing made in December 2010, thus formally meeting the 2010 plan. Overall, therefore, between the submission of the final agreed manuscript and the printing, the birth proved to be close to the norm of four to five months, although, according to Riverón, that was helped by the quality of Ajón's writing, reducing the need to correct text and style, and to his ready agreement to all major suggestions. Nonetheless, for Ajón, the whole gestation process was closer to three years. Moreover, the delays did not end there, since the continuing paper shortage meant that sufficient copies could not be produced to be sure of the novel's launch, as hoped, at the coming Feria. In the end, enough copies were printed to meet the demands of that launch and of the Feria's main bookshop, but were insufficient, until March, to meet the potential demands of other bookshops; hence, as is common, only those attending the Feria could acquire a copy. Nonetheless, the book was actually out.

The launch presented challenges. The original idea for *presentaciones* in summer 2010 had been grand: Ajón had asked for the Hotel Inglaterra, where his first book had been launched (with only eight friends present). As his public had grown with each publication, he now expected a better turnout for this novel, and proposed that the 'panel' include Matilde Salas (responsible for the hotel's public events), Rodríguez-Ojea, Riverón and someone else, as yet undetermined, to talk about the novel. Now, however, everything had to be downscaled and postponed, with the Feria as the main focus.

One feature of the Feria book launches, however, is that, unless the author is famous, they tend to cover groups of books; hence, Ajón had to share the limelight with three other authors being published in the same Letras series, *La novela del 2010*. Moreover, neither Riverón nor Rodríguez-Ojea could be at the launch, which was instead chaired by another editor and a presenter (both unknown to Ajón), the latter speaking about all four novels, largely by reading from the book covers. With the launch taking place in a cold room on a cold day (for which Cuba is always unprepared), it was a far cry from the August plans, but, if the actual first launch was something of a disappointment to Ajón, he did not show it; moreover, being launched at the Feria brought a larger audience, about sixty people (of whom Ajón only knew about twelve), to whom Ajón spoke for about ten minutes, explaining the book and its title. After the launch, Ajón also had the satisfaction of being approached by about fifteen readers asking for their books to be signed, most of whom had attended because they had liked his previous books – including one Frenchman who had long admired his work since reading a story in an anthology years ago. Clearly, therefore, Ajón's fame was greater than he had imagined, and publicity since publication (for the Feria, on the ICL website, through two television interviews and one radio announcement) ensured that more Cubans became aware of the novel's existence. Indeed, it sold out at both the Feria (launch and bookshop) and the sub-site in the Pabellón Cuba in the centre of Vedado; Ajón, as author, received sixty copies, ten free of charge and the others at cost price, as is normal. The Feria launch, however, was the only one in February or March, with the novel not being part of the subsequent *caravana* (literally, 'caravan', i.e. the Feria during its provincial tour), to the provinces. More launches were due to take place, but, with the Feria occupying everyone's attention, no plans were being made by the end of March 2011.

The final stage of the book's trajectory is, of course, reader reception. In all, nine readers' opinions were canvassed by various means. While a minority (usually older readers) felt that the novel's focus on the 'dark' side was inappropriate, exaggerated or inaccurate (one even suspecting the author of playing to stereotypical tastes), most responded positively to the book's evident humour; not only was this the most common trait identified, but even those more critical of its content found it a saving grace, responding especially well to the many moments where familiar episodes of normal daily life in Cuba are lengthily, but humorously, described. Surprisingly (considering the author's frequent use of unusual and even invented vocabulary, and his evident erudition), most readers found it easy to read, and everyone praised its acute awareness of slang, some even finding the juxtaposition of the highest linguistic register and the lowest patois to be especially attractive.

Conclusion

What, then, to make of this trajectory? Is it further evidence of an anachronistic and inefficient system which persists in subsidising book production in the face of the global trends measuring and shaping literary demand and supply? Is it further evidence of blindness to the realities of global cultural change, where printed literature is increasingly marginal to virtual spaces and more seemingly relevant mass cultural practices? Is it further evidence of the political forces underpinning the publishing of all literature in Cuba? Is it evidence, as is also often argued, that the Cuban system has created a haven of literary mediocrity for those who decide to support it, where literary quality is relegated to a secondary position behind political expediency? Was the novel in question too critical, too satirical, too ambiguous, at a fragile moment (the transition from Fidel to Raúl) when the system seemed vulnerable?

As always in Cuba, the picture is complex. Despite the delays and obstacles, this book clearly went through a rigorous process of checks and balances which indicated the importance of collective decisions – prize juries, committees, anonymous readers – rather than the tastes of individual gatekeepers. However, those processes were also prone to significant levels of flexibility, reflexivity and responsiveness, underpinned as always by the fragile and unpredictable economic backdrop, and by political considerations and forces, national and international. Indeed, this book's story illustrates vividly the complex negotiations and prioritisations that often come into play, with many different factors delaying the publication.

While it would be an exaggeration to claim that this trajectory is representative of the Cuban publishing environment, it does allow us to test the perspectives on Cuban literary culture outlined earlier in this study: while the post-2000 progress and expansion are impressive, the story of one book, a decade later, illustrates poignantly some important questions hitherto neglected in studies of Cuban literature.

Firstly, it confirms the death of the era of economic stability of the 1970s and 1980s, enabling long-term planning and large-scale editions. Secondly, it shows that the old complexity of pressures operating inside Cuba has been compounded by a whole new set of pressures, many unimaginable in the 'golden age' of Cuban publishing. Thirdly, however, it suggests that the traditional patterns whereby an underdeveloped country of only eleven million people could create a remarkably high number of published writers, responding to a highly literate and culture-hungry public, have not disappeared; indeed, those patterns may have become even more complex in the prevailing contradictions.

Hence, it also seems to show that, for all the often surprising similarities between the processes and decision-making motives in Cuba and in the outside (more evidently commercialised) world, literary culture in Cuba – the context for Ajón's book – remains unusual, underpinned still by the centrality of 'the book' in many Cubans' lives, as a space linking the potentially enclosed and rarified cultural elite (or 'vanguard') with the cultural consumers, at an individual level.

Beyond this, of course, the context in which the protagonist novel of this case study operated also suggests that the changes to Cuban publishing since 2000 have clearly enabled literary culture in Cuba to survive, if not flourish, the reorientation (towards the provincial and the local) creating space for writers and continuing to produce literature for readers, albeit at a much reduced level, but substituting variety for quantity. Equally, that context (and especially the priority given here to the Feria) seems to suggest that, by redirecting literary culture towards the reader (and thus the agents mediating the process), a sense of the diverse functions of literature may have been reinvigorated. In other words, by again reinscribing literary culture within a social project and within a hierarchy of value that is inclusive but that treads an ever-changing line between aesthetic, political, social and ideological concerns, it may be that Cuban literary culture is at its most complex, inclusive and diverse since 1959. Indeed, it suggests that, at a time of new strategies of economic prioritisation and rationalisation, the story of Ajón's book reminds us that literature in Cuba continues to be both a symbolic and a material object, demanding for its public existence the intervention of a range of agents along the individual–collective spectrum.

Notes

1 All details and quotations in the following section come from interviews with Ajón León.

8

The Feria Internacional del Libro de La Habana[1]

When analysing the complex nature of the evolving Cuban valorisation of literature, books and reading, the annual Feria offers a rich seam of evidence. In its post-2000 manifestations it offers, in purpose, scale, implications and impact, a repository of evidence of all that this study has argued. For, after 2000, the Feria was given new purpose and impetus, to develop as an event combining the commercial, publisher-focused nature of the conventional book fair with the author-focused literary festival, while simultaneously focusing more on the reader and the book (as an object to be valued), rather than on the writer and the publisher, and becoming a social phenomenon with the status of a national *fiesta* (being commonly referred to as a *festival de la cultura*, or festival of culture), with a range of political, cultural and social purposes.

Although the decision to mount a regular Feria began in the early 1980s, Havana was not unfamiliar with book fairs and literary festivals; given the emphasis on reading and literature, even before 1959, this was logical. Indeed, May 1937 saw a seven-day event, by the Punta fort (at the juncture of the Malecón and the Paseo de Martí, now the Prado), created by two historians in the newly established Oficina del Historiador de la Ciudad de La Habana (Office of the Havana City Historian) – the Historian himself, Emilio Roig de Leuchsenring, and José Luciano Franco. Organised with Havana's major bookshops (all of them with stalls), it also received support from the Education Ministry's Dirección de Cultura, the Jewish community, *Carteles* magazine and one publisher, Editorial Trópico. Although inaugurated by the mayor and the well-known writer Alfonso Hernández Catá, and closed by José María Chacón (then Director de Cultura), the event was ignored by the press, apart from *El País*, which lamented the implications of the public's lack of interest for Havana's claim to be cultured (Perdomo, 1996: 73).

In 1959, however, Carpentier, as President of the Imprenta Nacional, resurrected the idea, launching the Festival del Libro y la Lectura (Festival of the Book and Reading) with the slogan *Diez por el precio de uno* ('ten for the price of one'), as part of a strategy to bring reading within the reach of ordinary Cubans (*Boletín Cubarte*, 2009). Then, in 1961, explicitly supporting the Literacy Campaign, the ad hoc local government of Marianao *municipio* organised, through its Instituto de Cultura, a Primer Festival del Libro Revolucionario (first revolutionary book festival), in Almendares Park. Although a small event (almost certainly repeated in other *municipios*), this had several implications, particularly the explicit recognition of a necessary revolutionary commitment to the book (including the idea that the book itself could be part of a revolution), and the implicit recognition of the Revolution's need to go beyond reading ability and to encourage active reading of 'quality' (*Revolución*, 1961c: 3). In August 1961 (originally planned to accompany the postponed Congreso de Escritores y Artistas in the Palacio de Bellas Artes), Havana hosted a long Feria-Exposición de Libros, to allow readers and writers to meet each other, selling 5,000 books cheaply (provided by local bookshops and private collections, as a collective endeavour for the Revolution) and focusing on Cuban authors, new and old (*Revolución*, 1961d: 2). Finally, in July 1966, a ten-day Primer Gran Feria Nacional del Libro was held at the top of the Rampa, which, in length and scope, seems to have been an early prototype for the eventual post-2000 Feria, with over 250,000 books sold, and subsequent plans to take it out to the provinces, although with no clear plans about how much to take or precisely where to go (*Granma*, 1966: 6). However, this prototype was not followed, subsequent years instead seeing a series of one-off initiatives.

Then, in 1982, a regular Feria began its new, biennial, life, perhaps celebrating Havana's new prestige, following UNESCO's 1981 declaration of Habana Vieja as a World Heritage Site and the Cuban government's 1978 declaration of Habana Vieja as a Monumento Nacional. Certainly, the government gave the City Historian, Eusebio Leal Spengler, responsibility for restoration, generating public discussion of the city's condition and a growing call for a national effort to halt further deterioration (*Revolución y Cultura*, 1981).

The 1982 event was held in the Palacio de Bellas Artes, with a few Latin American visitors; in 1984, it moved to the Habana Libre Hotel and the nearby new show-space on the Rampa, the Pabellón Cuba; this time twenty-five countries were represented, with a new tradition in the awarding of the *Premio Nacional de Literatura* at the event itself. In 1986, with forty-four countries taking part and with a special focus on children's literature, it again moved, to the vast Palacio de las Convenciones, in Cubanacán in Havana's western outskirts, this being repeated in 1988. Notwithstanding economic problems, the 1990 Feria (by now in the large Pabexpo pavillion, also in Cubanacán) still had thirty-eight countries represented, although no Feria was held in 1992; however, the 1994 Feria saw similar numbers. Despite their smaller scale (in comparison with the later Ferias), these events were subsequently viewed with affection among the *literatos*, as small, un-massified and cosier events, selling Cuban books at affordable prices and more like a literary festival than a commercial fair [DE].

However, as the Special Period brought new commercial imperatives, the 1996 Feria took a new direction. Despite a modest scale (with only twenty-seven countries represented, and only 60,000 visitors over the six days, and 150 new titles), it had a clear commercial focus, outlined by the ICL President Omar González who, while talking of its cultural purpose and commitment to solidarity, specified the intention to make the Feria into a space to promote commercial relationships between small and medium enterprises in Cuban publishing and the 'grandes productores y exhibidores de libros' ('large book publishers and exhibitors'), thus emphasising the new international scope and commercial aims ('Una feria diferente', 1996: 73). Indeed, income reached an estimated $370,000 MN, thereby covering its costs. This new commercial imperative was also seen in plans to start collaboration with the Frankfurt and Guadalajara fairs and UNESCO, indicating the importance of relationships with the global book industry and the Feria organisers' conventional approach ('Una feria diferente', 1996: 73).

1998 saw a similar sized event, but with an innovation imported from Guadalajara: the naming of a *país de honor* – Mexico (Sánchez Espinosa, 2000: 9). The 2000 Feria seemed unchanged superficially, with thirty countries represented and around 300,000 books sold,[2] and, as with all post-1993 predecessors, with many books sold in dollars rather than Cuban pesos, confirming its outward-looking commercial focus and making it difficult for cash-strapped Cubans to participate effectively. However, three changes that became permanent were introduced then: it was relocated to the imposing Fortaleza de La Cabaña, the vast fort lining the eastern banks of the entrance to Havana Bay; a new permanent Martí-inspired slogan was created, *Leer es crecer* (to read is to grow); and it was decided to dedicate each event to a particular Cuban writer (Cintio Vitier, in this case).

Later that year, the decision was taken to launch a new Feria, changing its purpose, nature and scale. Henceforth, it would be a ten-day annual event, focused nationally rather than internationally, and with long-term plans to repeat aspects of the Havana event in an increasing number of towns and cities in the provinces, i.e. making the event national in its scope and its focus [DGS].

The sudden change in scale and ambition for a hitherto conventional book fair raises immediate questions about motives. As always in Cuba, there was no single explanation but, rather, a coincidence of factors, mostly arising from, or associated with, the simultaneous *Batalla de Ideas*. One underlying reason was, as already seen, the growing awareness of the damage to reading wreaked by the crisis and the reforms of the 1990s, the latter allowing the commercialisation of culture at home and abroad, benefiting some writers (who were able to publish and earn abroad) but leaving others behind, given literature's comparative inability to take advantage of the new freedom, unlike music or the visual arts. Since writers were increasingly driven to write for an overseas audience (responding to that market's tastes and preconceived expectations of Cuban literature), there was a risk of a gap between them and a potential Cuban reading public, unable to buy their work or to respond to their concerns. Meanwhile, of course, the shortages of the 1990s had reduced the availability of paper (and thus of books), of time for reading and of the means to travel to buy books [DGS], all of these raising growing concerns about the effects on reading.

Hence the idea of a larger, more nationally focused and more reader-focused, Feria responded to those concerns: while parallel reading programmes addressed the wider concern about reading habits, it was felt that attracting large numbers of readers and then taking the event out nationwide could go far in bridging whatever gap had developed [DGS; MR]. Furthermore, if the event focused on the provision and availability of children's literature, it could also start addressing the problem of youth alienation from reading [MR], and focusing on the provinces was part of the *Batalla*'s debt to the early Revolution, when the countryside had been prioritised to reject the traditional Third World focus on, and centripetal tendencies towards, the capital.

Certainly, although some writers remained nostalgic about the 'old' Feria, the new site alone made a powerful statement about the new importance of books and reading: not only was it imposing – the size of a small village and christened by Fidel Castro *la fortaleza de los libros* (the fortress of books) [FLJ] – but it was also much more accessible than the previous sites in the western outskirts, and even the Cabaña's slightly ruined and ramshackle buildings made a statement about the Revolution's characteristic ad hoc ethos [HC].

From this new base, the Feria developed, although the 2000 event had already indicated the new direction: eighteen cities and towns had been visited by some element of the Havana Feria, and the work of 612 Cuban writers was exhibited, confirming both the provincialisation imperative and the new focus on Cuban authors and Cuban readers (Sánchez Espinosa, 2000: 9). However, the significant thing about that event was not its scale but its ambition: a book distribution infrastructure weakened by a decade of the Special Period had the task of distributing in one month more books than had been distributed for the whole of the 1992–2000 period (Sánchez Espinosa, 2000: 10).

Thereafter, from 2001, the systematic expansion began, although only 200,000 attended the Feria in Havana itself, with 400,000 books being sold. In 2002, provincialisation accelerated, with seventeen places again being visited (over thirty-four days), but with fewer (twenty-seven) publishers, reflecting the Cuban focus rather than any international dimension (although with France as the *país de honor*). One version recounts Fidel Castro's influence in determining the provincial locations, when he unexpectedly decided to include Sagua la Grande, stimulating a panicky drive to gather sufficient materials and writers for that place [FLJ].

As an indication of the changed scale, 2002 saw 2,222,440 visitors to all iterations of the Feria, book sales reaching 2,419,731; clearly a completely new level of operation (and conception) had begun. 2003 continued the pattern, with 3,569,356 visitors and 2,911,996 book sales, with more towns and cities being included. Thereafter the pattern was multiplied steadily, in scale and scope: in 2004, 34 places were visited outside Havana, attracting 3,761,001 people and selling 3,154,706 books; in 2005, again in thirty-four places, attendance rose to 4,054,703, with sales also rising marginally to 4,800,000. The relevant figures for the following years confirmed this rising gradient: in 2006 (again 34 places), as many as 5,637,456 participants but sales falling to 3,104,393; in 2007, in thirty-nine places, 5,288,000 attendance and 5,193,677 sales, with the presence of only eighty-two (mostly Cuban) publishers (ICL, 2009).

Meanwhile, another pattern was being developed: having long

organised mass transport to ferry *habaneros* (residents of Havana) to the Cabaña, the Feria was now also taken out to the *habaneros*, extending its activities to other sites within the capital, including the Agricultural Fair south of the city and the Pabellón-Cuba exhibition space on the Rampa, and with books available in bookshops in different Havana *municipios* for those unable to travel. In 2011, this became even more evident, fully using the usual Vedado cultural centres, throughout, to host Feria-related book launches and discussions.

2008, however, had seen the start of a noticeable reduction in scale, responding to the economic effects of that year's three devastating hurricanes and the onset of the world financial crisis. Therefore numbers fell slightly, with 4,234,298 visitors and 4,389,643 sales, although thirty-five places all over Cuba were still visited. Indeed, this reduction initially only affected Havana (in terms of numbers of stalls and books), since a conscious effort was made, following Hurricane Ike, to pay attention to the provinces, as though, when little else was available to assuage the disaster's effects, there was a traditional reliance on the symbolic value of a literary festival. Hence, although the Feria's provincial iterations only lasted sixteen days, these were followed by a two-month drive to bring *miniferias* to all of Cuba's remaining 142 *municipios*, with special emphasis on those most affected by the hurricanes and those areas covered by the Plan Turquino and the Festival del Libro en la Montaña.

There was a similarly reduced operation in 2009, when only seventeen places were visited by the *caravana*, leading to significantly reduced attendance figures (2,012,264) and sales (2,594,178). The 2010 Feria still reached all provincial capitals and two other towns, aiming to sell five million books, including 250 new offerings and with special emphasis on the new edition of Martí's *Obras Completas*, printed unusually in 15,000 copies; however, actual figures were 2,383,245 books sold to 2,481,634 visitors. It is perhaps worth noting that the figures for Havana sales (946,852 in the Cabaña, the city's bookshops and other sites) are partly explained by a new (and popular) departure: the decision to place new books in Havana's bookshops one week before the Feria, meaning that 250–300 titles had already appeared before the main event, with total pre-event sales (150,000) equalling the 2000 figure [FLJ]. The 2011 event followed the same pattern of limited provincialisation, again explained generally as reflecting the acute economic crisis but also raising the possibility that a decision to downscale that key aspect more permanently might have been taken, even if only de facto.

Therefore, given the Feria's enhanced and expanded purpose, what does each Feria actually look like? How does it operate and what does it feel like for its participants?[3] Organisationally, each event comes under the auspices of the ICL's commercial arm, the Cámara del Libro (literally, 'chamber of the book'), which focuses on the external projection of Cuba's publishing industry and is responsible for each year's Feria, communicating with overseas publishers and arranging the Feria's different sites [JLM]. Nonetheless, despite this commercial focus and the attention paid by the Cámara to 'the economy of the book', it is careful not to be controlled by this value category, given the Feria's (and the book's) essentially social and political function.

The Feria, of course, consists of two elements: the (currently) ten-day Havana event, in the La Cabaña fortress and the two-to-three weeks of different provincial versions. Although some speculated that the special 2008 *miniferias* might eventually become a more permanent feature, the evidence from subsequent years points to them being a one-off experiment, a temporary part of local recovery operations.

The Havana event is the most impressive in size, scope and length. While its location (on the far side of the Bay from most *habaneros*) would normally present challenges for participants, involving long bus journeys, this has always been obviated by the daily fleet of free buses from different *municipios*. Moreover, for those unable or unwilling to travel (although many workplaces and schools arrange for their workers or pupils to be transported once during each Feria), all seventeen Havana bookshops (one in each *municipio* and others in the city centre) now house smaller versions of the event, and the Pabellón Cuba has an intermediate version for the whole period, including second-hand bookstalls (in Cuban pesos), high-priority shops for children's books and some sort of musical or dance performance.

The Cabaña event is clearly the focal point of efforts, organisation and investment, on a scale and with an efficiency usually only evident when the authorities mobilise voluntary labour for some one-off campaign. While the Feria may have been born out of the Elián González rallies, and while, until 2009, it was associated with the UJC (a mainstay of the *Batalla*), there is no evidence that it relies heavily on voluntary labour and mobilisation; instead the Feria's unusual efficiency (in delivering sufficient bulk transport, replenished supplies of fast food throughout, and other infrastructure for such a mass-focused event over ten days) seems to result from a mixture of experience and meticulous planning, and high levels of commitment from ICL workers and leaders. The

Feria's opening (Thursday or Friday) usually takes place either in Habana Vieja – typically in the city's historic centre, of the Plaza de Armas (by the pre-2011 ICL headquarters) – or in the Cabaña's own Plaza de Armas – and usually involves the President, the Minister of Culture, ICL luminaries and a leading representative of that year's *país de honor* (in 2006, this was Venezuela's Hugo Chávez, but when Russia (2010) and the ALBA countries (2011) enjoyed the accolade, lower-level emissaries attended.

What follows (from the Friday or Saturday) is the public event, buses bringing thousands over the first weekend; in the early stages of the 'new' Feria, only about 70,000–80,000 visitors would attend during the weekend, until the organisers decided to provide this transport [FLJ]. Typically, these buses start to bring visitors an hour before the gates open (at 10 am), leading to long queues, taking over an hour to enter; hence some will have waited for an hour and a half before entering the castle walls. From 2010 this was recognised by the organisers' provision of fast-food outlets outside the walls, catering for the waiting visitors. In all, some 5,000 attend the first morning. The weekends, logically, see peak attendance, weekdays being more peopled by workplace-organised outings and school visits. The entrance fee was, for some time, only two Cuban pesos per person (children entering free of charge), rising to three in 2010, although non-Cubans must pay around four CUC, over thirty times the cost for Cubans.

What they find are essentially three separate but closely linked events. Firstly, they find a standard book fair, with publishers' stalls spread throughout the larger buildings; these are now almost all Cuban, plus representatives of politically sympathetic foreign publishers. As all these books are sold in Cuban pesos, this represents an ideal opportunity for people to browse (somewhat frenetically at times, especially at the weekends), and to acquire large numbers of books, especially for their children.

Secondly, there is a parallel literary festival, mainly based on Cuban writers, who are typically present and available to be met, interviewed and seen at each day's full eight-hour programme. This consists of book launches (with the usual speeches, and opportunity to acquire signed copies of the book), discussions and round tables, prize presentations (the Feria usually hosting a well-attended event to award the national prizes for literary genres, social science, *crítica* and publishing), and poetry readings; the latter is occasionally held in the *Patio de la poesía*, between one entrance gate and the main buildings, in full view of, and with easy access for, the public. It is essentially this second 'event' which hosts the special celebrations of each Feria's dedicated writer; these have increasingly been writers who were victims of marginalisation in 1971–85, their selection seemingly becoming a formal apology for past treatment and adding another interesting purpose to the Feria.

The third 'event' is constituted by the continual entertainment created by the prevailing fairground atmosphere and driven by musical performances, face-painting, caricatures or similar stalls, and the mass picnic which inevitably materialises around lunchtime; until 2010, this was accompanied by food and drink outlets within the Cabaña, but this aspect then disappeared, replaced by more extramural outlets adjacent to the entrance queues and increased provision in the moat between the outer and inner walls – perhaps acknowledging writers' complaints that the 'fairground' dimension demeans the event's cultural nature. Despite (or perhaps because of) this entertainment, however, it is clear that what attracts the thousands is not the 'fun of the fair' but the festival atmosphere which is anticipated annually and to which large numbers go without evident peer pressure. Hence, each year thousands are prepared to stand for hours in long slow queues for certain bookshops; these tend to be those selling cheap editions or giving books away free, on behalf of the *país de honor*, but are more typically those selling children's books, for it is generally agreed that one prime motivation for attendance is the unusual opportunity to buy children's books, not so easily available at other times and in other places [MSM].

This patience raises all manner of questions about people's motives or tolerance. Although queuing for hours is all too familiar for most Cubans, having long been a basic part of daily life, the interesting question is why Cubans should be prepared to do this for books, going to the heart of the question of value which this whole study has highlighted. For it would seem that, each year and in each provincial location, Cubans queue, with a mixture of ingrained patience and evident eagerness, for the much-valued opportunity to acquire books – either specific books which they actively seek (because of the author in question or the media's advertising, or because they are actively interested in literature in general) or books per se. For the Feria seems to be demonstrable proof of the value which Cubans consensually accord to 'the book', where possession (and perhaps subsequent display) of a book, and preferably of many books, is valued, apart from any pleasure, benefit or education derived from it. It would seem, in fact, that this somewhat acquisitive approach to books is less about material possessions or commodities to be sold (although the Special Period did see an increase in the re-sale of recently purchased new books) than about demonstrating a visible sign of culture. One might go further, indeed, for it seems likely that such possession, and even such involvement in a mass literary festival, is linked in some way with the visitor's periodic need to register a visible belonging to the wider, national community. Hence, it seems very likely that the Feria is seen subconsciously as a cultural equivalent of the regular 'signing-up' implied by mass participation in more openly politicised events, such as each year's May Day or 26 July rally, or national demonstrations against specific US actions. In fact, since attendance at those latter events inevitably involves some peer pressure and institutional encouragement (although not sufficiently to explain all, or perhaps even most, of the scale of popular involvement, especially as large numbers of Cubans evidently stay away from them, with impunity), the attendance at, and patience shown during, each year's Feria would suggest that this is an even more significant, and willing, registering of belonging. Given that those attending also include several groups or pairs of young people who do not necessarily purchase books but who simply participate in what they see as a regular, and perhaps ritual, social event, this purpose may well be more significant than it seems.

In Havana, at least, therefore, we have some idea of the readers' motivation for repeated participation, confirmed by informal conversations. For some, of course, and certainly for the majority of the writers, it is the 'literary festival' event of the Feria which most attracts them and gives the event meaning. While a programme of events takes place daily, they are usually more prominent on weekdays, with public attendance much lower, shifting the focus away from the reader to the writer. Certainly, while the higher-profile events (prize-givings or addresses by renowned writers) take place when there is a larger public, weekdays generally see the less 'ritual' proceedings and the more genuinely intellectual discussions; although such Feria events are little different from the run-of-the-mill discussions or launches at any Havana cultural centre (many Feria book-launches actually reiterate earlier launches of the same book), there is a clear prestige attached to engaging publicly in such Feria gatherings. Moreover, this extends to non-literary writers too, such as critics, social scientists, journalists or historians; for, just as the Feria's focus on the book is largely through the deeper focus on the reader, so too is the focus on writing as much on the act of (any) writing as on the final written product or the writer.

That said, however, most writers, while perhaps occasionally paying lip-service to the importance of the Feria (and even maybe regarding their participation as a chore), do welcome the annual event, for a variety of reasons. Most see it as a unique opportunity to meet two classes of people: non-Cuban writers visiting especially for the event (to whom most Cubans do not have easy or affordable access [MR]), and the reading public, beyond those aficionados who frequent book launches and literary events; indeed some argue that it gives them the only opportunity for such an encounter, allowing some necessary feedback and perhaps bridging the potential gap between writer and reader [SH; GFL; HC]. Certainly all of those interviewed from 2006 tended to emphasise the value of such feedback, and welcomed the interaction between writers and readers. In this context, therefore, what seems to be important is the general recognition that the numbers attending, and the carnival atmosphere, make for a unique space for such interaction, without which they might feel marginal and readers might feel isolated from the literary community, other than reading in the privacy of their homes. In other words, all seem to value the event as a collective social gathering in which two sets of individuals (writer and reader) can find common ground, a common language and a common purpose: the book. There seems little doubt that, even if feeling obliged to participate, Cuban writers mostly value the event as providing something which is otherwise missing, at least in terms of scale and prestige. This also seems to apply to the opportunity which the *caravana* stage brings, both to meet and exchange views with otherwise unknown provincial writers and to 'perform' out in the 'sticks', among a public which might never have seen the writers whose work they have read.

Of course, ideology apart, one aim of the Feria (and also of all the subsequent book events) is to sell as many books as possible, not least to cover the ICL costs. Moreover, many have complained that, in order to ensure this, books have been held back from publication and even that some Havana bookshops have been closed for a week beforehand [MDO]. In fact, in 2011, this potential complaint was obviated by the decision to sell Feria-launched books in normal bookshops for several weeks before the event. However, this imperative comes partly because the political emphasis on the Feria leads to overproduction and then to the need to sell as much as possible to meet that figure in sales; certainly, however successful the Feria sales, it generally manages to sell only about half of the eight million or so books produced for the event [FLJ]. By 2011, this had changed. This is why each year's Feria is followed by a succession of smaller book-selling events, most notably the *Noche de los libros* (in Havana every September, complete with Feria-like entertainments and food-stalls) and similar events in several other provincial cities, all selling books at reduced prices. A similar enterprise, in 2009, was the celebration of the fiftieth anniversary of Carpentier's 1959 Festival del Libro y la Lectura, occupying all the same places as the original event in Centro Habana, Marianao and Habana Vieja, and selling over a thousand titles and 50,000 books (*Boletín Cubarte*, 2009).

What is also clear is that the Havana event becomes an opportunity for the cultural authorities to highlight other cultural forms and launch other initiatives, because public and media attention is so focussed on culture and books. Each year's event, for example, is accompanied by a daily programme of concerts, art exhibitions and films in the city; while many of these supposedly parallel programmes simply take advantage of the Feria to highlight otherwise routine events, the Feria does provide a cue for ICAIC, music venues and galleries to increase their programmes, using the cultural emphasis during the Feria. Equally, the 2010 event was immediately followed by a high-profile conference on anti-colonial thought and access to the book, in the AHS centre of the Pabellón Cuba, part of the general anti-globalisation campaign in Latin America of which Cuba was an enthusiastic participant. One interesting outcome of all this came in 2008 when international recognition of the Feria was accorded by the nomination of Havana as UNESCO World Book Capital for 2011, a title created in 1996 by UNESCO, as part of its annual International Book Day initiatives.

However, even statistically, it is the Feria's provincial iterations which are the real success story. What, then, do these look like, and how do they compare with the Havana event? Firstly, they are predictably much smaller; even the Santiago event (large though it is, in comparison with those in other cities) is a fraction of the parent event, although still filling the Palacio de las Convenciones and the adjacent park by the Plaza de la Revolución. They are also shorter, lasting three days at the most, and one or two days in some places. The *caravana* of dignitaries and writers, however, ensures that most major places see a significant representation of the Havana event, in terms of prestige, fame or political importance. In 2010, for example, the Minister, Abel Prieto, Miguel Barnet (UNEAC president), the leading poet Nancy Morejón and two of the foreign guests of honour constituted the delegation sent to Pinar del Río, clearly indicating a high level of official recognition of this particular sub-event. Moreover, 200,000 copies of 450 new books were displayed at the Pinar event, making it far from a small-scale side-show. In Cienfuegos, the celebrations included two of that year's dedicated writers and a few other Havana-based writers, while the Matanzas event (held appropriately in the Plaza de la Vigía, next to Ediciones Vigía), was addressed by the national Translation Prizewinner. However, this smaller affair (in comparison with Santiago and Pinar's more prestigious events) gave Matanzas a sense of second-rank importance, shared with Sancti Spíritus, which largely hosted local writers, although still selling 300 titles from ten outlets in the city.

Moreover, at least until the post-2009 downscaling, the provincialisation process has dramatically changed, or at least confirmed, the 'new' Feria's conception and purpose, not least in shifting the role of actor, from the centre (national and prestigious writers, publishers and critics) to the locality – thereby reaffirming the changed emphasis of the Revolution in the 1990s. Hence, it is left to the CPLL of each locality's Feria to agree with local writers, bookshops and the local governing bodies (OPP and Party) the details of maintenance, supply, sales and budget, rather than these things (as might have been true in the 1970s) being determined and imposed centrally [FLJ]. The process has, of course, also significantly changed the perspectives of many of those 'central' actors: some writers have commented on their delight in seeing copies of their work in small relatively isolated places [MR], while editors have observed that the experience of this diffusion has raised their national profile as a group [DGS]. The effect on the locality can only be imagined, since no serious sustained qualitative research has yet been carried out into this critical aspect.

In all of this positive coverage of what is unquestionably a remarkable phenomenon, some Cuban writers are clearly less enthusiastic about the event's scale, central importance and 'unseemly' razzamatazz, nostalgic for the former Habana Vieja event, when books were the main focus [JLM1]; while the organisers and authorities might extol the virtues of massification, some view it less positively, seeing the event as too large, with little time to relax. Another complaint (related to the reputed paucity of books in the build-up to each Feria) is that the Feria becomes the focal point of all literary activity, marginalising other events in the year. Indeed, it is clear that ICL managers are all too aware of the dangers of this, and talk of the need to seek a proper balance [DGS].

Where, then, does all of this fit into this study's central argument? Firstly, what has become clear is that the Feria's focus is not solely on the need for everyone to read more (the original motivation which helped spur the 'new' Feria) but rather on the intrinsic value of the book, and of the act and process of reading itself. One aspect of the importance resulting from this valuation refers to the rising price of books since 1991, compared with the universally acclaimed low-price books of the 1960s; for the common complaint that book prices are now inaccessible for most Cubans is echoed by readers and writers alike, the latter especially fearing the effect on declining reading habits, when a reader may have to choose between 'una libra de carne de puerco o un libro' ('a pound of pork or a book') and when Morejón's books are being sold in the bus terminal for fifty Cuban pesos each [HC]. Hence, it is clear that the Feria's emphasis on children is not only widely welcomed and even deemed essential, but also promises to create long-term habits of reading that might resurrect the 'heroic' early days of the Revolution [MHM].

What this means, therefore, is that the Feria is especially valued and seen as necessary both for avid readers to catch up and for realising the aim of creating an actively reading public, constituting a moment when people come into contact with so many books at one time that the collective and ambient experience awakens their curiosity and interest. Indeed, the collectivity of the experience is clearly fundamental to its impact; although it would be easier to distribute books to local bookshops, thereby avoiding the congestion, hassle and cost of transporting large numbers of people to the Cabaña, the act and process of gathering thousands together over several days may be anti-commercial [FLJ], but is essentially a moment to collectively value the book. It is in essence, as repeated by so many writers interviewed, 'Más que una feria de carácter cultural, es una feria de carácter popular y una suerte de fiesta' [VLL] ('more than a fair of the cultural kind, it is a popular kind of fair and a kind of party'), and, beyond that, of course, a national festival, as Cuba's biggest cultural event [EHL], a 'gran fiesta' [JLM1] ('big party').

If this is the writers' view, what role does the Feria, and perhaps implicitly the book, play in the lives of ordinary *habaneros*? This is an especially pertinent question when, every afternoon, crowds of people pour out of buses and make their way slowly up the hill to the castle gates, or throng the bridges into the castle; as this crowd invariably includes pairs and groups of young Cubans, not evidently – unlike the daily groups of schoolchildren – obliged to attend, one asks: what does it hold for them? This is even more pertinent when one sees some of those same young Cubans leaving the Feria later without having bought books; while one might marvel at the numbers leaving who *have* bought books, one's curiosity is also aroused by those other young Cubans who evidently have *not* bought anything, except perhaps for food or drink during the day. Since one can speculate that, in either the UK or the United States, it would be highly unlikely for such adolescents or young adults to go in groups or pairs to a book fair or literary festival, unless there were something else to attract them, what brings these young Cubans, otherwise so obviously attracted by the fashions of globalisation, to an event where the book is central to its existence but where they do not end up buying books?

In the absence of a scientific survey of such participants, some tentative conclusions might be drawn. The most obvious is perhaps that, for such people, books are simply not a 'problem' as they might be for some US or British youth. For, although experts in both countries, but also in Cuba since the mid-1990s, have long expressed concern about declining reading habits and a growing lack of youth interest in reading, let alone reading literary works, those British youngsters who do not generally read for pleasure would simply not be seen anywhere near a book-focused event; it would hold no interest for them, and there might even be an antipathy (perhaps class-based) against being associated with literature and reading. In Cuba, however, the evidence suggests that this is less so, and even that the book has become so integral a part of Cubans' daily lives – leaving aside the question of their values – that many young Cubans simply do not see it as a problem in the same way. One might draw a parallel with British youth, on a Saturday, choosing to go into the city centre and 'hang about' in a shopping centre with others, without necessarily buying anything, but simply seeing it as a place to gather and 'be themselves', and engage in some social bonding.

Of course, if that is true, then some Cuban writers' complaints that the Feria has become so massified and so 'commercialised' (with food stalls and entertainments) that it is no longer a book fair as they used to know it, may well be right. Yet is that in itself a problem? Is not the decision to massify (and then to supply the provisions and other attractions to draw people in and sustain interest and participation) doing something other than providing the writing community with a large-scale but essentially restricted space to 'be themselves'? Is it not creating an even larger space to allow readers, and even non-readers, to 'be themselves' alongside, and associated with, the writers' own spaces? If the book seemingly occupies an unremarkable and natural place in

Cubans' daily lives – so that, for some, going to the Feria to see and acquire books is seen as something that you do each year, or, equally, for others, simply going to the Feria is enough – then does this not mean that the book actually does have an unusual place which is not necessarily shared by other countries and cultures?

If that is true, then it is the extra-Havana dimension, the national process of 'provincialisation', which gives the Feria another special place in the Cuban political and cultural system. At one level, the Feria's ability to reach the furthest corners of the country has all manner of impact: integrating the most far-flung village with the capital in ways similar to the process of integration of 1961; bringing writers to the people in real and palpable ways [AGN]; creating new active readers in the *campo* (countryside) [RGZ].

Moreover, even without this nationwide dimension, the Havana event alone sees an unusual meeting of two separate cultural communities: the collective body of readers (collectivised in the event, as ritual and as celebration) and the smaller collective of the writing community, for whom – and from which – a great deal of mutual legitimacy arises. For the traditional and ingrained value accorded to the book (and its possession and appreciation) gives the readers some satisfaction and an opportunity to register their belonging to a reading (and, by Martí's standards, thus also *culto*) community, and, again echoing Martí by heart, aware that this somehow may be associated with 'freedom'. Hence, for all that the Havana Feria may seem, for many participants, to constitute little more than a massive 'state fair', accidentally associated with books, the reality is that the book is not accidental to its character, but fundamental to it. Quite simply, most participants come away from the event with some books, and those who have any antipathy towards books simply do not go. Equally, however, for the writers who participate, and (at least for a while and in small groups or at book-signings) meet the public, the Feria also helps to legitimise their place and role in that same reading community – either as 'stars' or simply as producers seeking feedback.

What this means is that the whole Havana Feria event succeeds on a number of different levels of collective identification. At the most basic level, the nature of the daily transport means that neighbours from a given *barrio* tend to attend together, travel home together and therefore share both a local and a capital-city experience. Equally, the whole event has become, as already argued here, a celebration of the capital city's emerging and revalorised identity, participation in the event thus also marking the participants as *habaneros*, sharing in a collective cultural celebration (Kapcia and Kumaraswami, 2010). Beyond that, of course, the Feria is now decidedly a national process of related events, rather than a single event, with each local manifestation in the provinces having at least the capacity to work on the same number of different levels: the *barrio*, the town, the region, and so on.

This brings us back to the issues addressed in the Revolution's early days, when both the '*Lunes* pole' and the 'radical pole', each in their different ways, conceived of cultural revolution as raising the cultural levels and aspirations of 'the people'; the former saw it in terms of giving Cubans the ability and the opportunity to gain access to the best of world literature (an ambition later matched by *piratería*), while the latter, although often sharing that same ambition – making that campaign a consensual phenomenon in an otherwise contested environment – might have tended to see the issue as making people's lives more rounded and fulfilling, and making them more complete and wholehearted citizens of the new society, associated of course with the whole 'cultural democratisation' drive. However, one of the things which the 'new' Feria may be demonstrating is that in Cuba 'cultural revolution' has been about neither of those two purposes alone, but about much more. For it is clear that, by combining the atmosphere and purpose of a book fair and a literary festival, and also a 'state fair' or city festival, all within a context where the book has long been valued as offering something special, and where possession of, and association with, books is seen as something normal and expected, the Feria may well be offering Cubans as a whole a series of different spaces for different groups, generations, tastes and even classes. In this respect, the Feria is thus not only unusual – one might say unique – in comparison with other similar events outside Cuba, but may well be a microcosm of the whole complex world of literary culture in Cuba. For it seems to achieve something which is difficult to achieve – to socialise a cultural form and artefact (the book), which usually implies an individual relationship between consumer and artefact, in ways that are not necessarily true of other cultural forms; reading is usually an individual activity, realised in private and silence (apart from book clubs and poetry readings, which, in Britain or the United States, tend perhaps to be activities associated with the better educated and with particular social groups). However, the Feria seems to demonstrate that the book can be socialised successfully, and, indeed, that it should be – for all manner of purposes, cultural, social and political – and has been, to the extent that the book occupies a space in Cuba – and thus does enjoy a value – which is special and perhaps unique.

Notes

1 Much of this chapter includes material from the fifteen email interviews (via questionnaires) with writers.
2 Information (from the OCLL) provided by email by Jaqueline Laguardia.
3 The following paragraphs are based on fieldwork carried out in Havana and Santiago in 2006, 2008, 2009, 2010 and 2011.

Conclusion

This study started by posing the question about the apparent contradiction between the fact that literature in Cuba since 1959 seems to have been both relatively privileged (e.g. in terms of the political profile of writers, the importance of the Feria, its special exemption from the original *instructores* idea) and also seen as problematic, even being marginalised in terms of the unusual degree of scrutiny and suffering of some of those same writers.

What has emerged clearly in the course of this study is that the question is an over-simplification of a highly complex reality, but also that the apparent contradiction arises in great part from the implications of the special value which literature (and, within that, reading of literature) has always held within the equally complex phenomenon of revolutionary change since 1959. Moreover, it has also demonstrated that the only way to understand questions such as these is, firstly, to consider literature as something going beyond texts and beyond supposedly key writers to incorporate everything which surrounds literary expression and the context in which it all takes place, i.e. literary culture. Without that it makes little sense. Including what happens around and beyond the literary text or individual author, however, reveals new directions for the exploration of the highly complex relationships between literature and politics in the Cuban Revolution, and also uncovers phenomena and interpretations which can only help to nuance more conventional approaches to literature.

Many of those conventional approaches to literature (as text/writer versus state) might be tempted to consider an answer to the original question as lying in the resistance paradigm which foregrounds the inherent potential and risk posed by the act of writing as a powerful counter-narrative to political discourse. In the Cuban case, the situation of an almost universally literate population that was created by the

Literacy Campaign and subsequent educational programmes (if only functionally literate in many cases, even that hailed the radical promise of literature becoming mass culture) would thus have heightened the desire to control the production of literature. Following this line, reading, including literacy, could be potentially dangerous since it is almost always an individual act, carried out in privacy, over which the system has little control. Of course, the solution to this threat would be a fairly simple one – for the state to oversee and regulate what is published, because an unpublished text has limited power to influence on a mass scale. Indeed, most conventional approaches argue exactly that: that the state-sponsored publishing infrastructure was always able to control hearts and minds through a coherent system of bureaucratisation which would facilitate censorship and self-censorship, prompting the exile or self-exile of many writers (who, using the same logic that keeps literature and politics firmly apart, must necessarily have been the 'best' representatives of Cuban literature, autonomous and untainted by political questions or responsibilities).

What this study has revealed, however, is that, although the relationship between the fields of literature and politics has been an intense and often confrontational one, with periods of acute tension throughout the entire trajectory of the Revolution, but especially in the 1970s, Cuban literary culture is built on a set of values which goes far beyond the 'form versus content' debate, and has developed a structure which is infinitely more complex than the model of 'monolithic state versus individual writer/literary group' which surfaces in many studies. Indeed, what has emerged from the extensive interviews and fieldwork that form the basis of this study is the importance of a more sensitive understanding of the relationality of the concepts of individual and collective in the case of Cuban society and thus, by extension, of literary culture. The underlying issue of the individual–collective continuum, the theme which has run throughout the book, has allowed us to identify the collective 'glue' which positions and binds individuals in and across time and space, and across the various mechanisms and processes that make up literary culture. Even the question of writing as opposed to reading, or vice versa, can be considered along this continuum – after all, while (in theory, and according to many conventional readings of post-1959 Cuba) one can easily 'collectivise' writers (in the bureaucratic structures of UNEAC, opposing small groups or magazines, the duty to communicate with the readership, and so on), reading remains an essentially individual act but can also become more collectivised through the development of phenomena such as the Feria del Libro or the *talleres literarios*.

More importantly, we can trace the evolution of the Cuban continuum (along individual/collective and national/international axes), more or less according to the trajectory of 'periods' identified in this study, always bearing in mind that a simple mapping of cultural and political trajectories does little more than to conceptualise culture as an instrument of politics and ideology, a simplistic model which ignores the complexity of the functions and uses of both politics and culture.

The focus that emerged empirically, rather than deliberately, during the early years was clearly on writers' conditions as individuals and as a self-contained group, their need for self-expression, and the centrality of writers' voices in early cultural and political decision making was critical. The only 'collective' that made real sense to many writers at this time was the old 'cultural community' of 'Western literature', based in New York or Paris. Readers, however, did not play a significant part in conceptions of revolutionary literature until mid-1960 and the start of the initiative that would culminate in the Literacy Campaign of 1961. But the gradual development of plans for that Campaign meant a steady and then rapid shift towards the collective, with the demise of *Lunes de Revolución* and the success of the Campaign heralding a new understanding of the place of the writer and literature in the Revolution (crystallised in the *Palabras a los Intelectuales*).

Building on the position emerging in 1961, the focus shifted overwhelmingly during this period to the collective. There were, nevertheless, varying – and often competing – definitions, of what was meant by the collective: in the internal context of nation-building, did it still refer to literary group, did it refer to generation (especially 'new' generations who had come of age with the insurrection and Revolution), or to the *pueblo*?; in the external context of being part – even the centre of – an international community, did it refer to Latin America or to the socialist world? In the midst of these debates, and against the backdrop of a rapidly changing revolutionary context now overlaid by a new sense of shared struggle and siege, itself given impetus by a new focus on mobilisation and mass organisation, the collective – whatever it was – was more important than ever.

From the late 1960s onwards, the developing focus defined the collective more clearly, but still with complex and seemingly unanswerable questions which explain, if not justify, the 'grey years' of the first half of the 1970s. Externally, the Third World assumed a new – and defiant – protagonism as the collective space to which Cuba should belong, while, internally and with a still inchoate state, the relationship or equivalence between *pueblo* and state was unclear and incoherent. Within that loose structure, the role of particular collective spaces – both institutional and informal – was critical, with some following a tendency to act as regulatory and restrictive mechanisms, while others evolved as permissive and protective spaces. In literary culture, moreover, a consistent commitment to collectivisation can be seen in the drive for cultural democratisation or the emergence and consolidation of the *talleres literarios* movement. With widespread institutional reform, the state strengthened in structure and accountability and those spaces which had played a key part in the first half of the 1970s weakened. The strengthening of state structures or institutionalisation, contrary to conventional approaches to Cuban literature, in fact ushered in a period of less restriction and more provision, permission and protection, with a relatively coherent internal vision of the collective. However, what was meant by the external collective became increasingly complex: no longer did it refer predominantly to Latin America, with new links being forged with other revolutionary leaders in Central America, and a new focus on the Third World, with the emergence of Cuba's internationalist agenda, but of course, also with a sustained economic and political relationship with the Socialist Bloc which provided the stability for the development and consolidation of sociocultural life on the island, described by both internal and external commentators as a 'golden age', but, as we have discovered, also benefiting from a drive for institutionalisation that had started in the 1970s.

The events of 1989 and Cuba's subsequent economic collapse brought that 'golden age' to an abrupt halt, and meant a clear crisis for the collective: internally, any collective sense of activity was weakened and challenged by individual survivalism, sanctioned by the inability of a weak state to provide for the population; externally, Cuba was now more isolated than ever, with no exogenous solutions being apparent. After years of severe austerity, mass emigration and social fragmentation, however, it was not external models, but the local, that provided a new definition of the collective. Thus, both organically and, eventually, as a result of state policy recognising the importance of this local level of activity, the national collective was reconfigured once again and given extra impetus with the *Batalla de Ideas*. This new emphasis on the national – meaning local and nationwide, as opposed to Havana-based

Conclusion

or reliant on the international – led to a new emphasis on the collectivisation of culture and reinvigoration of revolutionary ideology which, just as in the 1960s, recognised the centrality of literacy, reading and culture to the survival and success of the Revolution.

Under the surface of this trajectory, then, the importance of spaces – as the points where negotiations between individuals and collective take place, where tensions arise and are settled – is paramount in literary culture. For these spaces – whether small groupings, the symbolic spaces of literary movements or generations, the physical space of homes, local cultural centres and national networks of institutions – have not only offered protection to individuals against the 'crushing' collective of ideological commitment and service to politics, although at times of greatest crisis, they have undoubtedly served this function. More importantly, this network of informal and formal, real and symbolic spaces, have offered the individual ways of defining their relationship to the collective, and have assumed a special function when the collective is weak, inchoate, unclear or contested. In summary, spaces are how individuals understand and belong to the collective, in ways that makes sense and matter to them, and the need for this mechanism is as acute for a renowned and established writer based in the capital as it is for a reader – or potential writer – in one of Cuba's provinces. Crucial to a more complex perspective, then, is an understanding of the fact that the spaces created by individuals and institutions serve not just as spaces for prohibition, permission or protection but also as agents or brokers which negotiate the terms of each of the transactions that make up literary culture.

How each of these agents negotiates the spaces in which literary culture functions, however, is a more complex question. Here, the usefulness of the concept of 'value' comes to the fore, as a fluid and changing hierarchy of regimes which has been established through tradition and practice. These are regimes which come into opposition at moments, hence the underlying debates around 'art vs politics' and 'art vs money', which require complex negotiations in order for transactions between the regimes to take place. Thus, just as there is a dynamic movement along the individual/collective continuum, which is crystallised at certain moments of crisis or radical change, there is also a balancing act between the multiple regimes of value, with some taking precedence over others at certain points: in a perceived or real atmosphere of intensified political or economic siege, the aesthetic value of literature is forced to a more peripheral position in the network of types of value; with a weakened state and economic context, that aesthetic value has the opportunity to become more important, with writers and readers less tied to a shared ideological vision than ever, while the economic value of literary culture assumes a new importance as literature becomes for many a means of economic survival.

By tracing how the regimes of value interact with the wider context of the Cuban Revolution at any given time – whether through following the trajectory of one book from composition to reception, the multiple ways in which the Feria del Libro is understood and experienced by different actors, or the contradictory but ultimately rich interpretations of phenomena such as the *talleres literarios* movement – a more complex perspective on the place of literature within the Revolution can be achieved. Most importantly, the evidence gathered for this project, especially from interview material, has demonstrated that it is the humanist and social (though not necessarily socialist) value of literary culture that has provided the middle ground, a dynamic but always central commonality of vision and ideology which acts as a binding force when other types of value appear incommensurate or come into conflict. From writers who were marginalised during the 1970s to younger generations of writers, from editors to *promotores culturales*, critics and booksellers, from our observation of many book presentations and fairs, a vision of literary culture as a social space and a social force has been ever-present.

The equation since 1959 of *cultura* and *libertad*, that vision of education in the broadest sense first articulated by Martí (and which aims to go far beyond any instrumentalist vision) as the key to improving life for oneself and others, became a cornerstone of social, cultural and educational policies from the first days of 'the Revolution'. It was crystallised and put into practice, with seemingly outstanding results, with the 1961 Literacy Campaign, providing proof that any definition of *cultura* must include the ability to think, feel, express, escape and re-create imaginatively. Literacy and access to literature, of course, brought in an added dimension which distinguished it from other cultural forms, since the special power of the written word lies in its ability to encourage individual thinking in seclusion, at rest, in peace, and so on, which in turn encourages the ability to imagine, as well as the ability to interact with other cultural forms. The point is that the Literacy Campaign not only persuaded leaders that they could do the impossible and change people's *conciencia* (consciousness) – for those made literate and for the literacy workers (*alfabetizadores*)

Conclusion

– helping, for example, to give an empirical basis to Che Guevara"s ideas of *conciencia*, the New Man and the potential for transformation that subjective conditions could provide – but the Campaign also made the leadership aware that the ability to read imaginatively released what romantics would call 'the soul' in every reader, which itself created a basis for sharing collective moral principles, ideals, beliefs and a sense of loyalty and belonging on which the beleaguered Revolution depended.

Therefore, the creation of a literary culture – bringing shared faith, vision, hope, ideals – provided a mechanism for commitment which was infinitely more effective than mere propaganda (also, of course, an important sociocultural component of the Revolution).

Culture within the Revolution has thus been described, and often experienced, as a means of cultural self-improvement, of educational progress, of intellectual and spiritual evolution, of belonging to social or cultural communities, of political activism, of sociocultural agency, of personal and national development, of cultural or political resistance, of psychological survival, of re-creation and of refuge from the pressures of public – or private – life. To return to our opening question, literary culture – through its ability to attract prestige, to combine the individual (writing and reading) with the collective (participation), to act as stepping stone to many other kids of cultural experience and knowledge and thus de-colonise the individual and collective self-perception – has both suffered and enjoyed its special position in revolutionary culture. What this study illustrates, then, is the centrality of literary culture to the Cuban Revolution. The study ends with the words of a prominent editor, which sum up the complexities that we have aimed to analyse here:

> Entonces, eso te va haciéndote sentir a tu eres una gotita de agua dentro del charquito. Pero que no hay charquito sin ti. Y eso, es importante que el maestro lo sienta, el bibliotecario lo sienta, el tallerista lo sienta. O sea, si todos se sienten como la gotita del charco, el charco no se seca. Y eso es importante. Hacer que la comunidad trabaje para sí, pero trabaje para sí ¿a partir de qué cosa? A partir de que cada cual esté imbuido de que lo primero por quien tiene que trabajar es por su familia, después trabaja por el edificio, después trabaja por la cuadra, después trabaja por el consejo, después trabaja por el municipio, para integrarse a la provincia y a la nación. Cuando tú logras tener claro cada uno de esos estamentos, tú estás viendo resultados. [ELR][1]

Notes

1 'And so, all of this makes you feel like a drop in the ocean. But there's no ocean without you. And it's important that the teacher feels that, that the librarian feels that, that the *taller* participant feels that. In other words, if everyone feels like a drop in the ocean, the ocean never dries up. And that's important. Making sure that the community works for itself, but works for itself on the basis of what? On the basis of the fact that every individual is imbued with the idea that first you have to work for your family, then the building you live in, then for the block you live in, then for the People's Council, then for the *municipio*, then the province and finally the nation. When you are able to understand each one of those stages, you are guaranteed results'.

List of interviewees

Antoni Kapcia and Par Kumaraswami

Acronym	Name	Date of interview
AA	Arturo Arango	17 September 2008
AAB	Alejandro Alvarez Bernal	15 September 2007
AAG	Alpidio Alonso Grau	18 September 2008
AAL	Alberto Ajón León	29 September 2009; 27 February 2010
AAM	Antón Arrufat Mrad	19 March 2007
AAT	Aurelio Alonso Tejada	18 September 2006
AF	Ambrosio Fornet	15 September 2006; 14 September 2007
AFJ	Adelaida Fernández de Juan	9 July 2008
AG	Alberto Garrandés	13 September 2007
AGN	Alberto Guerra Naranjo	12 March 2007
AP	Alfredo Prieto	3 July 2008
ASC	Angela Soto Coyán	15 September 2006
BP	Basilia Papastamatíu	19 September 2007
CL	César López	13 September 2007
DAB	Dolores Agüero Boza	15 September 2008
DE	Doribal Enríquez	20 June 2006
DGS	Daniel García Santos	3 May 2006
ECP	Emilio Comas Paret	13 June 2006
EDL	Esther Díaz Llanillo	10 March 2007
EHL	Eduardo Heras León	21 September 2006
ELR	Esteban Llorach Ramos	10 May 2006
EM	Edel Morales	18 March 2007
EPD	Enrique Pérez Díaz	19 July 2006
FLJ	Fernando León Jacomino	14 July 2008

242 List of interviewees

Acronym	Name	Date of interview
FMH	Fernando Martínez Heredia	30 April 2006
FR	Fernando Rojas	28 April 2006; 27 September 2006
GFL	Gerardo Fulleda León	11 July 2006
GP	Graziella Pogolotti	3 July 2008
GRR	Guillermo Rodríguez Rivera	14 September 2007
HA	Humberto Arenal	15 June 2006
HC	Hugo Chinea	21 June 2006
IG	Ivonne Galeano	21 September 2006
IMR	Isabel Moya Richards	2 May 2006 and 18 September 2007
ISE	Iroel Sánchez Espinosa	14 September 2005
JAP	Jorge Angel Pérez	22 September 2007
JDC	Jesús David Curbelo	4 May 2006
JEL	Jorge Enrique Lage	21 September 2006
JF	Jorge Fornet	16 March 2007
JLF	José Luis Fariñas	16 March 2007
JLM	Jacqueline Laguardia Martínez	23 September 2009
JLM1	José Luis Moreno	7 July 2006
JTS	Julio Travieso Serrano	18 September 2007
LB	Laura Betancourt	3 May 2006
LC	Luisa Campuzano	20 September 2006
LO	Lisandro Otero	12 March 2007
LPF	Leonardo Padura Fuentes	21 September 2007
LRM	Laura Ruiz Montes	8 July 2008
MB	Marilyn Bobes	26 September 2006
MBN	Miriam Bajón Navarro	18 September 2008
MBR	Mirta Botana Rodríguez	10 September 2008
MDO	María Dolores Ortiz	9 September 2008
MG	Mirta González	15 September 2008
MHM	Mayra Hernández Menéndez	14 June 2006
MMC	Marcia Medina Cruzata	26 September 2006
MMM	María Mederos Machado	17 September 2008
MMP	Margarita Mateo Palmer	13 March 2007
MR	Marta Rojas	4 May 2006
MRA	Magda Resik Aguirre	16 September 2008
MSM	Mercedes Santos Moray	1 May 2006
MTG	Marta Terry González	25 September 2006
MY	Mirta Yáñez	4 May 2006

List of interviewees

Acronym	Name	Date of interview
NA	Nara Araújo	12 March 2007
NAG	Nancy Alonso González	21 September 2007
NC	Norberto Codina	14 March 2007
NRG	Nieves Rodríguez Gómez	22 June 2006
OMP	Olga Marta Pérez	12 September 2007
PAF	Pablo Armando Fernández	25 September 2007
PJG	Pedro Juan Gutiérrez	19 September 2010
PPG	Pedro Péglez González	6 July 2006
PPL	Pablo Pacheco López	14 September 2005
RFR	Roberto Fernández Retamar	21 March 2007
RGG	Rubiel García González	25 February 2010
RGZ	Reynaldo González Zamora	6 May 2006
RLA	Rolando López del Amo	1 July 2008
RM	Roberto Manzano	19 March 2007
RMR	Reina María Rodríguez	21 September 2006
RR	Rogelio Riverón	20 September 2006
RRC	Rogelio Rodríguez Coronel	8 July 2008
RRG	Rolando Rodríguez García	18 September 2006
RV	Ricardo Viñalet	9 March 2007
RZ	Roberto Zurbano	24 September 2007
SA	Salvador Arias	11 July 2008
SC	Sergio Chaple	2 May 2006
SH	Susana Haug	4 May 2006
SO	Sonia de la O	3 October 2009
VFC	Víctor Fowler Calzada	14 March 2007
VLL	Virgilio López Lemus	11 May 2006
WGL	Waldo González López	8 May 2006
YLG	Yannis Lobaina González	14 September 2007
ZCC	Zaida Capote Cruz	17 September 2007

Meesha Nehru

Acronym	Name	Date of interview
AB	Aida Bahr	18 April 2007 (by email)
ADM	Angela de Mela	26 February 2007
AE	Ahmel Echevarría	20 March 2007
AF MN	Ambrosio Fornet	9 March 2007
AGN MN	Alberto Guerra Naranjo	23 March 2007
ALV	Ana Lydia Vega	3 April 2007

Acronym	Name	Date of interview
AM	Arturo Mesa	27 March 2007
AO	Abraham Ortiz	16 March 2007
EE	Ernesto Ernesto	28 April 2007
EHL MN	Eduardo Heras León	29 March 2007
EPC	Ernesto Pérez Castillo	8 March 2007
ET	Emmanuel Tornés	2 March 2007
FR MN	Fernando Rojas	3 March 2007; 6 March 2007
IGC	Ismael González Castañer	17 April 2007
IG MN	Ivonne Galeano	27 March 2007
IH	Ingrid Hernández	27 February 2007
JDC MN	Jesús David Curbelo	3 March 2007
LC	Lizette Clavelo	7 March 2007
LCL	Lien Carranza Lau	8 March 2007
MB	Maysel Bello	15 March 2007
MB MN	Marilyn Bobes	27 April 2007
MM	Mercedes Melo	17 March 2007; 1 April 2007
MSM MN	Mercedes Santos Moray	24 March 2007
MY MN	Mirta Yáñez	25 April 2007
RGZ MN	Reynaldo González Zamora	5 May 2007
RHO	Raúl Hernández Ortega	6 May 2007
SC MN	Sergio Chaple	9 March 2007
SH MN	Susana Haug	3 May 2007
TFR	Tomás Fernández Robaina	11 May 2007
TH	Teresita Hernández	16 April 2007
VB	Viana Barceló	13 March 2007
VG	Viena García	16 March 2007
YLG MN	Yannis Lobaina González	7 March 2007
YM	Yohan Moya	13 March 2007

Bibliography

Abreu Arcia, A. (2007), *Los juegos de la escritura o la (re)escritura de la historia* (Havana: Casa de las Américas).
Acosta, E. (1998), 'Bibliotecas del Tercer Milenio', *Revista del libro cubano*, II:2, 5-9.
Aguiar, R., and J.M. Sánchez Gómez (2005), *Escritos con guitarra: Cuentos cubanos sobre el rock* (Havana: Ediciones Unión).
Aguila, R. de (1998), 'Pathos o marketing', *Caimán barbudo*, 31, 2-3.
Aguirre, M. (1963), 'Apuntes sobre la literatura y el arte', *Cuba socialista*, III:26, 62-82.
— (1980), *Dice la palma. Testimonio* (Havana: Letras Cubanas).
Álvarez, I. (1985), 'Del taller a los libros', *Revolución y cultura*, 3, 20-6.
Appadurai, A. (ed.) (1986), *The social life of things: Commodities in cultural perspective* (Cambridge/New York: Cambridge University Press).
Arango, A. (2009) 'Una mala escritura de la historia', *Gaceta de Cuba*, 1, 56-9.
Aróstegui, M. del C. and R. Zamora Fernández (1991) 'Televisión y actividades recreativas', *Ciencias Sociales*, 26, 89-99.
Barnet, M, M. Benedetti and A. Carpentier (1971), *Literatura y arte nuevo en Cuba* (Barcelona: Editorial Estela).
Bejel, E. (1991) *Escribir en Cuba: Entrevistas con escritores cubanos, 1979-1989* (San Juan: Editorial de la Universidad de Puerto Rico).
—(2001) *Gay Cuban nation* (Chicago: University of Chicago Press).
Benedetti, M. (1971), 'Situación actual de la cultura cubana', in Barnet M, et al, *Literatura y arte nuevo en Cuba* (Barcelona: Editorial Estela), pp. 7-32.
Bennett, T. (2008), *Culture and society: Collected essays* (Beijing: Guangxi Normal University Press).
Bernard, J.L. and J.A. Pola (1985), *Quiénes escriben en Cuba: responden los narradores* (Havana: Editorial Letras Cubanas).

Biblioteca Nacional José Martí (2002), *Programa por la lectura* (Havana: BNJM).
Birkenmaier, A. (2011), 'Is there a post-Cuban literature?', *Review. Literature and arts of the Americas*, 82:44:1 (May), 6–11.
Birkenmaier, A. and R. González Echevarría (eds) (2004) *Cuba: un siglo de literatura (1902–2002)* (Madrid: Editorial Colibrí (Colección Literatura)).
Blank, G. (2007), *Critics, ratings, and society. The sociology of reviews* (Lanham/Boulder/New York/Toronto/Plymouth: Rowman and Littlefield).
Boletín Cubarte (2009), 9:53 (18 de septiembre).
Bonachea, R.E. and N.P. Valdés (eds) (1972), *Cuba in revolution* (Garden City, NY: Anchor Books, Doubleday & Company).
Bourdieu, P. (1984), *Distinction: A social critique of the judgment of taste*, trans. Richard Nice (Cambridge, Mass: Harvard University Press).
—(1986) 'The forms of capital', in Richardson J.G. (ed.) *Handbook of theory and research for the sociology of education* (New York: Greenwood Press), pp. 241–58.
—(1990), *Reproduction in education, society and culture* (Theory, Culture and Society Series), with Jean-Claude Passeron (London & Thousand Oaks, CA: Sage).
Brenner, P., Jiménez, M.R., Kirk, J.M., LeoGrande W.M. (2008), *A contemporary Cuba reader. Reinventing the Revolution* (Lanham/Boulder/New York/Toronto/Plymouth/ UK: Rowman & Littlefield Publishers).
Brewer, J. (2002), 'Authors, publishers and the making of literary culture', in Finkelstein, D. and. A. McCleery (eds), *The book history reader* (London/NY: Routledge), pp. 241–9.
Bunck, J. M. (1994), *Fidel Castro and the quest for a revolutionary culture in Cuba* (University Park, PA: Pennsylvania University Press).
Cabrera Infante, G. (2003), 'Un mes lleno de Lunes', in Luis W., *Lunes de Revolución. Literatura y cultura en los primeros años de la Revolución Cubana* (Madrid: Editorial Verbum), pp. 137–53.
Campuzano, L. (1988), *Quirón o del ensayo y otros eventos* (Havana: Editorial Letras Cubanas).
Cantón Navarro, J. and M. Duarte Hurtado (2006a), *Cuba: 42 años de revolución. Cronología histórica, 1959–1982, Tomo I* (Havana: Editorial de Ciencias Sociales).
—(2006b), *Cuba: 42 años de revolución. Cronología histórica, 1959–1982, Tomo II* (Havana: Editorial de Ciencias Sociales).

Casal, L. (1971), 'Literature and society', in Mesa-Lago C. (ed.), *Revolutionary change in Cuba* (Pittsburgh: University of Pittsburgh Press), pp. 447–70.
Casanova, P. (2004), *The world republic of letters*, trans. M.B Debevoise. (Boston: Harvard University Press).
Casanovas Pérez Malo, A. (1997), *Participación y política cultural cubana. Una aproximación desde el sistema institucional de la cultura* (Havana: Centro Juan Marinello de Investigación y Desarrollo de la Cultura Cubana).
Castellanos, O. (1998), 'Defender todo lo defendible, que es mucho: César López, entrevistado por Orlando Castellanos', *Gaceta de Cuba* (marzo–abril), 29.
Castro Ruz, F. (1980), 'Palabras a los intelectuales', in López Lemus V. (ed.) *Revolución, letras, arte* (Havana: Editorial Letras Cubanas), pp. 7–30.
Castro, H. (2007), 'Una cultura de la política revolucionaria', *Tiempo de Cuba*, [Online]. Available at: www.tiempodecuba.34sp.com/modules. php?name=News&file=print&sid=1122 (accessed 6 November 2007).
Centro de Formación Literaria Onelio Jorge Cardoso (n.d.(a)), 'Introducción' (n.d.), *El Centro de Formación Literaria Onelio Jorge Cardoso*, [Online]. Available at: www.centroonelio.cult.cu (accessed 2 March 2009).
—(n.d(b)), 'Quienes somos', *El Centro de Formación Literaria Onelio Jorge Cardoso* [Online]. Available at: www.centroonelio.cult.cu (accessed 2 March 2009).
Céspedes, N. (2008), 'El Centro Onelio ha dinamizado la narrativa cubana', *Atenas: El Portal de la cultura matancera*, 20:10 [Online]. Available at: www.atenas.cult.cu/?q=node/5101 (accessed 2 February 2009).
Chanan, M. (1985), *The Cuban image* (Minneapolis: University of Minnesota Press; repub. 2004).
Chartier, R. (1989), *The culture of print: power and the uses of print in early modern Europe* (Cambridge: Polity Press).
Chomsky, A., B. Carr and P.M. Smorkaloff (eds) (2003), *The Cuba reader. History, culture, politics* (Durham and London: Duke University Press).
'Cinco años de revolución cultural' (1963), *Pueblo y cultura*, 17–18, 10.
CNC (Consejo Nacional de Cultura) (1973), *Folleto metodólogico: talleres literarios no. 1* (Havana: Consejo Nacional de Cultura, Dirección General de Literatura y Publicaciones).

CNC (1974), *Talleres literarios y círculos de lectura* (Havana: Consejo Nacional de Cultura, Dirección de Extensión Universitaria).
—(1975), *Bases para los encuentro-debates de los talleres literarios* (Havana: Consejo Nacional de Cultura).
CNCC (Consejo Nacional de Casas de Cultura) (2003), 'Valoraciones en torno a los talleres literarios de nuevo tipo', *Informe del equipo de literatura Consejo Nacional de Casas de Cultura* (unpublished).
—(2005a), 'Anexo I talleres y alcance poblacional de literatura', *Informe del Consejo Nacional de Casas de Cultura* (unpublished).
—(2005b), 'Análisis de las estadísticas de literatura 2005', *Informe del Consejo Nacional de Casas de Cultura* (unpublished).
—(2008), 'Talleres de creación', *Indicaciones metodológicas del Consejo Nacional de Casas de Cultura*. Available at: www.cenit.cult.cu/sites/cpcc/index (accessed 10 March 2009).
Codina, N. (2003), *Siglo pasado: Compilación de Norberto Codina*, Santa Clara: Capiro/Havana: Ediciones Unión).
Cohen, J.M. (1970), *En tiempos difíciles. Poesía cubana de la Revolución* (Barcelona: Tusquets).
Correa Cajigas, S., M.C. Alzugaray and C. Linares Fleites (1998), *Algunas tendencias sobre el consumo cultural de la población urbana en Cuba* (Havana: Centro Juan Marinello de Investigación y Desarrollo de la Cultura Cubana).
Coulthard, G.R. (1967), 'The situation of the writer in contemporary Cuba', *Caribbean Studies*, 7:1 (April) (offprint).
—(1975), 'The writer in the Revolution: literary development in Russia and Cuba since their respective revolutions', *Caribbean Studies*, 15 (July), 163–8.
Darnton, R. (2002), 'What is the history of books?', in Finkelstein, D. and A. McCleery, *The book history reader*, pp. 9–26.
Davies, C. (1997), *A place in the sun? Women writers in twentieth-century Cuba* (London: Zed Books).
De Certeau, M. (1984), *The practice of everyday life*, trans. Steven Rendall (Berkeley: University of California Press).
Del Duca, G.R. (1972), 'Creativity and revolution: cultural dimension of the new Cuba', in Suchlicki J. (ed.), *Cuba, Castro and revolution*, pp. 94–118.
Desnoes, E. (1967), *Punto de Vista* (Havana: Instituto del Libro).
Díaz Mantilla, D. (2006), 'De los alucinados de un mundo presente: reflexiones sobre el abuso de la crítica y las técnicas narrativas', *La letra del escriba*, 54 (Octubre), 1–2.

Du Gay, P. (ed.) (1997), *Production of culture/cultures of production* (London: Sage Publications/The Open University).
Du Gay, P. and M. Pryke (eds) (2002), *Cultural economy: Cultural analysis and commercial life* (London: Sage Publications).
Eagleton, T. (2000), *The idea of culture* (London: Wiley-Blackwell).
English, J.F. (2005), *The economy of prestige. Prizes, awards and the circulation of cultural value* (Cambridge, Mass/London: Harvard University Press).
Escarpit, R. (1971), *The sociology of literature*, trans. Ernest Pick and with an Introduction by Malcolm Bradbury and Bryan Wilson (London: Frank Cass and Co. (New Sociology Library, no. 4)).
Espinosa Domínguez, C. (2008), 'La pérdida y el reino', *Extramuros*, 28, 32–5.
Espinosa, N. (2008), 'Punto de referencia: Entrevista a Ambrosio Fornet', *Extramuros*, 27, 22–9.
Fagen, R.R.(1969), *The transformation of political culture in Cuba* (Stanford: Stanford University Press).
Fernandes, S. (2003), 'Island paradise: revolutionary utopia or hustler's haven? Consumerism and socialism in contemporary Cuban rap', *Journal of Latin American Cultural Studies*, 12:3, 359–75.
—(2006), *Cuba represent! Cuban arts, state power and the making of new revolutionary cultures* (London: Duke University Press).
Fernández Retamar, R. (1980), 'Caliban', in López Lemus V. *et al* (eds), *Revolución, letras, arte*, pp. 221–76.
—(2008), 'Opinión', *Extramuros*, 28, 18.
Fernández Robaina, T. (2001), *Apuntes para la historia de la Biblioteca Nacional José Martí de Cuba* (Havana: Biblioteca Nacional José Martí).
Foreign Office (1961), *American Department confidential report No 43 (1746/61 (S))* (28 August).
Fornet, A. (1971), 'El intelectual en la revolución', in Barnet M., *et al*, *Literatura y arte nuevo en Cuba*, pp. 33–7.
—(1994), *El libro en Cuba* (Havana: Letras Cubanas).
—(1995), *Las máscaras del tiempo* (Havana: Letras Cubanas).
—(1997), 'Entrevista a Ambrosio Fornet', *Revista del libro cubano*, 1:2, 28–30.
—(2008), *El otro y sus signos* (Santiago de Cuba: Editorial Oriente).
Fornet, J. (2006), 'Cuando Cuba comenzó a desaparecer', *El Cuentero*, 02 Año 00, 2–11.
Fowler Calzada, V. (2000), *La lectura, ese poliedro,* digital version

http://bdigital.bnjm.cu/secciones/publicaciones/libros/la_lectura/curso_frame.htm (accessed 3 April 2012).

Franco, J. (1970) 'Before and after: contexts of Cuban writing', *Caribbean Review*, 91:2195 (20 February), 104–7.

—(2002), *The decline and fall of the lettered city: Latin America in the Cold War* (Cambridge, Mass/London: Harvard University Press).

Frank, W. (1961), *Cuba: prophetic island* (New York: Marzani and Munsell).

Frow, J. (1995), *Cultural studies and cultural value* (Oxford: Clarendon Press).

Gallardo, E.J. (2009), *El martillo y el espejo: directrices de la política cultural cubana (1959–1976)* (Madrid: Consejo Superior de Investigaciones Científicas (Colección Difusión y Estudio)).

González Echevarría, R. (1985), 'Criticism and literature in revolutionary Cuba', in Halebsky S. and J.M. Kirk (eds), *Cuba: Twenty-five years of revolution, 1959–1984* (New York: Praeger), pp. 155–73.

—(2004), 'Oye mi son: El canon cubano', in Birkenmaier, A. and R. González Echevarría (eds), *Un siglo de literatura (1902–2002)* (Madrid: Editorial Colibrí (Colección Literatura)), pp. 19–36.

—(2011), 'Contemporary Cuban literature: a way out', *Review. Literature and arts of the Americas*, 82:44:1 (May), 12–19.

Goytisolo, J.A. (1970), *La nueva poesía cubana* (Barcelona: Ediciones Península).

Granma (1966), 2:190 (11 de julio).

—(1967), 3:172 (12 de julio).

Halebsky, S., and J.M. Kirk (eds) (1985), *Cuba: Twenty-five years of revolution, 1959–1984* (NewYork/Westport, Conn./London: Praeger).

Hall, S. (ed.) (1997), *Representation: Cultural representations and signifying practices* (London: Sage Publications/The Open University).

Hart, A. (1978), *Del trabajo cultural. Selección de discursos* (Havana: Ciencias Sociales).

—(1986), *Cambiar las reglas del juego. Entrevista de Luis Báez* (Havana: Letras Cubanas).

Harvey, D. (1990), 'Between space and time: reflections on the geographical imagination', *Annals of the Association of American Geographers*, 80:3 (September), 418–34.

Hennessy, A. (1963), 'Roots of Cuban nationalism', *International Affairs*, 39:3 (July), 345–59.

Heras León, E. (ed.) (1988), *Talleres literarios 1987* (Havana: Letras Cubanas).

—(2001), *Los desafíos de la ficción (técnicas narrativas)* (Havana: Casa Editorial Abril/ CFLOJC).
Hernández-Reguant, A. (2009a), 'Multicubanidad', in Hernández-Reguant A.(ed.), *Cuba in the Special Period: Culture and ideology in the 1990s* (New York: Palgrave Macmillan), pp. 69–88.
—(2009b), 'Writing the Special Period: an introduction', in Hernández-Reguant A. (ed.), *Cuba in the Special Period*, pp. 1–18.
Hoffmann, B. and L. Whitehead (eds) (2007), *Debating Cuban exceptionalism* (New York/London: Palgrave Macmillan).
Horowitz, I.L. (1977), *Cuban Communism* (3rd edn) (New Brunswick: Transaction Books).
Huberman, L. and P.M. Sweezy (1969), *Socialism in Cuba* (New York and London: Monthly Review Press).
Huertas, B. (1993), *Ensayo de un cambio. La narrativa cubana de los '80* (Havana: Casa de las Américas).
ICL (Instituto Cubano del Libro) (2004), *Memorias. Programa profesional XIII Feria Internacional del Libro de la Habana* (Havana: ICL/Ciencias Sociales).
—(2009), *Resumen estadístico 2009* (Havana: ICL).
—(2010), *Memorias, Ferias Internacionales del Libro de La Habana* (Havana: ICL/Editorial Científico-Técnica).
ILL (Instituto de Literatura y Lingüística) (1980), *Diccionario de la literatura cubana, Tomo I* (Havana: Letras Cubanas).
—(1984), *Diccionario de la literatura cubana, Tomo II* (Havana: Letras Cubanas).
—(2008), *Historia de la literatura cubana. Tomo III. La Revolución (1959–1988)* (Havana: Instituto de Literatura y Lingüística/Ministerio de Ciencia, Tecnología y Medio Ambiente).
James, C. (1996) 'Patterns of resistance in Afro-Cuban women's writing: Nancy Morejón's "Amo a mi amo" ', in Anim-Addo J. (ed.), *Framing the word: Gender and genre in Caribbean women's writing* (London: Whiting and Birch), pp. 29–34.
—(2003), 'Queering Cuba: male homosexuality in the short fiction of Manuel Granados', in Lewis L. (ed.), *The culture of gender and sexuality in the Caribbean* (Gainesville: University Press of Florida), pp. 251–74.
Jiménez, T. (1995), 'Los talleres literarios en México', en *Anales de Literatura Hispanoamericana*, 24, 251–58 [Online]. Available at: www.revistas.ucm.es/fll/02104547/articulos/ALHI9595110251A.PDF (accessed 3 June 2007).

Jolly, R. (1964), 'Education', in Seers D. (ed.), *Cuba. The economic and social revolution*, pp. 161–282.
Kapcia, A. (2000), *Cuba. Island of dreams* (Oxford: Berg).
—(2005), *Havana. The making of Cuban culture* (Oxford: Berg).
Kapcia, A., and P. Kumaraswami (2010), 'The Feria del Libro and the ritualisation of cultural belonging in Havana', in Young R. and A. Holmes (eds), *Cultures of the city: Mediating identities in urban Latin/o America* (Pittsburgh: University of Pittsburgh Press), pp. 204–29.
Kirk, J.M. and L. Padura Fuentes (2001), *Culture and the Cuban Revolution: Conversations in Havana* (Gainesville: University Press of Florida).
Knauer, L.M. (2009), 'Audiovisual remittances and transnational subjectivities', in Hernández-Reguant A., *Cuba in the Special Period*, pp. 159–77.
Kumaraswami, P. (2006), '"Pensamos que somos historia porque sabemos que somos historia": context, self and self-construction in women's testimonial writing from revolutionary Cuba', *Bulletin of Hispanic Studies*, 83:6, 523–39.
—(2007), 'Cultural policy, literature, and readership in revolutionary Cuba: the view from the 21st century', *Bulletin of Latin American Research*, 26:1 (January), 69–87.
—(2009a), 'Cultural policy and cultural politics in revolutionary Cuba: re-reading the *Palabras a los intelectuales*', *Bulletin of Latin American Research (Special Issue)*, 28:4, 527–41.
—(2009b), '"El color del futuro": assessing the significance of the Encuentros of 2007', *Journal of Iberian and Latin American Research*, 15:2, 103–20.
'La distribución del libro: ¿un dilema?' (1996), *Revista del libro cubano*, 1:1, 74–5.
La lucha ideológica y la cultura artística y literaria (1982) (Havana: Editora Política).
La política cultural del período revolucionario: memoria y reflexión. Ciclo de conferencias organizado por el Centro teórico-Cultural Criterios. La Habana, 2007 Primera parte (2008) (Havana: Colección Criterios).
La revista del libro cubano (1998), II:3.
Lefevbre, H. (1991), *The production of space* (Oxford: Blackwell).
Lewis, J. and T. Miller (eds) (2003), *Critical cultural policy studies: A reader* (Oxford: Blackwell Publishing).

Linares, C., Y. Rivero Baxter and P.E. Moras Puig (2008), *Participación y consumo cultural en Cuba* (Havana: Instituto Cubano de Investigación Cultural Juan Marinello).

Linares Fleites, C., P.E. Moras Puig, and Y.Rivero Baxter (eds) (2004), *La participación. Diálogo y debate en el contexto cubano* (Havana: Centro Juan Marinello).

Linares Fleites, C. and P.E. Moras Puig (2004), 'Universos para la participación: su concreción en el ámbito de la acción cultural', in Colectivo de autores (2004), *Participación social en Cuba* (Havana: Centro de Investigaciones Psicológicas y Sociológicas), pp. 73–106.

'Los intelectuales extranjeros: Declaración del Primer Congreso Nacional de Educación y Cultura, 30 de abril de 1971' (1971), in Montaner C.A. (1976), *Informe secreto sobre la revolución cubana* (Madrid: Ediciones Sedmay), pp. 147–53.

López Calvo (2008), *Imaging the Chinese in Cuban literature and culture* (Gainesville: University Press of Florida).

Loss, J. (2009), 'Wandering in Russian', in Hernández-Reguant A., *Cuba in the Special Period*, pp. 105–22.

Luis, W. (2003), *Lunes de Revolución. Literatura y cultura en los primeros años de la Revolución Cubana* (Madrid: Editorial Verbum).

McKenzie, D.F. (2002), 'The sociology of a text: orality, literacy and print in early New Zealand', in Finkelstein, D. and A. McCleery (eds), *The book history reader*, pp. 189–215.

Marqués Ravelo, B. (1985), 'Informe personal sobre el olvido', *Caimán barbudo*, 211 (junio), 20–1.

Mario, J. (1969), 'Novísima poesía cubana', *Mundo Nuevo*, 38 (August), 63–9.

Martín Rodríguez, A. and A. Jiménez (1992), *La Casa de Cultura de Centro Habana: la labor de sus especialistas como promotores culturales* (Havana: Centro Juan Marinello de Investigación y Desarrollo de la Cultura Cubana).

Mas Zabala, C.A. (1994), *Space, place and gender* (Oxford: Polity Press).

—(2000), 'Las nuevas del libro en Cuba', *Revista del libro cubano*, III:1: 49–51.

Massey, D. (2005), *For space* (London and Thousand Oaks, CA: Sage).

Medin, T. (1990), *Cuba: the shaping of a revolutionary consciousness* (Boulder, Col.: Lynne Reinner).

Medina, M. (2001), 'Bibliotecas nacionales: el breve espacio en que sí estás', *Correo del libro*, IV:13, 10–12.

'Mensajes de intelectuales al taller' (2002), *La Jiribilla*, 18:10. Available at: www.lajiribilla.co.cu/2002/n78_noviembre/1841_78.html (accessed 10 October 2007).
Menton. S. (1964), 'La novela de la revolución cubana', *Cuadernos americanos*, XXIII:CXXXII:1 (January–February), 231–341.
—(1975), *Prose fiction of the Cuban Revolution* (Austin: University of Texas Press).
Mesa-Lago, C. (ed.) (1971), *Revolutionary change in Cuba* (Pittsburgh: University of Pittsburgh Press).
Mills, C. Wright (1960), *Listen, Yankee. The revolution in Cuba* (New York: Ballantine Books).
MINCULT (n.d.(a)), 'Instituciones adscriptas', *Ministerio de Cultura de la República de Cuba*, [Online]. Available at: www.min.cult.cu/loader.php?sec=ministerio&cont=adscriptas (accessed 1 May 2008).
—(n.d.(b)), 'Objetivos: Centro de Formación Literaria "Onelio Jorge Cardoso", *Ministerio de Cultura de la República de Cuba*, [Online]. Available at: www.min.cult.cu/ (accessed 20 January 2008).
Miranda, J.E. (1971), *Nueva literatura cubana* (Madrid: Taurus).
Morales, E. (1998), 'Literatura y mercado', *Revista del libro cubano*, II:3, 4–8.
Navarro, D. (2006), *Las causas de las cosas* (Havana: Letras Cubanas).
Nehru, M. (2010), 'A literary culture in common: the movement of *talleres literarios* in Cuba 1960s-2000s' (PhD dissertation, University of Nottingham).
O'Connor, J. (1970), *The origins of socialism in Cuba* (Ithaca and London: Cornell University Press).
Ong, W.J. (2002), *Orality and literacy: The technologizing of the word* (London: Routledge).
Ortega, J. (1973), *Relato de la utopía. Notas sobre la narrativa cubana de la Revolución* (Barcelona: La Gaya Ciencia).
Otero, L. (1997), *Llover sobre mojado: una reflexión personal sobre la historia* (Havana: Letras Cubanas).
—(1999a), *Llover sobre mojado. Memorias de un intelectual cubano (1957–1997)* (Mexico: Editorial Planeta).
—(1999b), *Llover sobre mojado: una reflexión personal sobre la historia* (Madrid: Ediciones Libertarias).
—(2003), '1961, Cuando de abrieron las ventanas a la imaginación', in Codina N. (ed.), *Siglo pasado*, pp. 78–87.
Pacheco, P. (2000), 'La Editorial ARTE y LITERATURA y la cultura cubana', *Extramuros*, 4, 47–9.

Padilla, H. (1989), *La mala memoria* (Barcelona: Plaza & Janes Editores).
Pardo Lazo, O.L. (2011), 'Has there been any Cuban literature since the Revolution?', *Review. Literature and arts of the Americas*, 82:44:1 (May), 126–30.
Pawley, L. (2008), 'Cultural citizenship', in *Sociology compass*, 2:2, 594–608.
Perdomo, O. (1996), 'La primera Feria del Libro en Cuba', *Revista del libro cubano*, 1:1, 73.
Pérez, L.A., Jr. (1999), *On becoming Cuban. Identity, nationality and culture* (Chapel Hill: University of North Carolina Press).
Pérez, O.M. (1998), 'La lectura: ¿tarea de quién?', *Revista del libro cubano*, II:2, 10–11.
Pérez Castillo, E. (n.d.) 'Llegando tarde y mal', *Cubaliteraria*, Available at: www.cubaliteraria.com/delacuba/ficha.php?Id=2738 (accessed 2 May 2009).
Pérez Chang, E. (n.d.), '¿A la escuela hay que llegar puntual?', *Cubaliteraria*, Available at: www.cubaliteraria.com/delacuba/ficha.php?s_Seccion=12&Id=2670 (accessed 4 October 2007).
Pérez Cruz, F. de J. (2001), *La alfabetización en Cuba. Lectura histórica para pensar el presente* (Havana: Ciencias Sociales).
Pérez Prats, G., M.V. Prado Ramírez and N.J. Sosa Zayas (1991), *Resumen de los estudios realizados sobre la oferta cultural dirigida al turismo internacional* (Havana: Centro Juan Marinello de Investigación y Desarrollo de la Cultura Cubana).
Pflaum, I.P. (1962), *Tragic island: How communism came to Cuba* (New York: Prentice-Hall).
Pogolotti, G. (ed.) (2006), *Polémicas culturales de los 60* (Havana: Letras Cubanas).
Política Cultural de la Revolución Cubana. Documentos (1977) (Havana: Ciencias Sociales).
Portuondo, J.A. (1963), *Estética y revolución* (Havana: Ediciones Unión).
—(1965), *Crítica de la época* (Santa Clara: Universidad Central de las Villas).
—(1979), *Itinerario estético de la Revolución Cubana* (Havana: Letras Cubanas).
Prats, D. (2003), '1967', in Codina N. (ed.), *Siglo pasado*, pp. 130–6.
'Punto 4' (2007), *El Cuentero*, 4:2, 1.
Rama, A. (1996), *The lettered city*, ed. and trans. John Charles Chasteen (Durham/London: Duke University Press).

Resik Aguirre, M. (1997), 'Memorias de libreros', *Revista del libro cubano*, I:3, 42–5.
—(1998), 'Cada libro es un hecho cultural', *Revista del libro cubano*, II: Suplemento Especial: 'Instituto Cubano del Libro: 30 años por el libro y la lectura': 4–8.
Revolución (1961a), IV:767 (5 de junio).
—(1961b), IV:796 (8 de julio).
—(1961c), IV:773 (12 de junio).
—(1961d), IV:817 (2 de agosto).
—(1961e), IV:833 (21 de agosto).
—(1961f), IV:863 (25 de septiembre).
Revolución y cultura (1981), 107 (julio).
Rodríguez, C.R. (1984), *Palabras en los sesenta* (Havana: Ciencias Sociales).
Rodríguez, R. (2001), 'Génesis y desarrollo del Instituto Cubano del Libro (1965–1980): Memoria y reflexión', *Debates americanos*, 11 (enero-diciembre), 65–80.
Rodríguez Rivera, G. (2007), *Canción de amor en tierra extraña* (Havana: Ediciones Unión).
Rojas, R. (2008), *El estante vacío. Literatura y política en Cuba* (Barcelona: Editorial Anagrama).
Rosales Rosa, M. (2002), 'Los novísimos', *Revista Proceso México*. Available at: www.amirvalle.com/comentarios/articulos/proceso.htm (accessed 3 March 2009).
Salazar Navarro, S. (2008), 'El Centro Onelio estrena sitio web', *La Jiribilla*, VI (enero/febrero). Available at: www.lajiribilla.co.cu/2008/n351_01/351_20.html (accessed 3 May 2009).
Sánchez, W. (1998), 'Plaza de Armas: otro avance y nuevos compromisos', *Correo del libro*, 1:3, 8–9.
Sánchez Espinosa, I. (2000), 'Los saldos de una feria mayor', *Correo del libro*, III:10, 9–10.
Sánchez Mejías, R. (2006), 'Literatura y violencia', *La Habana elegante, segunda época*. Available at: www.habanaelegante.com/Spring-Summer2006/VerbosaDos.html (accessed 16 April 2009).
Santiesteban, A. (n.d.), 'Siempre puntual, con el peor de los ciegos', *Cubaliteraria*. Available at: www.cubaliteraria.cu/delacuba/ficha.php?sub=2&Id=2759 (accessed 20 January 2007).
'Saramago en el Centro Onelio' (2005), *El Cuentero*, 00:00, 24–5.
Sartre, J.-P. (1961), *Sartre on Cuba* (New York: Ballantine Books).

Seers, D. (ed.) (1964), *Cuba. The economic and social revolution* (Chapel Hill: University of North Carolina Press).
Serra, A. (2007), *The 'New Man' in Cuba: Culture and identity in the Revolution* (Gainesville: University Press of Florida).
Shatzkin, L. (1985), 'Book publishing in Cuba. How it works', *Publishers Weekly* (12 April), 36–9.
Simo, A.M. (2006), 'Respuesta a Jesús Díaz', in Pogolotti G. (ed.), *Polémicas culturales de los 60* (Havana: Letras Cubanas), pp. 369–82.
Smorkaloff, P.M. (1987), *Literatura y edición de libros, 1900–1987: la cultura literaria y el proceso social en Cuba* (Havana: Editorial Letras Cubanas).
—(1997), *Readers and writers in Cuba: A social history of print culture, 1830s–1990s* (New York/London: Garland Publishers).
Soler Cedre, G. (1997), 'Pinos Nuevos en la balanza: ¿Ser o no ser?', *Revista del libro cubano*, I:4, 20–3.
Stevenson, N. (ed.) (2001), *Culture and citizenship* (London: Sage).
—(2003), *Cultural citizenship: Cosmopolitan questions* (Maidenhead: Open University Press).
Stock, A.M. (2008), 'Tradition meets technology: Cuban film animation enters the global marketplace', *Cuban studies*, 39, 1–24.
Suardíaz, L. (2003), '1965', in Codina N. (ed.), *Siglo pasado*, pp. 98–102.
Suchlicki, J. (ed.) (1972), *Cuba, Castro and revolution* (Coral Gables: University of Miami Press).
Tompkins, J. (2002), 'Masterpiece theatre: the politics of Hawthorne's literary reputation', in Finkelstein, D. and A. McCleery (eds), *The book history reader*, pp. 250–8.
'Una feria diferente' (1996), *Revista del libro cubano*, 1:1, 73.
UNEAC (1993), *Memorias del V Congreso de la UNEAC* (Havana: UNEAC).
—(2000), *La difusión masiva de la cultura* (Havana: Consejo Nacional de la UNEAC).
Uxó, C. (2009), 'Internet, veinte años después', *Journal of Iberian and Latin American Research*, 15:2 (December), 121–43.
Valladares Ruiz, P. (2005), 'Lo especial del período: políticas editoriales y movimiento generacional en la literatura cubana contemporánea', *Neophilologus*, 89:3, 383–402.
Weyl, N. (1961), *Red star over Cuba: the Russian assault on the western hemisphere* (New York: Devin-Adair).
Whitfield, E. (2004), 'Narrando el dólar en los noventa', in Birkenmaier, A. and R. González Echevarría (eds) (2004), *Cuba: un siglo de*

literatura (1902–2002) (Madrid: Editorial Colibrí (Colección Literatura)), pp. 391–405.
—(2008), *Cuban currency: The dollar and 'Special Period' fiction* (Minneapolis: University of Minnesota Press).
—(2009), 'Truths and fictions: the economics of writing, 1994–1999', in Hernández-Reguant A. (ed.), *Cuba in the Special Period*, pp. 21–36.
Wilkinson, S. (2006), *Detective fiction in Cuban society and culture* (Oxford/New York: Peter Lang).
Williams, R. (1981), *The sociology of culture* (Chicago: University of Chicago Press).
Wright, A. (1988), 'Intellectuals of an un-heroic period of Cuban history, 1913–1923. The Cuba Contemporánea group', *Bulletin of Latin American Research*, 7:1, 109–220.
Zeitlin, M. (1970), 'Cuba: revolution without a blueprint', in Horowitz I.L. (ed.), *Cuban communism*, pp. 117–30.
Zurbano, R. (1997), 'Revistas de movimiento', *Revista del libro cubano*, 1:3, 4–6.
—(1998), 'Hacia una búsqueda de sí y de las(s) poéticas(s) del fin de siglo', *Revista del libro cubano*, II:3, 17–22.

Internet sources

www.bnjm.cu/bnjm/espanol/acerca/info_general/minerva.htm (accessed 26 September 2006).
www.min.cult.cu/loader.php?sec=legislacion&cont=decretoley145 (accessed 3 April 2012).
www.cubanradio.cu/index.php/cuban-radio-history/24–radio-memories/933–dr-maria-dolores-ortiz-cepero-brito-offered-me-the-job-as-a-panelist-for-escriba-y-lea-television-show- (accessed 18 August 2011).
www.ecured.cu/index.php/Plan_Turquino (accessed 7 July 2011).
http://entretenimiento.terra.com.pe/cultura/publicacion-de-libros-en-cuba-cayo-un-82–en-cinco-anos,bb1bda88f41e0310VgnVCM400000 9bf154d0RCRD.html (accessed 7 July 2011).
www.granma.cubaweb.cu/eventos/19ferialibro/sedes/04_matanzas/matanzas-04.html (accessed 21 April 2010).
www.juventudrebelde.cu/secciones/ujc/htm/jovenes_cubanos/ahs.htm (accessed 24 April 2011).
www.oei.es/cultura2/cuba/06.htm (accessed 22 July 2011).

Index

Abreu Arcia, Alberto 102–5, 124–5
Acosta, Eliades 142, 168–9
Adorno, Theodor 49
aficionados movement 30, 89, 115, 179–80
Agüero, Luis 71
Aguiar, Raúl 183
Aguirre, Magda Resik 77, 163
Ajón León, Alberto 194, 205–10 *see also Qué bolá*
Almendros, Néstor 71, 85
Alonso, Alicia 2
Alonso, Alpidio 124
Alonso, Aurelio 91, 110
Alonso, Nancy 98–9
Alvarez, Alejandro 107, 110–11
Angola 15
anti-colonialism 13
Antuña, Vicentina 71–2
Appadurai, Arjun 57–8
Arango, Arturo 103–4, 120
Araújo, Nara 34
Arenal, Humberto 78
Arias, Salvador 114
Ariel, Sigfredo 124
Arrufat, Antón 77, 94, 109
Asociación Hermanos Saíz (AHS) 124, 156, 168, 190

Ateneo bookshop 201, 203
La Azotea group 132–3

Barnet, Miguel 226
Batalla de Ideas 17–21, 32, 153–6, 161–2, 169, 172, 218, 221, 236
Bay of Pigs 11
Benedetti, Mario 92
Biblioteca Nacional José Martí (BNJM) 6, 25, 65–7, 71, 91–2, 95, 122, 140–3
black consciousness 19
Bobes, Marilyn 99
book launches 200–1, 211–12
book prices 203–5, 228
book production 97, 122–3, 172, 198–9, 213, 225
bookshops 98, 139, 141, 161, 201–3
Bourdieu, Pierre 45–8, 56–7
Brewer, John 43, 61
Brigadas Hermanos Saíz 88, 101

Cabrera Infante, Guillermo 24, 69, 71, 72, 77, 209
Caimán group 88–9, 102–3, 106
Campuzano, Luisa 34, 133
Carpentier, Alejo 7, 10, 78, 85, 198, 209–10, 216

Carter, Jimmy 14
Casa (magazine) 64–5
Casa de las Américas cultural centre 2, 23–4, 64–5, 86, 89, 94, 107, 113, 115
Casal, Lourdes 6
Casanova, Pascale 42, 56
Casas de Cultura 32, 155
Castillo, Belarmino 105
Castro, Fidel 11–12, 18, 22–3, 25, 40, 44, 68, 71–2, 75, 84, 90, 96, 105–6, 123, 126, 141, 153–4, 198, 210–13, 219
Castro, Raúl 5, 18, 56, 169, 172, 211, 213
Catá, Alfonso Hernández 215
Catholic Church 21
censorship 71–2, 234
Centro de Estudios Martianos 30
Centro de Formación Literaria Onelio Jorge Cardoso ('Centro Onelio') 5, 178–93
and cultural citizenship 186–8
Cevedo, Sergio 183
Chacón, José María 215
Chartier, Roger 60
Chávez, Hugo 222
children's literature 139
Ciclón (magazine) 8
'circuit of culture' (Du Gay) 47
Círculo de la Crítica 169–70
Clinton, Bill 16–17
Club Minerva 142–3, 203
Clubes de Amigos del Libro 164
Codina, Norberto 118, 163
Comas Paret, Emilio 100
Comisión Revisora de Películas 71
Communist Party of Cuba *see* Partido Comunista de Cuba

Consejo Nacional de Cultura (CNC) 23–4, 29, 50–1, 65, 79, 90, 95, 98, 101, 104, 107, 120–2, 179
Consejos Populares 16
copyright 84–5, 101, 166
Cortázar, Julio 99
Council for Mutual Economic Assistance (CMEA) 13, 15
criticism, literary 92–3, 152, 169–70
Cuba Contemporánea (magazine) 8
Cuban Missile Crisis 12
Cuban Revolution 1–4, 82–3
and literary culture 22–33, 46, 49, 55, 63, 182, 233, 239
political and economic trajectory of 11–18
social trajectory of 18–22
cultural attachés 26–7
cultural citizenship 186–8
cultural imperialism 28
cultural policy 22, 30–2, 92, 121
cultural revolution 79–80, 83, 231
cultural studies 45, 59
'cultural value' (Frow) 57
culture industries 49

Darnton, Robert 44
Davies, Catherine 35
de Juan, Adelaida 86
del Casal, Julián 10
Desnoes, Edmundo 27, 85
Díaz, Jesús 88–9
Díaz Mantilla, D. 185
'discourses of value' (Frow) 59
Distribuidora Nacional del Libro (NDL) 139–40, 169, 199, 202

Index

'domains of value' (Appadurai) 57–8, 102
Domenech, Joel 84
Don Quijote, publication of 65, 68, 77
Du Gay, Paul 47

Ediciones Cubanas 199
Ediciones Revolucionarias 84–5
Ediciones Territoriales *see* Sistema de Ediciones Territoriales
Ediciones Unión 195–7, 200
Editorial Cultural 6
Editorial Lex 6
Editorial Nacional 2, 66, 88
Editorial La Verónica 6
education 19–20, 82–5, 105, 112
El Puente group 3, 87–8, 94–5
emigration of Cuban writers 7, 18–19
emigré memoirs 40–1
employment policy 20–2
Enríquez, Doribal 115
Escarpit, Robert 43
Escuela de Artes y Letras 86, 91, 111–12
Escuela de Periodismo 113
Ethiopia 15
European Union 17
exceptionalism, Cuban 45
Extramuros 160

Feria de Guadalajara 166
Feria Internacional del Libro de La Habana 5, 132, 156, 161, 172, 189, 200, 203, 211–32, 234–5, 238
Fernández, Pablo Armando 69, 74–5, 113

Fernández Retamar, Roberto 27, 34, 86, 106, 149
Fondos Territoriales 150
Fornet, Ambrosio 26, 30, 34, 38, 76, 83, 85, 90, 97, 101, 115, 118–21, 197
Foucault, Michel 50
Fowler, Víctor 110, 143
Franco, José Luciano 215
Frankfurt school of cultural studies 49
Franqui, Carlos 24, 69, 72–3, 77
Freyre de Andrade, María Teresa 66–7
Frow, John 57–60
Fulleda León, Gerardo 87

Gaceta de Cuba 25–6, 72, 106, 163
Galeano, Ivonne 178, 189
García Buchaca, Edith 90
García Márquez, Gabriel 93
García Santos, Daniel 142, 165, 194
Garrandés, Alberto 116
Gente Nueva (publishing house) 117
Ginsburg, Allen 88
globalisation 49
González, Elián 17, 153, 182
González, Omar 139, 217
González, Reynaldo 107–8
González Echevarría, Roberto 36, 41, 61
Gorbachev, Mikhail 15
Granma (newspaper) 27
Guevara, Alfredo 2, 23, 26, 77
Guevara, Che 11–14, 27, 64, 72–4, 239
Guillén, Nicolás 10, 26, 78

Gutiérrez Alea, Tomás 101
Gutiérrez, PPedro Juan 146, 167–8

habitus (Bourdieu) 47–8
Hall, Stuart 45
Hart, Armando 29, 64, 123–4
Havana Book Fair *see* Feria Internacional del Libro de La Habana
healthcare 21–2
Helms-Burton Act 16–17
Heras León, Eduardo 109, 116, 178, 181–6, 191–2
Hernández-Reguant, Ariana 35–7, 41–2, 45–6, 62
Huracán 97

Imprenta Nacional 2, 65, 68
individualism 53, 234–7
institutionalisation of the political establishment 125–6
Instituto Cubano de Artes e Industrias Cinematográficas (ICAIC) 1, 8, 23–6, 53, 64, 71–2, 75, 78–80, 86, 101, 105, 107, 111
Instituto Cubano del Libro (ICL) 122, 155–60, 164, 167, 171–2, 195
Instituto de Literatura y Lingüistica (ILL) 93–8, 101, 113
instructores de arte 2, 30, 89
internacionalistas 14
internet resources 60–1

Jiménez Leal, Orlando 71
journalism 91, 133–4

Laguardia Martínez, Jacqueline 159, 161, 194
Lam, Wilfredo 10
Lea y Escriba (television programme) 115
Leal Spengler, Eusebio 216
León Jacomino, Fernando 194
Letras Cubanas 195–7, 200, 209–11
Leyendo Espero programme 157
libraries, use of 67, 91–2, 140–1, 203
Literacy Campaign (1961) 44–5, 48, 73, 76, 79–80, 82–3, 90–1, 114, 124, 206, 233–5, 238–9
literacy levels in Cuba 10, 19
literary culture
    changes in 87, 94–6, 99, 104, 111, 118, 125, 141, 146, 153–5, 161–2, 172, 214
    definition of 46
    foci and methods of 60–2
    and the *individual–collective* continuum 234–7
    national strategy for 5, 10
    social value of 79, 94, 120, 143–4, 157–8, 172, 228, 237–9
    see also Cuban Revolution, and literary culture
Llorach Ramos, Esteban 117, 239
López, César 95, 108
López Sacha, Francisco 178
Loss, Jacqueline 55
Luis, William 70, 73, 75
Lunes film project 71–2
Lunes group 3, 8, 25, 27, 30, 53, 69, 74, 79–80

Index

Lunes de Revolución (magazine) 22, 24, 68–75, 235
Lunes en Televisión 70–1

McKenzie, D.F. 44, 47
magazines, literary 7–8, 68–70, 163
Manzano, Roberto 116
Mario, José 87–8
Márquez, García 93
Martí, José 2, 9, 30, 85, 143, 220, 230, 238
Mateo Palmer, Margarita 135
Melo, Teresa 124
memoirs by writers 39–41
Méndez, Roberto 122
mentoring 121
Ministry of Culture (MINCULT) 29, 98, 121–3, 142–3, 158–9, 164
Ministry of Education (MINED) 23, 64–5, 105, 142–3
Morejón, Nancy 226, 228

newspapers 27
Nicaragua 123
Noche de los libros 225–6
novísimos 134–7, 144
Nuestro Tiempo group 8, 23–4, 77, 79

Observatorio Cubano del Libro y la Lectura (OCLI) 158–61
Oliver Labra, Carilda 124
Ong, Walter 60
Organisation of American States 13
Organizaciones Revolucionarias Integradas (ORI) 12

Orígenes (magazine) 8
Ortiz, María Dolores 34, 115, 164
Otero, Lisandro 28, 39, 72, 78, 91

Pacheco, Pablo 119
Padilla, Heberto 3, 28, 72, 78, 102, 105–6
Padura Fuentes, Leonardo 38, 146, 171, 198
Papastamatiu, Basilia 99
paper shortages 133, 198
parametración process 109, 122
parlamentos obreros 16
Partido Comunista de Cuba (PCC) 12–14
Partido Socialista Popular (PSP) 11, 24–5, 30, 72, 75, 79, 90
Pavón, Luis 29, 104–7, 168
Pawley, L. 181
Pensamiento Crítico (magazine) 27
Pérez, Olga Marta 144, 171
Pérez Castillo, Ernesto 183
Pérez Chang, Ernesto 184–8, 192
Piñera, Virgilio 7, 72, 88
Pinos Nuevos collection 137
Plan Turquino 140
plaquettes 144–5, 149
Pogolotti, Graziella 65–6, 69
Portocarrero, René 10
Portuondo, J.A. 87, 92–3, 102–3
presentaciones 158–9, 162, 200
prestige of literature and literary figures 9–10, 91, 147, 164
Prieto, Abel 30, 108, 111–12, 121–2, 153, 169, 226
Primer Congreso 82
print culture 60

prizes, literary 85–6, 136, 146–9, 166, 169–70, 195
promotores culturales 158–9, 199–200
provincial writers 162
Qué bolá (novel) 208–14
Quesada, Armando 168
quinquenio gris 29, 92, 95, 119–20
Rama, Angel 103
Ramonet, Ignacio 198
Ramos, Sidroc 92
Randall, Margaret 121
Reader's Digest 6–7, 9
reading habits 138–9, 142, 229–31
Reagan, Ronald 14
Redonet, Salvador 183
'regimes of value' 57–9, 105, 145
regulation of literary activity 125, 167
Revista de Avance (magazine) 8
Revolución (newspaper) 27
revolutionary movement *see* Cuban Revolution
Revolutionary Offensive (1968) 12–13
Ríos, Soleida 124
'RISO' publishing 150–2, 160, 171
Riverón, Rogelio 194, 209
Roa, Raúl 23
Rodiles, Javier Jomarrón 140
Rodríguez Coronel, Rogelio 197
Rodríguez, Reina María 132, 167
Rodríguez Rivera, Guillermo 121
Rodríguez, Rolando 84, 95–6
Rodríguez-Ojea, Anet 209–12

Rojas, Fernando 168–9
Rojas, Marta 209
Romay, Suleika 172
royalties 199

Sacha, Francisco López 134
Salas, Matilde 211
Sánchez Espinosa, Iroel 159
Santamaría, Haydée 23
santería 21
Santos Moray, Mercedes 112
'scenes of value' (Frow) 59
Serguera, Jorge 29, 168
Simo, Ana María 88–9
Sistema de Ediciones Territoriales (SET) 150–2, 160, 170–1
Smorkaloff, Pamela 43, 65–6, 98
socialisation, literary 155–6, 231
Soviet Union 15
space, concept of 49–51
Suardíaz, Luis 85, 92

talleres literarios 2, 5, 30, 76, 89, 100, 114–18, 121, 123, 151, 162–3, 167, 178–81, 234–8
talleres de vanguardia 180–1
television 70–1, 163–4, 168
Terry, Marta 115
tourist industry 137–8
trabajadores sociales 21
26th July Movement 24, 79

Unidad Militar de Ayuda a la Producción (UMAD) 26
Unión de Escritores y Artistas de Cuba (UNEAC) 25–6, 30, 50, 79–80, 85–8, 94–5, 101, 106–7, 123–6, 134, 146,

153, 156, 158, 165–8, 179, 185
United Nations Educational, Scientific and Cultural Organisation (UNESCO) 216, 226
Universidad de La Habana 8–9, 84, 98, 121
Universidad Para Todos 183
university entrance 20–1, 76
university textbooks 83–5

Venezuela 17
Vitier, Cintio 210

Whitfield, Esther 146
women, role and status of 21

Yáñez, Mirta 38, 112–13, 169

zafra crisis 28
Zeitlin, Maurice 63
Zurbano, Roberto 68–9, 122–3

Lightning Source UK Ltd.
Milton Keynes UK
UKOW06f0756121215

264584UK00001B/51/P

9 780719 099953